TOUGH SELL

TOUGH

SELL

Fighting the Media War in Iraq

TOM BASILE

Foreword by John R. Bolton

```
HV6432.B375 2017
Basile, Tom, 1975- author.
Tough sell : fighting the
media war in Iraq
[Lincoln, Nebraska] :
Potomac Books, [2017]
```

Potomac Books | *An imprint of the University of Nebraska Press*

Library of Congress Cataloging-in-Publication Data
Names: Basile, Tom, 1975– author. | Bolton, John R.,
writer of foreword.
Title: Tough sell: fighting the media war in Iraq / Tom
Basile; foreword by John R. Bolton.
Description: Lincoln, Nebraska: Potomac Books, an
imprint of the University of Nebraska Press, 2017. |
Includes bibliographical references and index.
Identifiers: LCCN 2016032572 (print) | LCCN
2016053430 (ebook)
ISBN 9781612349008 (cloth: alk. paper)
ISBN 9781612349077 (epub)
ISBN 9781612349084 (mobi)
ISBN 9781612349091 (pdf)
Subjects: LCSH: War on Terrorism, 2001–2009—
Personal narratives. | War on Terrorism, 2001–2009,
in mass media. | Coalition Provisional Authority.
Classification: LCC HV6432 .B375 2017 (print) | LCC
HV6432 (ebook) | DDC 956.7044/31 [B]—dc23
LC record available at https://lccn.loc.gov/2016032572

Set in Lyon Text by John Klopping.

For Sgt. Joseph T. Basile, USMC,
who by example gave me the discipline
to embrace a sense of duty.

—————

For all those, both military and civilian,
who sacrifice to protect America from
terrorism.

—————

For my wife and children.
May they live in an America that
is free and free from fear.

CONTENTS

FOREWORD

AMBASSADOR JOHN R. BOLTON

Those who define today's "conventional wisdom" in Washington would have us believe that the second U.S.-Iraqi war was a failure. So pervasive is this mindset that, as a presidential candidate, even Jeb Bush, former president George W. Bush's own brother, fled in horror from the prospect of defending the 2003 decision to invade Iraq and overthrow Saddam Hussein. And from this conventional wisdom about Iraq, supplemented by cherry-picked data from public-opinion polls, flows the further conventional wisdom that, in the years ahead, the American public will simply not abide similar U.S. national-security policies.

Notwithstanding its pervasiveness, this conventional wisdom about Iraq is wrong. It is wrong in its factual description of what actually happened in Iraq, wrong about the appropriate conclusions to draw from that experience, wrong about American public opinion (and correspondingly wrong about how to shape that opinion), and wrong about the international policies necessary to protect American citizens and interests in a time of growing uncertainty and indeed growing chaos.

This is not to say that mistakes—indeed, serious mistakes—were not made in Iraq both before and after the invasion and overthrow of Saddam Hussein.

Of course there were mistakes, large and small, primarily the assessment of Iraq's capabilities in weapons of mass destruction (WMD). Without rearguing this issue, which has and will fill volumes for years to come, Saddam's WMD threat was not well explained before the invasion. Neither was it understood well, let alone explained well, once the evidence available failed to meet the expectations raised before the conflict. Unfortunately for sensible national-security analysis, the WMD-related errors about Iraq became public contemporaneously with post-invasion mistakes (often only seen in 20/20 hindsight) that came to dominate the ongoing international, mass-media news coverage of events on the ground in Iraq.

What is perhaps most disturbing about today's conventional wisdom is the careless, intellectually sloppy, and often flatly disingenuous way that mistakes made after Saddam's fall have been used to attack the initial policy decision to oust him. In fact, many post-invasion circumstances were neither inevitable nor even reasonably foreseeable before military hostilities began. There is simply no basis in historical causality to assert that everything that happened following the successful removal of Saddam was dictated by the initial decision. To make that point, as the conventional wisdom does, is to contend that the entire course of events in Iraq (and the broader Middle East) flowed solely and unalterably from the 2003 decision to remove Saddam. The conventional wisdom must also posit that, absent the U.S. military action, life in Iraq would have continued essentially unchanged from what it was before 2003. Neither assumption is accurate or even reasonable.

For well or ill, the historical reality is that the U.S. government is good neither at empire-building nor at nation-building. (The government is often not good at nation-building at home either, but that's a debate for a different time.) The notion that some combination of the American political leadership, State and Defense Departments, USAID, and private contractors could re-create a fractured and despoiled country like Iraq was always fanciful. That job was always for the Iraqis themselves. What America did do successfully, up until Barack Obama's catastrophic decision to withdraw all U.S. forces in 2011, was provide a stabilizing and protective presence in Iraq so that Iraqis could make their own decisions. That they made a variety of serious mistakes after decades of crushing authoritarian rule should have surprised no one—except, of course, the mainstream American and international media, which seemed almost willfully determined to misunderstand and misreport what was actually happening in the country after Saddam's overthrow, as Tom Basile compellingly demonstrates in the pages that follow.

No one book, especially a personal memoir, can resolve these complex issues, but *Tough Sell* is a critical contribution to the literature of what actually happened in Iraq and more broadly in the region during the post-invasion years. These kinds of first-person narratives are essential for American decision-makers today and tomorrow to understand the fog of war they will encounter not only on the battlefield but also from the media, especially their own fellow countrymen. It is not a pretty sight. Any U.S. president contemplating a controversial, complex policy decision has to recognize that what the media will report will at best often be only coincidentally related to the reality that U.S. personnel on the ground—civilian and military—themselves experience.

Much of what follows is truly the nitty-gritty of post-conflict communications and media relations, but it must form an essential part of any politico-military strategy. Some will find it completely realistic, others will wonder at the ordinariness of it, but others will ask how anything so bizarre could exist outside of the pages of a novel. That is why *Tough Sell*'s narrative is so important. Until American policymakers and analysts fully understand what it is like out at the tip of the spear, not only in military but also in political terms, there cannot be an adequate appreciation of the consequences of decisions made back in Washington.

Even experienced government hands, including many who were involved in some way in the broader events Tom Basile describes, will learn from this memoir. And let's hope the learning sticks until the next conflict.

ABBREVIATIONS

BIAP   Baghdad International Airport

CAC   City Advisory Council

CJTF7   Combined Joint Task Force 7

CPA   Coalition Provisional Authority

CPIC   Coalition Press Information Center

DAC   District Advisory Council

FSO   Foreign Service Officer

ICDC   Iraqi Civil Defense Corps

ICE   Iraqi Currency Exchange

JOC   Joint Operations Center

KBR   Kellogg, Brown, and Root, a subsidiary of Halliburton

NAC   Neighborhood Advisory Council

NSC   National Security Council

TOUGH SELL

INTRODUCTION

If policymakers do not effectively articulate policy, manage their message strategy, and counter misinformation, they soon will find themselves unable to execute policy. That places America and freedom at great risk.

A ll I could think was that I was going to die. It wasn't the first time, but I really wondered whether this was it as I clutched the bottom of my jump seat with both hands. As the countermeasures deployed, I watched the cargo lift off the deck and felt weightless during the plane's steep plunge toward the earth. I looked over at the lieutenant colonel seated next to me and he was white as a sheet. There was fear in his eyes. We had been fired upon. It all happened so quickly, but that incident stays with me. It remains a stark reminder that no matter what the politicians or headlines say, make no mistake, we are a nation at war.

It is a constant struggle between those who believe that government exists to provide a few with privilege and those who believe it is a mechanism to enhance the freedom of all individuals. It is a fight between those who use power to control absolutely the destinies of millions and those who seek to enhance the right of self-determination. It is a war between those who use ignorance as a tool to produce violence and those who bring the tolerance and empowerment that secure peace.

The current conflict with radicalism in the form of the Islamic State of Iraq and Syria (ISIS), Al-Qaeda, and dozens of other groups is a new world war against a lethal, unconventional enemy called Islamic extremism. No single movement or philosophy in the world today has the aim of killing more Americans, more Westerners, more Jews, more Christians, and certainly more Muslims than Islamic extremism. This

1

conflict wasn't born out of the imagination of a group of "neocons" huddled in the basement of some Washington-based think tank. It's real, and free nations (including the United States) are still fumbling in their efforts to counter the threat.

This global conflict, like all modern warfare, is waged with different resources. Territorial wars fought by militaries and nation-states are evolving into something more dangerous and more complex. For millennia, the causes of war and the strategies associated with it were defined within particular margins, involving a combination of resource and territorial acquisition aimed at the subjugation or oppression of conquered populations. I suggest that, for most people, this paradigm continues to drive perceptions of war. One nation invades another, plants its flag, rapes the land of resources, and controls the population until another nation or the indigenous people eject it.

What we witnessed in the rise of Al-Qaeda during the Clinton administration, and the decision-making of the United States in the aftermath of September 11, 2001 (9/11) during the Bush years was a sharp departure from the usual war-making paradigm. In fact, we are still in a transitional phase regarding the way this country handles both its military and diplomatic strategy to account for this shift.

Gone are the days of the Cold War when mutually assured destruction kept the world in a state of relative stability. Today, we face different enemies around the world who are non-state actors and who call no set of boundaries home. The state aggressors are still there to be sure and, since the 1990s, many have assisted the growing and emboldened Islamic extremist movement through acts of commission and omission.

This more complex paradigm and the rise of pervasive digital media require governments to evolve also in the way they execute and articulate policy. Now more than ever it takes a broad assortment of people with wide-ranging specialties to execute effective wartime strategies. Now more than ever civilians are a critical component of winning a war on the battlefield and here at home. Our heroes in uniform are increasingly dependent on the expertise and sacrifice of civilians. Civilians are playing often unseen roles in the aftermath of conflict in everything from getting the lights back on and the phone lines up to developing new government institutions and furthering democratic reforms. They also play key roles in articulating and defending policy in our age of digital media. Their contribution to the success of our foreign policy objectives diplomatically, politically, and militarily both at home and abroad was felt more distinctly during our engagement in Iraq than in any other mission in history.

It's been more than a decade since the United States–led coalition toppled Saddam Hussein. During those difficult years, we've seen all too clearly that warfare is now more than ever a blend of policy, politics, and the business of journalism. The challenges faced by the coalition were not merely between the terrorists and the U.S. military or insurgents and Iraqi forces. The coalition wasn't merely engaged in a fight to build a more tolerant, participatory society against incredible odds. It was also in a constant clash with forces that affected public perception about the mission. There are those who will dispute the existence and impact of these forces, but they were real and present. Serious, unbiased observers must agree that winning the war at home was vital to the success of the Iraq policy. We also must accept that our government was not sufficiently aggressive in defending its policy or combating that editorial filter. Certainly, anyone who doubts that the Western media utterly failed to present a balanced view of the mission to the detriment of the West's ability to fight terrorism is simply kidding themselves.

If policy makers do not effectively articulate policy, manage their message strategy, and counter misinformation, they soon will find themselves unable to execute policy. That places America and freedom at great risk.

It is vital for us to consider that, regardless of one's views on the Iraq War, we may very well engage in a mission like this again. Our ability to counter terrorism requires our active engagement and that requires our ability to sell and sustain policy. Within the context of this war against Islamic extremism, we will likely be forced to engage in extensive political, social, and economic reform in another country at some future time. That could involve an extended military obligation. It may not. Either way, it is important for us to examine the Iraq War both from an operational and communications standpoint to assist policymakers in the future. Our failure to win the media and communications war in Iraq has, even in just these last few years, adversely affected our response as a nation against ISIS and its affiliates.

This country cannot afford to be timid in the face of threats to its security and the values that keep us free. These pages recall my time as an advisor to the Coalition Provisional Authority (CPA) in Iraq. More than merely being a chronicle about one person, a critique of the media's reporting, and an assessment of the Bush administration's home-front communications strategy, this writing is meant to serve as a tribute to civilians from the United States and other coalition nations who lent their talents to the cause of establishing an Iraq that was free. By way of my own experiences, it is meant to deliver the untold story of these ordinary people who, of their own accord, left the safety of everyday life to do extraordinary things for the Iraqi people. By and large, these men and women who served alongside our heroes in uniform deserve our respect, admiration, and appreciation for the risks they took, the price they paid, and the tireless efforts they made to protect America, the Iraqi people, and the world. Regardless of age or background, they made personal and professional sacrifices, placing themselves in harm's way to help the coalition achieve its goals.

For more than a decade, we've spent an enormous amount of time and energy debating whether we should have invaded Iraq in the first place. The more relevant question for discussion is, "What was the rationale for our policies that guided the aftermath of the initial military operation and led to the creation of the Coalition Provisional Authority?" From there, we need to assess fairly the decisions of those first fourteen months.

Once the decision was made to invade Iraq, we had three primary choices in terms of the direction of our policy in the aftermath. The United States and the coalition had three options:

1. Remove Saddam and simply leave the country. I believe that was a false choice;
2. Remove the leadership, then grab some general or expatriate and impose him as a new leader with absolute power—simply

replacing one tyrant for another. The moral or political argument fails there as well; or

3. Attempt to secure the country and build institutions that could support not what some have suggested was the goal—an American-style democracy—but rather a participatory, pluralistic, and tolerant government.

The Coalition Provisional Authority in Iraq was developed to execute option three. This historic gathering of now often-maligned civilian and military personnel had the responsibility to establish a security and political framework that would accomplish this goal working together with the Iraqi population. The CPA and its advisors tackled this extraordinary task with great passion and commitment. They sacrificed much and their efforts went unnoticed as the security situation worsened due to the rise of Al-Qaeda in Iraq and sectarian violence. The challenge was compounded by a failure to effectively counter media and political opposition on the home front.

This book isn't meant to serve as a justification of the Iraq War or to delve into a lengthy defense of the complex decision-making process that led to the invasion. However, it has been suggested that invading Iraq was not justified because no direct link was proven between Saddam's regime and the 9/11 attacks. The War on Terrorism is not about 9/11. That tragedy should have served as a catalyst for change in the way we deal with the gathering threat of hate directed by the likes of Al-Qaeda and now ISIS and its affiliates. It was supposed to change the way we fight and deter this modern enemy. Suggesting, as many critics have, that the War on Terrorism is about 9/11 and, therefore, only about Al-Qaeda would be like claiming that World War II was only about Pearl Harbor. Of course, no one would agree today that our actions in the larger conflict should have been governed by the events of a single day.

When it came to the War on Terrorism (of which Iraq became a central front), the Bush White House was faced with the challenge of handling both the traditional territorial and institutional impacts of war. These were namely that external forces such as terror groups were embedding in and influencing the governments of state actors—along with the viral nature of the radical Islamist terrorist movement and the exploitation by governments of the new global paradigm that emerged after the end of the Cold War.

President Bush believed that addressing the freedom deficit in the Middle East and in countries that serve as incubators for these groups—however long-term and complex that strategy might be—was essential. He believed it was an avenue toward ensuring a more peaceful world and furthering international cooperation to interdict terrorist networks. He also understood that it was necessary to employ a policy of active deterrence not only with respect to countering terror groups but also regarding the nation-states who support them. Iraq became part of the War on Terrorism and part of a larger effort of active deterrence.

Where the Iraq strategy fell short was how to fight and manage all of the various components simultaneously while maintaining public support at home. This mission was not the ejection of one state power from within the borders of another, or protecting territorial integrity. The mission became the fighting of a foreign insurgency and former regime elements while attempting to rebuild physical infrastructure and new government institutions. The administration also had to attempt to prevent other state actors like Iran from exploiting regional instability and supporting the efforts of the terrorist enemy. Of course, there was a media war to be fought as well.

The manpower issues that plagued the Iraq mission early on were real. For our part, nearly every civilian and military liaison I worked with—from Ambassador L. Paul Bremer on down—agreed from the outset that we needed an increase in the number of troops on the ground to accomplish the mission. Despite poor intelligence regarding the state of the Iraqi infrastructure, the mass looting, and a lack of indigenous security forces, the Iraq mission realized a range of successes often not sufficiently promoted by the Bush administration and frequently ignored by the media.

As we look back, many issues can be analyzed and debated, and, certainly, lessons can be learned. A few things are certain that must inform our thinking: The world has changed. The challenges we face have changed. Yet giving people a chance to be free and self-govern is the surest way to a greater peace.

We are a nation at war. Unlike wars of the past, this War on Terrorism will require the service of a broader range of participants. Among them are our neighbors, coworkers, friends, and relatives—people who don't wear the uniform but who nonetheless will be driven to fight with their minds, their passions, their experience, and their talents. Their boot camp is the battlefront, their bullets their expertise, their uniform their convictions. Through the successes and failures of the Iraq mission, history should record the unbending purpose of many a coalition civilian as a triumph of spirit and sacrifice. I hope it will.

PARACHUTING

These tired young men and women in uniform, sweating in the sun, knew so much more than I did about war, about Iraq, and about the challenges that were waiting a short plane ride away.

New York City is one of those places where things happen. It's what makes it one of the greatest places on earth. The city bustles around you at a fever pitch and, at the end of the long days of playing whatever game dominates your life, you feel a sense of triumph just for being part of the greatness of the city. Every once in a while, the influencers of Gotham manage to drag themselves away from their offices on a weeknight, put on black tie, and pause to reflect. On this particular night in June 2007, the Economic Club of New York was holding its Centennial Gala, celebrating a hundred years of contributing to American discourse on economic and foreign policy. The three-story ballroom at the fabled Waldorf-Astoria was aglow, as much from the candles and chandeliers as from the sparkling elite of New York's financial powerhouses. The gathering storm of the coming economic collapse didn't appear to be on anyone's mind. Hollywood has the Oscars. Washington has the Alfalfa Club and the Gridiron dinners. Although many prestigious functions of note happen every year in the Big Apple, the Economic Club of New York is clearly one of the oldest and most venerable institutions for the wealthy and successful—not that I claim to be either. I was the guest of a client. Alan Greenspan, Pete Peterson, John Whitehead, and Harold Burson were there. So were the likes of John Hennessy and Bill McDonough. The guest list read like the pages of the *Wall Street Journal* and the *Financial Times*. In fact, Paul Gigot was on the dais. As I sat there at table thirty-five with bunch of private equity and venture capital folks, talk of Iraq swirled around. I couldn't help but think that the scene was about as far from the Middle East as you could get while still being on this planet.

About a half hour into the program, former commerce secretary Barbara Hackman Franklin introduced the keynote speaker. Interestingly, it was not some economist, captain of industry, or Wall Street financial wizard but a political scientist. Secretary of State Condoleezza Rice stepped up to the ostentatious cherrywood podium and gave her best analysis of where we'd been, where we were, and where we were going as a nation. As she spoke in her characteristically even and amiable tone, the audience began to listen intently, momentarily forgetting their marinated baby artichoke tarts and parmesan herb salads. Rice spoke of what she called American Realism as "an approach to the world that arises not only from the realities of global politics, but from the nature of America's character." She said,

> America has always been, and will always be, not a status quo power, but a revolutionary power—a nation with New World eyes, that looks at change not as a threat to be feared, but as an opportunity to be seized.

She continued with a refreshing simplicity of word to say that "American Realism deals with the world as it is, but strives to make the world better than it is: more free, more just, more peaceful, more prosperous, and ultimately safer."

She did what she could to inform and impress, extolling some little-known facts about the Bush administration's foreign aid record. She reminded everyone that in 1946 the question on everyone's minds was not "Would communism be stopped in Eastern Europe?" but "Would Western Europe survive communism's advance?" After all, the communists won 48 percent of the vote in Italy and 46 percent of the vote in France just after World War II. More than two million people were starving in postwar Europe because of failed reconstruction programs. In the late 1940s, the Turks were embroiled in civil conflict, and Greece had erupted in civil war. The years that followed the Nazis' defeat saw post–World War II Germany permanently divided, Czechoslovakia fall to a communist coup, the Soviet Union explode a nuclear weapon five years ahead of schedule, and the Chinese embark on communist revolution. "Few would have thought," she said, "that freedom was on the march in those days," but because our decision-makers "kept faith with our highest principles, supported them with national power, kept their optimism, and practiced a brand of distinctly American Realism," we defeated a great collective threat to freedom. The comparisons to the War on Terrorism were straightforward and direct for the sophisticated audience.

The speech was striking. It was striking not because I hadn't heard the pitch before or didn't know the facts she offered but because I suspected that few of the influencers in the room, let alone the general public, knew them. *How many of these folks*, I thought, *actually know that between 2001 and 2007 the United States nearly tripled foreign assistance worldwide and quadrupled aid for sub-Saharan Africa? Do people realize that over the past four years this nation dedicated $1.2 billion to fight malaria and $30 billion to fight AIDS, the largest effort by one nation in history to fight a single disease? Did they realize that the Bush administration was working to interdict terrorism in more than 160 countries around the world with unprecedented cooperation from other governments?*

To my mind, her remarks underscored the critical knowledge gap that represents one of the most significant problems faced by the United States' Iraq policy and American foreign policy generally. There is a public diplomacy crisis to be sure. America's good work gains little attention overseas in comparison to persistent criticism leveled by liberal activists, the press, and foreign governments. Yet, much more significantly, the knowledge gap has also reached crisis levels in the United States among Americans.

The War in Iraq had proven to be the front line not just in the War on Terrorism but also in a struggle to articulate and defend American policy on the home front. At its core, the issues were bigger than George W. Bush and his administration. They are not about Republicans or Democrats. The crisis of effective communication is about the future ability of the United States in its role as the world's preeminent force to craft, sustain, and defend a foreign policy that will keep us safe. The future of American hegemony is directly related to the capacity of policymakers to articulate and win the battle for public opinion, particularly here at home.

Watching the historic events of the first decade of the twenty-first century living in Washington and New York, I have often thought of how Harry Truman met with Franklin D. Roosevelt only twice before the presidency was thrust upon him in 1945. The man from Kansas had become the vice presidential nominee at the Democratic National Convention the year earlier, not because of his relationship with FDR or for that matter his leadership ability but because of one of those backroom deals that just happen in presidential electoral politics. History records that it even took a phone call from FDR himself to convince Truman to join the ticket. Yet there he was in 1945, president of the United States during World War II, having only met with Roosevelt once subsequent to the inauguration and bearing on his shoulders the decisions that could decide the fate of the world. Truman was a visionary and performed well under very difficult circumstances, but there is little doubt that in many ways he was wholly unprepared for the job when he took office. That's the way Washington works. In many ways, that's the way history is made: unsuspecting, often unprepared people being thrust into extraordinary circumstances and forced to prove their mettle by rising to the challenge.

That's the way it was for so many American civilians who came to be part of the Iraq mission. It was certainly much the way I became an advisor to the Coalition Provisional Authority and, consequently, the fight to effectively articulate policy in the age of the new, digital media. I'm not comparing myself to Truman or anybody who made such a substantial contribution to history. Yet, again, it's Washington and it works all the same way, whether you're a White House intern, a political staffer at a federal agency, a press secretary on Capitol Hill, or the president of the United States. I've come to learn that there is a certain formula to getting a job in our nation's capital, most of it having to do with luck and circumstance. In fact, it's really safe to say that in Washington, advancement is based primarily on who you know, luck, and then (a distant third) what you know. To be sure, I must have done something right in my career, but clearly I was in the right place at the right time. I am thankful for it. I always will be. History is replete with examples of someone in that odd, obsessed little town on the Potomac being propelled into the middle of historic events by death, resignation, scandal, knowing the right person, or just being in the right place at the right time.

On a hot and muggy late morning in July 2003—the kind of morning that makes your shirt stick to your body from the humidity—I was sitting in my office at the Environmental Protection Agency on Pennsylvania Avenue when I received an unexpected phone call. My assistant, Tracy, came into the office and told me with a wry smile and a roll of her eyes that somebody was on the phone claiming to be calling from Iraq. Though she often thought that I was a little uptight about things, like insisting that my staff show up to work on time, Tracy had a good sense of humor. She liked to smile and loved to laugh, especially at my expense. I thought maybe she was being sarcastic. Like any rational human being in the midst of a busy day, I thought I was about to be the victim of a practical joke. *Perhaps it is one of my old buddies from college*, I thought, *checking in with their phantom friend who had abandoned them for the Washington game*. I was late for lunch with a former colleague of mine from the White House. I told her to take a message, and I went on my way.

As I walked past the lush green North Lawn of the White House in the heat, I slowed a bit, as I usually did, to peer through the high iron fence and the sprinklers showering the grass with a cool spray. Standing on the sidewalk in the midst of the usual flock of tourists taking photographs, I happened upon someone I knew from the Office of Presidential Personnel. Upon seeing me, he gave me a rather strange look. Of course, I asked why the reaction, to which he replied, "I didn't think you were still here." I pressed him for an explanation, but he didn't elaborate. His comment concerned me. After all, I was a political appointee, and his office was responsible for my continued employment. I decided to at least temporarily shrug it off and continued my brisk walk through the typical thick air of a Washington summer day. At the restaurant, I met up with Greg Jenkins, who at that time was director of the Office of Presidential Advance, and somebody whom I worked with during the 2000 presidential campaign. Greg had returned several months earlier from a tour of duty in Afghanistan working for the White House communications operation during Operation Enduring Freedom. He made several trips to Afghanistan to help coordinate the international media and message development about the progress of the war against the Taliban and Al-Qaeda following the 9/11 terrorist attacks. Upon his return, he accepted the job as director of advance (which took him out of the game, so to speak) on the administration's message development and communications planning for the Global War on Terrorism.

During lunch, we talked extensively about his experience in Afghanistan, and I happened to mention the phone call that I received just before coming to meet him. He noted that the White House and the Defense Department were building a staff for Ambassador Bremer, who had recently taken over as administrator of the Coalition Provisional Authority. Over his sandwich and my salad, he posed the question, "What if they ask you to go?" To which I of course responded, "I don't know," not thinking for an instant that it was actually an option. Besides, leaving my job and being deployed over to a war zone for an indeterminate amount of time would be a major life change and a substantial risk. It would be enough of a risk to give anyone pause. He said essentially, "If they offer you something and you don't take it, you're crazy."

I returned to the office a few blocks away, hauling my body through the midday sauna, to find that Tracy had vanished and a new voicemail was waiting from this mysterious person from Baghdad. The female caller, in a rather firm voice with a German or perhaps Austrian accent, said that they had a request for me to join the communications team that Ambassador Bremer was assembling in Baghdad. She also pointed out that when "they" called, "they" expected the phone call to be returned. "They" turned out to be Special Assistant to the President Katja Bullock from the office of Presidential Personnel at the White House, who had been asked to help staff the CPA. "They" apparently needed an answer quickly. I needed to sit down.

For several months, I had been looking for a new challenge in my life. Since the inception of the Bush administration in January 2001, I had been working at the Environmental Protection Agency under former New Jersey governor Christine Todd Whitman. I had been frustrated at the agency for quite some time and found myself increasingly butting heads with several members of the senior staff who, in my opinion, failed to promote aggressively the president's agenda. I saw promoting the president's agenda as my job after all. We simply weren't articulating the positive achievements of the Bush administration on the environment, most notably sharp increases in funding to clean up thousands of toxic sites, historic diesel fuel regulations, and other clean-air proposals.

No, I'm not kidding. Environmental groups expected Bush to do everything short of shutting the agency down after he took office. Of course, the programs, the research, and the work went on. Surprisingly, they were actually accomplishing some important things on the environment. It was just that nobody was listening. The environmental lobby, the Democrats, and the media of course had long before made up their minds that the "oilman from Texas" was going to be a mockery of an environmental leader. I'm not saying his agenda was very ambitious, but there was certainly more going on than people realized. After all, Bush even proposed a historic reduction in greenhouse gases that the Democrats killed because they didn't want him getting the credit and because the regulations were not draconian enough for their taste. Bush environmentalism was a hard sell to say the least.

You're probably not going to buy it either. Suffice it to say, for a number of reasons, the agency was a frustrating place to work.

I appreciated the opportunity to work for Whitman, who was a dynamic leader with an impressive ability to grasp numerous and difficult policy concepts. As a New Yorker, I had followed her career closely and, when the Bush transition team asked me to join her staff, I jumped at the opportunity. Most of the folks coming off the campaign wanted to work anywhere but the EPA (for obvious reasons), and I actually ended up being one of the only appointees at the agency who previously had a full-time commitment to the president's campaign. For two years, I served as director of the Office of Communications for the agency and then later supervised the public liaison team within the administrator's office. It had been difficult working with some of the "politicals" whom I felt were not playing on the White House's team. When Whitman finally announced her resignation in June of 2003, I definitely knew it was time to leave.

Some opportunities had come my way in the months preceding that phone call from Baghdad, but nothing really sparked my interest. It was July, and I was getting impatient, as I often am about the progress of my career. A couple of months earlier, Brian McCormack, a colleague of mine from the 2000 presidential campaign, and I had a few drinks at Shelley's Backroom, a bar near the Treasury Department that was frequented by White House and administration staffers. Actually, he had a beer and I had a Coke as we sat in the back of the dimly lit, smoke-filled cigar bar. We talked about his preparations to go over to work for Bremer, who at that time was about to take charge of the coalition's effort in Baghdad. Brian had served as the personal aide to Vice President Cheney since the inauguration in 2001. He too was looking forward to a change, a challenge and the opportunity to broaden his horizons.

I remember sitting there at the bar conveying my frustrations to him about the EPA and we both reminisced about the 2000 campaign and the Republican National Convention in Philadelphia, where we had worked together, he on the Cheney side and I on the Bush side of the operation. I wished him luck and we went our separate ways, he to Baghdad and I back on the hunt for what might come next. *What an exciting opportunity*, I thought as the adventurous part of my brain perked up. *How amazing.* I admit I was a little envious.

Around Independence Day, I attended a birthday party for my friend Marty Molloy, who at the time was living in California with his wife, Meredith. Marty is a good friend and, despite his politics, a good soul. Friends of ours often joke about the "lost causes" he has involved himself with over the years. All kidding aside, he has done a great deal of good work helping those in need. A big heart gets you far in my book—even if, as in his case, you happen to be a borderline socialist. He and I both see ourselves as people who want to make a difference. That vision we share is a big part of the bond we have as friends. A number of us who went to college together were at the birthday barbecue in Maryland on the same sprawling lawn where Marty and his wife had been married the weekend before 9/11. We reminisced about a time long gone in our lives over the grill filled with hamburgers, hot dogs, and chicken. It was your typical college reunion scene filled with talk of who's getting married, who's had a baby, who's changed jobs, and the usual catching up that old friends do after having been apart for too long. As the evening drew on, Marty and I stood in his in-laws' kitchen and talked about the future. He and I often talked about the future. Marty, perpetually frustrated at work, was thinking of coming back to the East Coast. I told him it was time for me to move on as well, but I wasn't sure to where. As the conversation went on, I told him I had this feeling that I was going to be given an extraordinary opportunity—one that would change my life both professionally and personally. I had this deep-seated belief that something meaningful would come along, which only added to my frustration about the professional stagnation I continued to experience.

When the phone call came in from Baghdad a week later, I knew I'd been right. Now I didn't know what to do. That night, I turned on the TV to watch the coverage of what was happening in the aftermath of major combat operations in Iraq. I considered what it would be like to live and work in that environment. I believed that, given the intelligence, going to war in Iraq was the right thing to do. I obviously supported the policy, not just because I was a member of the Bush administration but also because the president's vision made sense to me. Addressing the freedom deficit in the Middle East was something that we needed to do as a nation to defeat the terrorists that continue to plot against free people of the world. Yes, I "drank the cool-aid," so to speak, on the administration's line, but I have always been a big believer that the expansion of freedom and participatory, pluralistic societies helps create security and stability.

My being a New Yorker, 9/11 hit home, and this new conflict seemed real and very personal right from its inception. Not because I ever envisioned that I would be living and working in Iraq but because I had a cousin my age in U.S. Army who was stationed in the Middle East. The night that major combat operations began, I was on the phone with his father, my cousin John. Neither one of us knew exactly where his son John was, or what his duties entailed, but we knew that he was potentially in harm's way. Throughout the war, not a day went by when I didn't stop and pray for John and the other men and women in uniform who were freeing the twenty-seven million people of Iraq.

More than that, however, we as a nation were pursuing a strategy that I believed could help strike to the core of the terrorists' ability to recruit, train, and kill.

As it turns out, unbeknownst to me, several people in the Bush administration knew about my deployment before I did. Folks at the White House and Pentagon, some of whom I saw regularly, had put my name forward for consideration in the early days after Bremer's arrival in Iraq. I assume that it was also helped by my interest in being deployed to Qatar earlier that year. During the war, the White House was looking for someone to serve as a press aide at Central Command. I sent my resume over, but the job went to someone else. On the day of that first phone call from Baghdad, I was still surprised, although apparently nobody else was.

I had a decision to make. Whenever I have a decision to make, I usually pick up the phone and call my old friend Conrad Eberstein. Conrad is a former Democrat political fundraiser and mentor of mine back in New York. I knew in my gut what to do. I knew that I had to take the job. I knew that this was the opportunity I had been waiting for. I just needed somebody to confirm it. Conrad was always good for telling me to stop overanalyzing and accept the decision that I had already made before I placed the phone call to him. Everybody needs someone to put things in perspective for them every now and then. People often overanalyze life decisions. What they don't realize is that they often come to a decision the moment the options are presented and are just too scared to take the risk or make the changes necessary to capitalize on those opportunities. In the end, I believe one should always go with one's gut instinct. It's typically the first, and typically correct.

I also managed to call Brian, now nearly two months into his tour of duty in Baghdad. After a few questions about security and living conditions, I asked him to sum it up for me in one sentence. He replied, "It's like the campaign on crack." Brian knew I would understand what he meant. We were both veterans of the long days of the 2000 presidential campaign and subsequent Florida recount. We had both pulled the all-nighters and gone months without a break to help play our small roles in executing a successful presidential campaign. It was exhausting and exhilarating all at once. Most of all, we were working to achieve something historic—electing a president of the United States. For anyone involved in such an undertaking, be they Democrat or Republican, it is a thrill to play a small part in making history. Iraq too would run the spectrum of emotions. Iraq too would be to live and work as part of a truly historic purpose.

Now I realize that, right off the bat here, it appears I'm fueling the fire of a popular criticism of the Iraq mission: that those of us who served in the Green Zone were nothing more than a bunch of neoconservative political hacks who were unqualified, unfocused, and unprepared. I will get into this issue more later on, but let me state for good measure at this point that the critics' archetype for the ideal CPA staffer simply didn't exist. The model wasn't grounded in reality. It would have been great if everyone spoke Arabic. It would have been terrific if everyone had some experience working in Iraq or in the region. It would have been beneficial if the most prominent people from a wide range of fields had simply dropped their lives and boarded C-5 transport planes to Baghdad. It would have been fantastic if every CPA staffer had previously participated in a large-scale democratization and reconstruction project in a country with deep religious divides that had been under authoritarian rule for three decades.

Many of those who came close to the critics' model in fact served with the CPA in some fashion. To be sure, their numbers were far fewer than what was required to execute such a broad mission. They didn't exist by the thousands.

As it turns out, making the decision to go overseas was the easy part. The first real challenge was going to be explaining the move to my family and friends. I had to explain to my loved ones that I was going to live and work voluntarily in one of the most dangerous places on earth. I've done some crazy things in the past, but my family always understood. They understood when I left law school to travel full time on a presidential campaign. They understood when I came home one evening and told them I was going to be the youngest candidate in history to run for supervisor of our town. They understood when I told them that, at seventeen, I was going to fight my way onto the school board, while still in high school. *Would they understand that, within ten days, I was going to be living in a combat zone?*

The first question I had to anticipate and prepare for was the inevitable, "When will you be coming home?" I had no idea. In fact, most of the civilians who went over to Iraq didn't have a God's honest clue. If you were going to commit to work for the CPA, you didn't ask a lot of questions or set timelines or conditions. What the White House, Pentagon, and coalition needed were people who were willing to get over there and do whatever it took to help accomplish the mission. They needed people to parachute in and get to work. The term "parachute" was a legitimate term of art that the human resources folks in Baghdad were using as they worked around the clock to staff the CPA. I just assumed they'd feed me and house me somewhere and I would work out my return according to the needs of the organization and my specific duties. The only thing I did know was that I was going to be working in the Strategic Communications Office, although there was also some talk of me going to work with the Governance Team, specifically to handle the communications effort for a possible Iraqi Constitutional Convention.

From some conversations that I had with a good friend already overseas and the personnel folks in Baghdad, I came up with the concept of telling people that it could be as little as two months. I knew that it would probably be longer, but I also knew that this was a chance a lifetime that I couldn't pass up. Okay, so maybe I obfuscated the truth a little. I certainly didn't want to go off to Iraq with the people that I care about feeling that I was being inconsiderate of them or being reckless with my own life. Like I said though, this was an opportunity of a lifetime and there was a genuine need. Once I had decided to go, I placed the first call to my brother, Joseph, who was understandably concerned. He probably thought I was nuts, but he was nonetheless and surprisingly supportive, perhaps because he could hear in my voice that this was a challenge I wanted to take. Whatever the reason, it was nice to have him on my side, as I knew I would need his support to get my mother through what would certainly be a difficult time.

When you're single without kids, as I was at the time, your mother, especially if she's an Italian mother, is naturally the person who requires the most attention at times like these. Needless to say, she had a much different reaction than my brother. Who could blame her? My father had died when I was a kid, and her entire existence from that moment forward revolved around making sure her two boys grew up in an environment where they could achieve their goals. Now, I had told her essentially that I was going to risk my future, my very existence, for a mission that neither she nor many Americans fully understood or endorsed. It didn't go over well. After a cooling off period, she came to realize that I had made up my mind and, as my departure rapidly grew closer, she put on a brave face. Of course, she didn't know that the two months would become seven.

Naturally, you couldn't just pick up, get on a plane, and go to Iraq. For civilians, especially, there is a need for preparation. Certainly, the government wasn't going to send civilians with no training or preparation over to a combat zone? It seemed a logical assumption. I was a political appointee to the Bush administration who went to work in a suit in an office three blocks from the White House. I grew up in one of the safest suburban neighborhoods in the country, just outside New York City. The closest thing I'd seen to a war zone was being in the middle of a massive union protest during one of Bush's 2000 campaign events in Pittsburgh. Despite the logical need for some training, the CPA intended for me to be on the ground in Kuwait awaiting transportation to Baghdad within only ten days. My preparation and adjustment period was going to be, to say the least, abbreviated—very abbreviated.

About a week before I departed, after having cleaned out my office at the EPA and filled out a mound of paperwork at the Pentagon, I reported to "training" at Fort Belvoir, just south of Washington. I put the word training in quotation marks for a reason. This wasn't as much a training program as it was more equipment distribution and a medical screening. I thought I was going to get weapons instruction and a rundown of techniques that would be useful in situations where my safety was in jeopardy. What I got was a bunch of shots, a set of desert camouflage gear (DCUs), a sleeping bag, mosquito netting, a pair of desert boots, a flak vest, a Kevlar helmet, and a hearty "Good luck!"

I really think that the first time it hit me that I was actually going was when I looked in the mirror after trying on my gear in a cramped little dressing room with a torn green curtain in the cavernous equipment warehouse at Fort Belvoir. The person staring back at me wasn't wearing that Italian suit but was in full desert military dress, minus the M-16 or anything that could result in injury to me or anyone else. Of course, they didn't point out that the flak vest—which was issued without armor plating I might add—could only stop 9 mm rounds. In Iraq, I would later learn, almost anyone who wanted to shoot you used an AK-47 that fired its 7.62 mm rounds at higher velocity. If you got hit without plates, you were screwed.

We did actually get trained on how to use our gas masks in the event of a chemical attack. Needless to say, they would never be used. The staff at the post also distributed a variety of chemical and biological weapons antidotes in a series of injectors, neatly conveyed in an unmarked brown paper bag. The training session for the antidotes went something like this:

> ME: "How do I use these?"
> NURSE: "Read the directions."
> ME: "But when should I . . ."
> NURSE: "Someone will tell you."
> ME: "Before or after I'm dead?"

The only instruction that I was actually given was not to sleep with the injectors under my pillow. It turns out some young enlisted soldier had recently stuck himself in the head accidentally. Apparently, that's not a good thing. I never did find out what happened to the poor kid.

I took my not-so-bulletproof vest and brown paper bag filled with chemicals that I knew nothing about and found my way over to the medical facility for my physical and shots. Truthfully, I had been more nervous about the medical exam and the shots than actually being deployed. I hadn't seen a doctor for years—twelve to be precise—and I promptly informed the nurse that I was a bit of a chicken when it came to needles. After looking at me with an expression that said clearly, "What a pain in the ass," she had me lie down. She took a couple of vials of blood, I promptly turned white as a sheet and began to lose all feeling in my fingertips and legs. They rushed me to the emergency room, where I sat in a wheelchair drinking orange juice for about fifteen minutes before they let me leave to continue my "training." Yes, very embarrassing. But wait, there's more.

Then it was time for the shots. Joy. I was determined to take it like a man. I had to. In less than a week, I was going to be in Iraq. If I couldn't take a few of shots, how could I survive Baghdad? I strode confidently into the room and kept my cool, as the nurse stuck me four times in my right arm. Not bad, I thought. It didn't hurt at all. I was waiting for my smallpox vaccination when the medic asked me how I felt. I looked over him, nodded, and muttered something unintelligible and collapsed. The next thing I knew I was flat on my back on the cold and unfortunately hard linoleum floor, staring at a fluorescent light. It took over two hours, several Twinkies, and a bottle of Coke—not to mention the patience of several medical personnel—to get my heart rate and blood pressure to the point where they could get me up off the floor. At least it got me out of the anthrax and smallpox shots.

The medics were fantastic. *Embarrassing!* I kept thinking as I was lying there. They must be really concerned that the government was sending these soft civilians over there to help take charge of the mission. Just before I deployed, I brought each of them a gift from the White House. They deserved it. I'm a terrible patient.

As I prepared to leave, I also had to think about the possibility that I wouldn't be coming back. Much like members of the military and the other civilians who went before me and since, I began taking stock of my life, and while I didn't want to dwell on the possibility that I could get killed over there, it was certainly on my mind. Perhaps it was a bit melodramatic, but I sat down and wrote a will, laying out the distribution of my estate. This is not to say I had that much, but I wanted to make sure certain people had something to remember me by. It wasn't a validly executed will, but more like a guide for friends and family, detailing what items I wanted given to which people, and a rather long list of preferences for funeral arrangements. The document, which I sent to my very good friend and fellow lawyer Chris Caruso, contained everything from the music I wanted played at the church service to certain gifts I wanted made in memoriam to my law school and other organizations.

You think I'm being overdramatic, I know, but civilians didn't prepare mentally and physically for deployment the way members of the military are trained to do. As time wore on, there were folks attached to the CPA who would pay the ultimate price for the mission. So yes, it was a bit morbid and melodramatic, but I felt it was necessary.

It also made me think about all the service men and women who have left families behind. If they were reservists, they left their businesses, professions, and entirely separate careers as well. These people go off to defend us and those they've never met, not knowing whether the next time they go home it will be to their loved ones or into the waiting arms of God. I would be joining them soon. This was a dramatic moment. It was one of introspection. It was a time when I realized just how much of a sacrifice people were making to fight our very real War on Terrorism and defend freedom.

A couple of days before my departure, I found myself getting anxious. I paced around my townhouse in Alexandria wearing down the carpet. I just wanted to leave. The more I tooled around town saying goodbye to people, the more nervous I got. Yet, when you are in a situation like that, you have to prepare. I spent a day with my lifelong friend Brian Walsh. Brian and I grew up together in New York, but he had moved to Washington after graduating from college. We'd known each other since we started first grade and I consider him to be like a brother. He's one of those people you couldn't imagine your life without. When I was growing up, I spent a great deal of time with Brian and his family when my father was fighting cancer. The Walsh house was a kind of escape for me as a child, away from the harsh reality of a home that was filled with the kind of uncertainty and emotional upheaval no kid should have to experience. We were close then and remain so. As a friend, he had always been there for me and I for him. On this occasion, however, I would ask him to be there—if I suddenly wasn't.

We were visiting his brother Kevin who not long ago had moved with his wife to Maryland. Kevin was a recent Harvard Law graduate and his wife was a resident at Johns Hopkins Medical. They were expecting their first child and just bought a nice little Cape Cod with a white picket fence. It was the kind of house we always pictured Kevin buying—conservative, understated, and as American as baseball and apple pie. We had a nice time. They pinged me with questions that I couldn't answer about the environment that I was about to enter. I reminisced with them about the simpler days of life when we played together as kids in the woods behind the Walsh home in the Hudson Valley.

The evening grew late and Brian walked me to my car. I almost couldn't get the words out, but I grabbed the shoulder of my oldest friend and asked him for his strength and his help should anything happen to me over there. Looking at his face, I think he realized for the first time, that there was a chance that this might be the last time we saw each other. Brian isn't one for expressing himself, unless he has a few beers in him, but I knew as I hugged him that he would help in any way he could. As I drove home, I thought about his reaction and began to grasp just how much my going over there was going to affect the people I cared about here at home. I wasn't even thinking about how the media coverage of relentless carnage would affect them. It wasn't much of an issue at the time. The odds were clearly in my favor that I would be fine. The operation had produced the lowest number of casualties of any military operation of its size in history. This remained so even after the violence began to escalate following my arrival, continuing for years afterward. I also was going to be in the coalition headquarters compound and better protected than our soldiers or even many other coalition civilians working in the field.

Little did I know that, as I arrived in Baghdad, the security situation would worsen and the need for more troops would become painfully apparent. Little did I know that those realities would be amplified by a news media that would all but give up giving an accurate account of the Iraq mission and an administration that would falter in the defense of its own policy.

Just before I left, my mother, Jo Ann, my brother, Joseph, and my friends Chris Caruso, David Berez, David Goldstein, Ken Winkelman, and Jared Kindestin all came by the house to send me off. Colleagues from the White House Brad Blakeman, Andrew Ciafardini, and Jason Recher also took time to say goodbye in their own ways. People stopped in, helped me pack, and just spent some time.

Speaking of packing, when you accepted a job with the CPA, the Pentagon provided you with a packing list of recommended items to bring when being deployed to Iraq. When I left the States for the Middle East, I had an entire suitcase filled with toiletries unavailable at the time in Baghdad, including boxes of baby wipes, bug spray, hand sanitizer, and tissues. I also had about thirty pairs of tube socks for my boots. I didn't know this until then, but apparently when it is 125 degrees your feet sweat and swell so much that you go through socks like crazy. Now, if you are a member of the military reading this, you're thinking, "big deal." You have to remember, for me and many others like me, the week before this I was buying ties and dress shirts at Nordstrom, not foot powder and baby wipes in bulk at Target. When it was all zipped up and ready for the airport, the luggage amounted to one large army-issued duffle bag, three suitcases ranging in size from thirty inches to twenty-two inches, and two shoulder-carry bags.

Finally, it was time to join history in progress over in Iraq and, I hoped, play some small role that would help achieve the mission's goals. As I waited in line at the ticket counter at Dulles International, I peered through the windows of the terminal at the American flag waving proudly in the breeze and wondered about all that I might see, all that I might do, before I again saw the Stars and Stripes on my native soil. It remains the only time that I have ever been content to stand in a stalled line at the airport.

After two uneventful commercial flights, I landed in Kuwait City and took a cab to the Kuwait Hilton, the home base for civilians heading to Baghdad. It was one night in a resort on the Persian Gulf before you left what Americans consider "civilization" behind. The villas were run by Kellogg, Brown, and Root (KBR), a subsidiary of Halliburton that held the U.S. government contract to provide pretty much everything you could think of to sustain the massive deployment of people and resources to Iraq. From the very beginning, Halliburton and KBR have been roundly criticized for their performance and their price tag. There was waste to be sure. Yet, the Bush administration came under fire almost immediately for awarding them the contracts in the first place. At the outset here, it is important to mention two things. First, Halliburton and KBR weren't perfect and had their problems. Second, there simply is no American company, and arguably no other company in the world, that can provide the range of services that Halliburton offers for a mission of this scope and conforming to the tight timetable required. It is an indisputable fact that the critics cannot refute and they have never offered a viable alternative. Had the Federal government gone through the usual bidding process for everything or awarded multiple contracts to multiple vendors who would have then have had to coordinate their activities between each other, supplies would have taken months to arrive, and more importantly, it would have cost American lives. I've often wondered whether the critics of Halliburton thought about it in those terms. I also wondered whether they would have preferred the money go to a foreign firm.

On my first full day in the region, I awoke to the bright blue of the Persian Gulf outside my window and a warm breeze flowing through the villa from the beach just beyond my patio. The ceramic tile floor cooled the soles of my feet as I walked over to the window and stood looking out at the palm trees and the oilrigs in the distance. I spent the day eating well, walking on the beach, and swimming in the warm waters of the gulf. It was a time to reflect and wonder. It was a time to relax before the work ahead. It was the calm before the storm.

The following morning, I woke up early, gathered my bags, and jumped on the shuttle bus to the military side of the Kuwait Airport. When we arrived, the small group that I was traveling with left our luggage next to the ramp in the area where they loaded the pallets onto the planes. I was worried that the contents of my baggage, especially all those toiletries, might melt, as it was well over 120 degrees on the tarmac. I sat on my suitcase in the blazing sun for a moment before walking over to the small building that served as the military air terminal. It was then that I caught sight of something that brought home the fact that I would soon be in a war zone: soldiers—a lot of them. They were wearing their DCUs and sleeping on the ground. Some were propped up against the pillars of the overhang just outside the terminal, their green duffle bags piled high on pallets nearby. They looked hot and exhausted. I later learned that they were thankfully heading home. I caught myself just staring at them. I guess I was a little in awe and rightly so. I was curious and even a little envious. I wondered about their experiences. *Had they seen combat? Did they lose anyone? How were they dealing with being away from home? Were they in the desert, a village, or a city?* These tired young men and women, sweating in the sun, knew so much more than I did about war, about Iraq, and about the challenges that were waiting a short plane ride away. As a group, we more political civilians might have represented the Bush administration, but we clearly knew little of the sheer depth of despair and dysfunction that awaited us in the "liberated" Iraq. We sure could have learned a lot from these brave Americans. Indeed we did as we groped our way together through this extraordinary mission.

After about three hours of waiting in the heat, I finally boarded a brutish, gray C-130 cargo aircraft en route to Baghdad. I should mention at this point that I'm not the best flier either. In fact, I strongly dislike it. Flying on a commercial airline on a domestic flight is comparable for me to being locked in a sardine can. Flying in a combat zone was, as was seemingly everything at this point, a new experience for me.

I was nervous. I boarded the plane and took a seat on the far side of the aircraft near the front. The C-130 is not made for anything except hauling stuff. That stuff on this particular morning happened to be me and about thirty soldiers also being transported into theater. Everything on a C-130 is cargo, whether it has a pulse or not. The C-130 is a propeller-powered aircraft and is essentially a flying tin can. Inside, passengers sit on red mesh benches along the fuselage, which are jump seats designed for paratroopers. It's not comfortable. It's functional. There are virtually no windows, save a couple near the front and rear. The back end of the plane opens to permit the loading of cargo. When it's on the ground, the interior is like an oven. When it's in the air, it can be an icebox. The C-130 is loud and uncomfortable, but truly it is a workhorse of the skies. I would make many trips strapped into the belly of those planes over the next seven months and came to respect the machine and its importance to the success of the military and civilian mission.

As we got moving, I put my earplugs in and said a prayer. Although most of the passengers had dozed off before we were airborne, I don't sleep well on airplanes, so I was wide awake for the two hours into Baghdad. As we began our descent into Baghdad International

Airport (BIAP), the plane began to twist and turn in ways that made me look feverishly for the motion sickness bag in the seat pocket in front of me. As there were no seats, there were consequently no seat pockets and therefore no bags. I closed my eyes and concentrated on not getting sick while the crew performed what I later learned was a corkscrew landing into the military side of the airport. I said another prayer.

I had arrived at last—and alive. *A real plus*, I thought. As the doors to the plane opened and I stepped onto Iraqi soil for the first time, the heat hit me like a hairdryer. The sun was bright and the sand-colored landscape seemed only to intensify its effect. It was a world of beige, contrasted with the clear blue sky above. We were escorted over to "baggage claim" to wait for the pallets with our luggage to be offloaded. Baggage claim at this point was a canopy made out of camouflage netting where soldiers and other travelers would wait for planes and cargo to arrive. Eventually two large air-conditioned tents would be erected on the site, complete with big-screen televisions, but in July 2003, we made do out in the heat.

The airport was bustling with activity. A C-17 had landed just prior to my plane and was being off-loaded. There were convoys arriving and departing, cargo shipments coming in, and helicopters landing for fuel, spraying sand through the air. There were forklifts, busses, Humvees, trucks, and, of course, soldiers.

You couldn't go ten feet in Iraq without feeling KBR's effect on your life, so the bags were loaded onto a truck and I boarded a KBR bus for the trip to the Green Zone. There was one catch. The road between BIAP and the Green Zone was closed that day because it was too dangerous to travel. The folks on the ground called it the "road of death." No, it wasn't a terribly original name, but it got the point across. All of us on the bus were asked rather loudly by the crusty and obviously southern contractor driving the bus to don our flak jackets and helmets for the trip. We had no choice. He wouldn't move the bus until we did as he instructed. As we drove out the gates of the airport, a sign caught my eye. It didn't say "Welcome to Iraq." It read essentially "ATTENTION! DO NOT LEAVE THE AIRPORT UNLESS ALL WEAPONS ARE LOADED AND PROTECTIVE GEAR IS WORN." *Just great*, I thought.

The trip to the Republican Palace located in the Green Zone usually takes fifteen minutes. The route had been altered, so it took more than an hour. About halfway through, I noticed that visibility was decreasing rapidly along our route. Off in the distance I witnessed an overpass disappear from view as what was identified as a sandstorm kicked up. In retrospect, it was a small sandstorm; we drove through it in a couple of minutes. For me at the time, any sandstorm was a big sandstorm and made for a tense ride. After all, former regime loyalists could take advantage of the phenomenon to attack the bus.

Once we emerged from the dust cloud, we drove through some of the worst poverty I've ever seen. The road made the Cross Bronx Expressway seem like a freshly paved surface. Through the sweat pouring from under my helmet and into my eyes, I caught my first real glimpse of Saddam Hussein's Iraq. Iraqis were collecting water from stagnant pools on the side of the road and living in mud huts with no windows. Piles of garbage served as playgrounds for children, while chickens and donkeys roamed between the shanties that lined the road. As we jostled about in the bus, I could see people selling produce on the side of the road, not more than a few feet from what looked like raw sewage. I would later come to understand that the scene I witnessed in that hour on the bus was common across Baghdad and throughout the country. I thought, *My God, how could a government permit this? How could a country with oil resources like these let this happen?* When I finally arrived at the Presidential Palace, it was then I saw clearly where much of the money and much of those resources had gone.

IN THE SHADOW OF THE TYRANT

It was where significant social, political, and economic change would take shape or collapse on itself. It was our White House, our capitol, our Pentagon, our Downing Street, but more than that, our refuge.

The center of daily life for many civilians who worked in Iraq was the Republican Palace, home to the headquarters of the Coalition Provisional Authority and one of the most impressive structures in Baghdad. It was one of the jewels in Saddam's crown and in many ways more of a showplace. Unlike other palaces and government buildings, this one was actually protected by the former regime in anticipation of the invasion. Prior to the coalition bombing campaign during the war, the furnishings were taken to storage and the windows and doors were removed to allow the concussions from dropped ordnance to pass through the building more easily. This helped preserve the structure. The sprawling complex on the banks of the Tigris River was a sight to behold with its four mammoth busts of Saddam looking down over its façade. No matter where one was in front of the building, you stood beneath the gaze of the tyrant. Contrary to popular belief, this palace was more of an office building than a residence during the time of the regime. Saddam was not a regular resident of the building in the way the president of the United States occupies the White House. In fact, he usually moved around so frequently that he rarely spent more than a night in any one location.

For an American on his first trip to the Middle East, its design was completely foreign. The size, the architecture, the décor, and the landscape were unlike anything I had seen before. On that first day, my bus and the baggage truck pulled up to the rear portico of the building. Sweaty and dusty, I got off the bus, unsnapped and removed my helmet, and wiped the grime from my face. My eyes burned from the salt of my perspiration. Soldiers and other civilians coming and going at the rear of the palace looked at us as they went about their business, perhaps thinking that the chow line was going to be a little longer tomorrow. I collected my luggage piece by piece as it was handed off the baggage truck. I lugged them up the stairs into the building and walked into the rotunda for the first time. I stood for a moment, soaking in the recently repaired air conditioning, trying desperately not to look like I didn't know where I was or what I was doing, though both happened to be true. To the left was a ballroom that had been converted into a workspace. It was called the Green Room, the muddled bullpen that was home to the Strategic Communications Office. With the help of someone who recognized a deer in headlights when she saw one, I placed my bags near the room's large sliding pocket doors and asked for Dan Senor. She pointed him out and off I went to meet my new boss.

Tall, lanky, and unassuming, Dan had a desk in the middle of the room and worked away on his laptop while activity buzzed around him. I approached and found him typing. Not wanting to interrupt, I kept a distance of a few of feet and waited for him to acknowledge that someone was there to speak with him. After a few moments, I moved closer and waited again. He finally looked up to see this strange face staring back at him. He kept typing. He looked up again and I introduced myself as a new member of his staff. He kept typing, now looking at me with a confused countenance. His fingers finally stopped. Scrambling through a few of the papers piled on his desk he said, "Sorry I had no idea you were supposed to be here today. Actually, I didn't know you were coming at all." This is the kind of organization that I like to see when starting a new job in a war zone. Dan wasn't joking or being obnoxious. He wasn't a manager. He was an "ideas person." He had been told by the Pentagon and the White House personnel representative, and forgot. Dan was and is a very focused and intense individual. He had to be. On the American side, he was shockingly the only senior-level civilian communications strategist we had on the ground immediately after the war. Dan also often doubled as Bremer's political advisor, and his counsel was sought on a variety of issues. One time, his whole staff sat in his office for our morning meeting for five minutes before he realized we were there. Like I said, he was focused.

I had a copy of my resume with me and gave him a quick rundown of what I thought I could bring to the operation. He sent me over to Naheed Mehta, a British Foreign Service Officer (FSO) with a pronounced accent who was the chief of the press office at the time. We had a brief conversation, during which I was distracted by another Brit up against the far wall of the room yelling at someone on the phone. That was my introduction to Charles Heatly, the chief CPA spokesperson in July 2003. I was immediately concerned that although Dan was clearly closer to Bremer and the leadership, the British appeared to be in charge of the press operation.

Charles was a remarkably capable individual. He spoke Arabic fluently and had spent the last several years working in the Middle East for the British government. He knew the Middle Eastern reporters and the Arab mindset very well. He had been dealing with the likes of Al Jazeera and Al Arabiya for some time by then and handled the regional media effectively. Charles was the exact opposite of what you would expect from a British diplomat. High-strung, profane, disorganized, moody, a little disheveled, and loud, Charles always seemed on the brink of a breakdown. He would take some getting used to.

Naheed also introduced me to Pearse Marchner, the CPA's webmaster and the office jack-of-all-trades. Pearse was an American Marine Corps reservist who came to Iraq as a civilian by way of the defense department. He was not connected with the Bush administration but was hired after doing some work for an American intelligence agency in Washington. As you might imagine, Pearse was a resourceful guy and very helpful. He took me down to the D-Fac, short for dining facility or chow hall, for the first time. Over dinner, he gave me a rundown on the operation and the folks in the office. Perhaps even more helpful, he began to clue me in to the process of getting housing at the Al Rashid Hotel. Like a prisoner smuggling contraband, he said to me, "Give me a few days. I'll work it out." I was the contraband.

After dinner, I hit a wall. It was time for my first night in Baghdad. The first week or so that I was in Iraq, I lived in the palace. I used to laugh out loud at journalists who would glorify life in the palace suggesting that members of the CPA were living in the lap of luxury beneath the ornate domes and chandeliers of Saddam's old seat of power. In fact, the palace was in many ways the exact opposite. When I arrived, most of the north wing of the expansive complex was being used by the CPA and the Combined Joint Task Force 7 (CJTF7) as a barracks facility. Residents entered their living space by ascending the steps that led from the old original portion of the building to the newer north wing, finding themselves in a great marble space that originally served as the anteroom to the largest reception hall. There was ornate carved wood-work around the chandeliers and light fixtures in the ceiling. Marble columns and frescos framed the large doors that led to the ballroom. Inside the massive ballroom, which was easily one hundred feet long and sixty feet wide, eighteen bronze statues looked down over the space and the high ceiling was illuminated by enormous diamond-shaped chandeliers. The eighteen statues represented the eighteen provinces of Iraq. At the far end of the room, on the second floor, was an ornate balcony undoubtedly reserved for Saddam and other senior members of the regime during official functions.

Sounds luxurious, I'll admit. Now add to your mental picture several hundred beds in the foyer and ballroom no more than three feet apart, mountains of luggage, green military duffle bags, foot lockers, a maze of hanging laundry, and drying towels. There were whirring oscillating fans and flip-flops, balled up clothes, and of course, snoring civilian contractors, next to snoring soldiers, next to utterly exhausted Washington types who parachuted into the strange scene much more accustomed to anything but this. As I lugged my bags to bed, I was careful to be quiet, though it was only about 8:00 p.m. The lights in the north wing were almost always off or dimmed because people were sleeping at various times due to the shift work that often comes with soldiering and other duties. I managed to find a quiet place on the far side of the foyer next to one of the windows to lay my head. The bed was open, and the area looked to be deserted save a couple of enlisted men who had "racked out" there before me. This is not to say the other beds weren't taken, just that their occupants were not yet snoring away. I'm a light sleeper and I thought myself lucky to get to bed before the rest of them. I got changed and laid out my army-issued sleeping bag, since KBR had run out of sheets and pillows. Good thing I brought my pillow from home. My earplugs went in and, thanks to a combination of the heat and jetlag, I slept like a log straight through the night. Such a solid sleep would not be the norm.

I awoke about 5:00 a.m. on my first full day in country. The palace was still and quiet. My internal clock was on East Coast time, but I figured I'd get an early start. The other added incentive to getting up early in the palace was the ability to take a hot shower. Another thing about the "luxury" of Saddam's palace was that almost none of the bathrooms worked following the war. That's right. The hundreds of CPA civilian and military personnel that lived and worked there used bathroom and shower facilities in trailers out back of the building along the service road that ran the length of the compound.

In one of the most surreal moments of my time in Baghdad, I grabbed my towel and shaving kit, put on my shower shoes, and in a pair of lacrosse shorts and an undershirt shuffled off to find the shower. It was dark outside, and the hallways were ghoulishly silent. My footsteps on the marble floors echoed against the plaster walls and high ceilings. As I walked I thought, *If I listen, perhaps I'll hear the ghosts of Uday and Qusay howling in disgust at the sight of this young American, roaming the halls in his shower shoes and living in what was once part of their playground.*

I made it to the trailer and checked the sign out front twice before entering. There were two shower trailers out back. One converted from a "male only" shower to a "female shower" between certain hours. I had been warned about this. I wanted to make sure I hit the right trailer at the right time or else some unsuspecting woman might get the shock of her life. The shower trailers were a recent improvement. At the beginning of July, the CPA staff was showering only a couple of times per week. Just after the war, water trucks would come by the palace every so often so staff could shower and shave. The shower trailers accommodated six people at a time in tiny molded fiberglass stalls on either side of the trailer. Between the stalls was a wooden bench. The floor was usually soaked, which made getting dressed while keeping dry exceedingly difficult. More than that, however, it was also usually filthy. Iraq after all is a country where sand and dirt unavoidably form a thin layer over everything. The folks at KBR ultimately hired Pakistani workers to clean the bathrooms, which wouldn't have been a bad thing except for the fact that the workers were *always* in there, taking advantage of the air conditioning. I also often suspected that the cold air wasn't the only thing that attracted them to the place.

When there was water, the pressure was good. When there was hot water, it was hot. It wasn't that bad. It just took some getting used to a naked Gurkha from Nepal being the first person you saw in the morning. The Gurkhas were contract soldiers who, prior to the arrival of the U.S. Marines, guarded the palace grounds.

A couple of months earlier, I was in Poland helping plan President Bush's visit to Krakow. The White House staff stayed at a nice hotel and ate at some fantastic restaurants. The year before, I was in Rome and spent nearly two weeks at the Excelsior Hotel, meeting with Vatican officials before being part of the president's audience with Pope John Paul II. Now I found myself showering in a trailer and trying to get dressed on a sopping wet floor in front of a bunch of strangers. If life has one constant, it's that it changes. You never know where it will take you. You just have to roll with it.

After I got dressed, I spent the early morning hours exploring my new surroundings. The palace was a gargantuan building divided into three sections: the north wing, the south wing, and the main building at its center. The main building was a pink sandstone structure that was rather plain with the exception of the large, dusty blue-green dome rising high above its center. There were porticos on the east and west fronts of the building. The main building dated back to the time of King Faisel in the 1950s, although Saddam made a number of changes to the building's interior after it sustained damage during the first Gulf War. On either side of the main section were the much larger and newer north and south wings. I was astonished to learn that the two wings had been built in the last ten years, since the first Gulf War. It was widely believed that they were built with money from the UN Oil for Food Program that was intended to meet the needs of the Iraqi people. In contrast to the main section, these wings were much more ornate. Sheathed in white and green marble, two curved colonnades hugged the exterior walls of the L-shaped structures. Each had matching porticos with a frieze of an eagle keeping watch over the entryways. The most striking elements of the north and south wings were those thirty-foot bronze composite busts of Saddam that were placed atop towers at the four corners of the building. Beneath the Saddam heads were modern architectural elements suspended between the columns of each tower. We all lived and worked for months in the shadow of the deposed dictator, whose towering image kept watch over our every move. The sight of them was eerie at times, but it more often generated a sense of pride in what we were trying to accomplish for the people there, the region, and the folks back home.

The palace was impressive from afar, but upon closer inspection, the buildings were thrown together and the materials and workmanship were not of the quality that one would expect in a building of its kind. In fact, most of Saddam's palaces were like this. He had so many built in such a short period of time (thank you Kofi Annan and the UN) that crews focused much more on getting the job done and making it look good rather than on getting it done right. Additionally, Saddam designed many of the elements of his palaces himself. Through the eye of even the casual observer, it was obvious that these buildings were built "on the cheap." Which is not to say that Saddam wasn't spending lavishly to build these homes, many of which he never used. Although he was spending less than one dollar per person per year on health care, he undoubtedly spent hundreds of millions on more than fourteen palaces over his last decade in power.

I once had the opportunity to speak with a member of the construction team that was hired by Saddam for the sole purpose of building palaces throughout the country. They worked for months at a time, often leaving their families for extended periods to fill Saddam's grotesque need for these symbols of his absolute power. The team would be brought to an audience chamber where Saddam would explain his vision for the new edifice. The architects and engineers had no choice but to accept the timetable and design specifications. There was certainly no arguing about the practicalities of design elements. On one occasion, the chief architect was brought before dictator to receive his orders for a new project. After Saddam explained that he wanted a palace that would be entirely surrounded by water in western Baghdad near the airport, the foreman dared to question the feasibility of such a building in a place where little water existed. One of Saddam's aides promptly took him aside and whispered in his ear words that made him visibly shaken. He then approached the dictator and gave his assurances that the palace would be built. Indeed it was. This mammoth structure, called the Al-Faw Palace, surrounded by a manmade lake stocked with bass and carp, became Saddam's hunting resort. After Operation Iraqi Freedom it served as the Joint Operations Center (JOC) for the coalition forces. It is a grossly ornate building, boasting twenty-nine bathrooms and one of the largest chandeliers in the world, which still hangs in its towering rotunda.

Occasionally, when material shortages threatened the timetable, the engineers and architects would risk improvising. In the Republican Palace one of the large ballrooms is decorated with alternating columns of green and beige marble. During a renovation when the columns were installed, the builders exhausted their supply of the marble. The tops of many of the columns in the room were actually completed with wood that was painted to look like marble. The workers matched the grain and color almost perfectly, and Saddam never knew the difference. They took a tremendous risk with their improvisation. Had Saddam realized what they had done, they risked being put to death.

Upon entry to the main section of the CPA headquarters, the visitor ascends several steps into a cross hall that leads to the north and south wings. Moving forward one sees, toward the rotunda, on both ends of the building, small parlor rooms with gaudy furniture and mirrored walls. The CPA used these rooms as lounges and meeting spaces. One was eventually incorporated into the CPA Protocol Office and another into the Strategic Communications Office. These parlor rooms were either green or red and the mirrors ran floor to ceiling. The furniture was gold-colored and looked to be an ornate French or Italian style. At any given time, CPA staff were catching quick naps on the sofas, taking a break during their sixteen-plus-hour work days, or using the rooms for meetings. The garish rooms were also a favorite among the soldiers, who constantly took photographs of each other sprawled out on Saddam's ornate furnishings.

Beyond the parlors was the centerpiece of the palace—the rotunda. The rotunda and the dome above were a cream color and simple in decoration with the exception of a large mural on the far side. This mosaic tile mural was installed by Saddam and features the dictator handing a brick to an "everyman" Iraqi building a wall. Pure propaganda for visitors to the palace, the mural was designed to present the impression that Saddam was a man of the people dedicated to helping build a strong nation and better future for his citizens. To a Westerner arriving in the palace after the fall of Baghdad the symbolism seemed absurd. It illustrated how Saddam helped erect a barrier between his people and the outside world. It depicted how his brutality used the people of Iraq as tools to help retain and attempt to expand his own power. The mural was covered in a blue tarp shortly after the CPA occupied the palace, and it remained out of view.

On one side of the rotunda through a solitary metal detector was Ambassador Bremer's front office. Soldiers stood guard outside around the clock joined by a post-stander from Blackwater, the contract security firm responsible for Bremer's protection. The dark paneled doors to the front office never quite closed right and either slammed shut or hung open refusing to latch. The outer office, where the ambassador's support staff was located, was a long, narrow, wood paneled room with small, cheap-looking chandeliers every few feet. The ceiling was a dark, heavily carved design that incorporated the seven-pointed star pattern adopted by the Ba'ath Party that was a common architectural element in virtually all buildings.

The first person everyone saw when entering the outer office was Ambassador Patrick Kennedy, one of the U.S. representatives to the UN in New York, who temporarily traded his office at the U.S. mission on First Avenue for a broken desk in Baghdad. Kennedy was Bremer's chief of staff and a senior foreign service pro. He had a reputation as a good manager of people and was a fantastic operations guy. If there was a problem, Kennedy was the one to fix it. Most of the time, one would enter the front office and find Kennedy sitting behind his desk staring back through his thick, black-rimmed glasses at a person or persons with a problem. His job was to find a solution. The CPA needed to work. It needed to grow and change and operate—and it needed to do so without dragging Bremer into all of the personnel, personality, and facilities issues that can seriously detract from the type of high-level, policy decision-making that occupied most of his precious time. Kennedy filled that role well. Pale, thin, and unpretentious, he was one of the highest-ranking American officials on the compound, yet he refused security on most occasions, shared a room in a trailer out back of the building, and drove a beat-up Suburban with bad breaks and a torn-off side view mirror.

Off to the left and opposite Ambassador Kennedy sat Ambassador Clayton McManaway. McManaway was an older former ambassador who served as one of Bremer's senior counselors through to the end of 2003. He was in his seventies and had been a mentor of Bremer's for many years. As a former ambassador to Haiti, he brought a range of valuable experience to the front office in dealing with unstable political situations. He was not a warm and fuzzy personality. He was a curmudgeon. He was a bulldog. Even if he was happy with your work, he seemed a little annoyed to be talking to you. He expected prompt answers when he asked questions and expected people to perform. On one occasion, as we were responding to a crisis, he peeked out of Bremer's office and asked me a question about a damage assessment. I ran across the rotunda and posed the question to the military, who gave me a very weak response. I made the mistake of thinking he would be satisfied. He stuck his head back through the office door and promptly told me, "That's not an answer. Get me a real answer." Slam went the door. McManaway negotiated the deal between the CPA and the Jordanian government that led to the establishment of the Jordan International Police Training Centre outside Amman. The facility was intended to play an important role in the training of Iraqi security forces. One day, the *New York Times* was snooping around, naturally to find some dirt on funding for the project, and I logically went to the seasoned diplomat for the answers. He didn't have a lot of time for the press, or for press people for that matter. He gave me a ten-minute briefing and a bunch of paperwork to read and essentially told me to figure it out. You just had to like this guy. He was legit.

On the same side of the room, at least initially, was Brian McCormack, Bremer's overworked, overstressed scheduler, travel aide, and ten-minute advance guy. Brian was thriving in his new role after our chat at Shelley's Backroom a few weeks earlier. He was always in the office, usually pulling his hair out about booking helicopters and flights around Iraq or back home to Washington. He was one of the principal people who saw to it that Bremer kept to schedule, that the events were well planned, and that the ambassador and his security were able to get not only from point A to point B but often also to the unexpected point C. Later on in my time in Baghdad, Brian and I worked closely when Senor asked me to begin making proposals for long-range media events for the ambassador. Brian's duties were far ranging and he handled them all, sometimes playing the part of the shrewd diplomat, other times acting like Napoleon. He was probably better known for the latter, but the job got done, and he served Bremer well.

There was also Olivia Troye and later Alex Zemek, Justin Lemon, Matt Fuller, and Sue Shea, who sat outside Bremer's office door, keeping watch over the comings and goings and the ever-changing daily calendar of meetings, travel, and interviews.

Through double doors at the far end of the room was Ambassador Bremer's office. About fourteen feet by twenty feet, the office was ringed with built-in bookcases. It had a surprisingly warm feeling with its mismatched furniture and dusty bookshelves. It was the scene of many a historic moment during that critical year Paul Bremer helped guide the new Iraq. It was not a large space and certainly understated. The bookcases were mostly empty, though some of them contained gifts presented to the ambassador from various Iraqis during the course of his travels throughout the country. There was the commission from President Bush naming him administrator of the CPA, photos of him with the president, and, of course, pictures of the family that he left behind to become the most marked man in the Middle East. Maps were tacked up over the bookcases to be used during briefings. In the corner was a coat rack, usually adorned with a conservative red tie or extra sport jacket. On his desk was a large sign that read, "Success Has a Thousand Fathers" (a phrase spoken by JFK in the aftermath of the failed Bay of Pigs invasion in 1961 that has its origins in an Italian proverb). There was also a small picture of the Virgin Mary, whose eyes perhaps lent daily strength to this deeply committed man charged with doing the near-impossible.

The man who sat behind the desk during that time was the single most powerful American aside from the president and the secretary of defense. He alone possessed executive authority in Iraq. Bremer had the power to create laws, establish institutions of government, and move millions of dollars all with the stroke of a pen. During meetings, he would sit with the other participants around an octagonal black onyx and marble coffee table and prop his now famous desert boots up on the mosaic top. Meetings were typically short and numerous.

Bremer, as former Iraqi Governing Council member Muafak Al-Rubaei once commented, was "shockingly brilliant." He had a mental and physical stamina that seemed to be uniquely suited for the job. There were a hundred decisions to be made each day, and he made them in a very deliberate way. He was not an outwardly passionate and emotional man, but you could definitely see it in his eyes. This wasn't a cold, dispassionate autocrat. Several hours after the bombing of the UN headquarters in August 2003, we received the news that Sergio de Mello, the UN envoy, had died of his wounds from the attack that destroyed his office. Charles went into Bremer's office to read him the official statement written to be released under Bremer's name about de Mello's death. Halfway through the statement, Bremer's eyes watered and he told Charles to stop and just send it out. Later that night, I was with the ambassador as he and Iraqi Governing Council member Dr. Akila Hashimi did a series of interviews about the bombing. During one live interview with CNN, his voice hesitated as he said, "I've lost too many friends to terrorism over the years." He and Hashimi spent a great deal of time together that night discussing the impact of the bombing on the Iraq mission. Interestingly, some of the American networks wanted nothing to do with the woman Iraqi Governing Council member that evening. For all my cajoling, for some reason they didn't see the importance of putting an Iraqi on television that night, let alone an Iraqi woman. Within six weeks, she too would be dead, the victim of assassination and another martyr for the cause.

Bremer made those hundred decisions a day with the help of a slew of advisors and confidants, civilian, military, coalition, and Iraqi. He had a drive that was simply astonishing. Bremer had an innate ability to size up the environment and the playing field. He knew from the beginning he was shoehorned into a unique and often frustrating role. He knew from the beginning he was given a near-impossible task.

Scott Carpenter, the senior advisor for governance and State Department official, who was one of the first people involved in constructing the CPA, once recalled to me his first meeting with Bremer. In that meeting, the ambassador told Scott and the staff that one of the first priorities would be to convince the U.S. military to start killing the looters. Bremer was right, but the Bush administration was afraid to give the green light. He wasn't suggesting killing all of them, but lawlessness breeds lawlessness. If Iraqis didn't think they could get shot for robbing stores, government buildings, and the homes of their fellow citizens, they would keep doing it. We've seen this phenomenon in the United States. It frankly happens all the time. Why would we think it would be any different in Iraq, where the security had collapsed and the legal system was offline? One would think that folks back in Washington were concerned about the optics and impact on "hearts and minds," but their priorities were clearly misplaced.

Although I'll discuss the controversial decision allegedly to disband the Iraqi Army later on, one can't discuss the record of Paul Bremer without also addressing the CPA's much maligned de-Ba'athification policy codified in CPA General Orders 1 and 2. The genesis and importance of the policy remains lost to history because of the barrage of shallow criticism leveled against the coalition and the Bush administration that often went unrefuted. The media refused to report and the administration often failed to articulate effectively several key elements of the policy mentioned earlier. Here's a quick primer:

Bremer, Carpenter, and others, including experts on both sides of the aisle, believed that de-Ba'athification was one of the best things we did. The press and the global foreign policy cognoscenti helped ingrain in the minds of anyone who would listen that the move was a disaster.

They ignore basic facts. I will discuss the rationale for the policy concerning the Iraqi military angle later on, but in a general sense, the policy worked, was supported by the population, and is one of the lasting contributions of the CPA to Iraq.

First, the policy wasn't created out of thin air, as so many critics have led Americans to believe. Discussion was going on in the Pentagon for weeks (if not months) about the policy between former Clinton administration undersecretary of defense Walt Slocumbe, Undersecretary of Defense Douglas Feith, and Deputy Secretary Paul Wolfowitz among others. Any suggestion that Bremer unilaterally made the decision without anyone at the White House or Defense Department being consulted is pure bull. Paul Bremer wasn't even a glimmer in anyone's eye when they started talking about de-Ba'athification. The rhetoric was a deliberate attempt to deflect blame for the looting that was a direct result of the lack of troops. Washington ran away from the policy, and that affected the CPA's credibility as an organization in the ongoing discourse back home about the conduct of the mission.

Second, the de-Ba'athification policy was popular with Shiites, Kurds, and even a large number of Sunnis who, despite being of the same slice of Islam as Saddam, were in tribes that did not reap the spoils of the Ba'ath Party. Essentially, if you weren't in the Hussein clan, so to speak, you weren't getting the benefits.

Third, the process of de-Ba'athification was the first thing that the coalition handed over to the Iraqis to control. It was their process. They managed it with oversight from the CPA. The Iraqis set up internal processes and review committees in Baghdad and in the provinces. Locals knew who was a "good Ba'athist" and who was a "bad Ba'athist." The program largely worked smoothly.

Fourth, only government employees of a certain rank were affected by the policy and many of them just disappeared to begin with. General Order 1 affected only Firqua-level officials and above. Firqua level was a civil service designation that meant that you were a member of the party who was high enough in rank to receive a state pension or other benefits. Exceptions were made for teachers who, under the former regime, all had to be members of the Ba'ath Party at the Firqua level.

Lastly, although several successive Iraqi governments have had the opportunity to reverse the coalition's outlawing of the Ba'ath Party, none have chosen to do so. It is one of the most popular decisions among the population that was instituted by the coalition.

You didn't hear much of any of that from watching CNN or reading the *New York Times*. Your history professor won't mention it either.

The senior British official and deputy administrator, Ambassador Jeremy Greenstock, had an office on the opposite side of the long outer office. He too had several staffers who often noted that Bremer was in his office long before they—let alone their boss—had arrived at work every morning. Bremer stayed late, too. One could always tell when Bremer was in his office by the post-stander from Blackwater outside in the rotunda. Many a night, I'd walk out of the Green Room well past ten or eleven o'clock to see the bodyguard still at his post. Bremer was still working.

When it came to the Iraqis, Bremer wasn't out to win a popularity contest. He neither wanted nor needed people to like him. They needed to respect him. Bremer was deemed by the press to be Iraq's imperial "viceroy," as if he were the head of *Star Wars'* evil trade federation. It was a mischaracterization to be sure. It is true though that he never saw himself as some benevolent savior of the Iraqi people. He walked a tightrope, while pushing hard for action on the complex issues we faced. He worked to understand the intricacies of reform and reconstruction, dedicating himself with every fiber of his being to bring people together who had never contemplated cooperation. Bremer was a visionary who looked to stay ahead of the issues and make decisions not just to improve the situation on the ground for the day but also for the long-term success of a free Iraq.

The Bush administration gave him little credit for what he accomplished in the year he ran the country. In fact, there were some on the White House staff who were looking for someone to blame who threw Bremer under the bus, taking steps to discredit his efforts.

Across the hall from Bremer's office was the Green Room, and around the corner, through the cross-hall heading into the south wing, was the JOC. This was the military's command post in the Green Zone and the domain of Lieutenant General Ricardo Sanchez. The JOC was also a converted ballroom as large as the Green Room except the military had built stadium-style classroom seating in nearly two-thirds of it. A security clearance was required for entry. In the front were three large screens that were constantly updated to include various operational data, including troop activities. Below the screens were desks littered with secure telephones and seats for the commanding officers of the CJTF7. Ascending the steps through a center aisle, military personnel with specific areas of responsibility worked at desks and laptops on each level. Their stations were manned in most cases around the clock. From the U.S. Army chaplain to communications and security forces training and public affairs to combat operations, if you had a major function you had a seat in the JOC.

In the south wing, down three broken white marble steps, was the central hub of palace activity—well at least three times a day. The dining facility was a mammoth room with large doors that were inlaid with hand-tooled bronze. It was a bright room with a large chandelier hanging in the center of an ornate canopy of carvings. The walls were decorated with white tiles. Red and green marble arranged like abstract date trees reached from nearly floor to ceiling, ringing the room with color. The palace dining facility at its height, before additional cafeterias were brought online, served more than two thousand people per meal. The lines often stretched down the halls, nearly spilling over to the main building. The food was trucked in from Kuwait and prepared by Pakistani workers who had supposedly been vetted by KBR and judged to not be a threat. Feeding the workforce was a daunting task for KBR. They had to ensure that the food was safe and not tainted by those wishing to harm coalition personnel. They also needed a lot of it.

The fare was typical soldier food. Dr. Atkins would have rolled over in his grave at the amount of carbs served with every meal. It was necessary. For the first six months or more of the CPA's existence, many of the soldiers stationed in and around the Green Zone also ate at the palace dining facility. Wearing forty pounds of gear while working in the searing heat required the energy from an endless parade of pasta dishes and potato this or that, which filled the trays at the serving stations. It was a big treat when they started serving ice cream in the fall of '03. KBR eventually began serving "mid-rats" or midnight rations for those of us who were still working after 10:00 p.m. and wanted another meal. It was basically just leftovers from dinner and breakfast cereal, but it was a good excuse to get out of the office and take a break.

The basement, accessed by a staircase to the rear of the main building, was home to one of Saddam's private movie theaters and, more important, just down the hall, the check-cashing service. Whether you wanted to go out to eat downtown, get a haircut at the Al Rashid, take advantage of a great deal on a handmade wool rug, or purchase souvenirs, if you wanted to spend money, you needed cash. Throughout the entire country, neither credit cards nor checks were accepted. The only place where you could use a credit card was the large post exchange built out at BIAP in the closing months of 2003. Contractors and vendors located in the country didn't bill you for services or supplies either. That made it a challenge to obtain materials quickly from inside the country.

Incidentally, also located in the basement was the palace vault. Many people have read stories about the vault, about how millions of U.S. dollars in cash were stacked in its thick steel shell—millions of dollars that, according to the CPA's inspector general, were doled out irresponsibly. It is true that the CPA controlled large amounts of American taxpayer money and often paid in cash for shipments of needed supplies and equipment. It is true that sometimes these disbursements were made in advance of delivery. What the critics routinely fail to acknowledge are realities that existed on the ground that necessitated unorthodox spending practices. The regulations regarding the expenditure of U.S. federal government funds exist to protect against abuses and fraud. They also ensure that the procurement process takes time. The regulations are voluminous and justifiably so. One such regulation gives the U.S. federal government the right to withhold payment until ninety days after the merchandise is delivered. This is done to ensure conformity with the contract. Imagine trying to do that in Iraq! Imagine trying to bid contracts for equipment and supplies! It would have taken months to procure needed materials, some of which were critical to ensuring progress toward important CPA goals like the equipping of new Iraqi security forces and repair of essential services. It would not have been possible. Not having some of the usual protections, of course, presents real risks of fraud or abuse, but overall, the percentage of alleged waste or fraud in comparison with the overall amount of money expended was estimated in the low single digits. It was remarkable under the circumstances yet almost universally ignored by the talking heads on television. In Iraq, if you needed something, you presented a need, found a vendor who could deliver to the specifications in the time required, and you hired him. Sometimes it worked out. Sometimes you got less than what you wanted. The sense of urgency necessitated the risk.

The north and south wings as well as the main building housed what were called ministry offices. It is important to point out that during the early days following the war, the coalition not only held executive authority, but it was also was also responsible for the running of every Iraqi government agency. Before the Iraqi Governing Council installed the first cabinet in September 2003, the coalition appointed interim ministers or senior advisors who ran the day-to-day operations to ensure some continuity of government. These ministry offices came to occupy virtually every square foot of spare space in the building. Ballrooms were turned into office suites. Larger rooms and even hallways were converted into cubicles and bullpens with rows of desks. Over the space of a few short months, the palace again became much more of an office building than anything else. Even most of the beds were moved out and personnel were billeted in trailer parks that had sprung up like weeds where the date palms once grew undisturbed behind the building. A CPA support office, which corresponded with every Iraqi ministry and staff for additional government and security functions, was housed in the sprawling complex—all beneath those four giant busts of the butcher of Baghdad.

Most evenings, either standing outside the palace, taking a break, or walking over the pockmarked driveway of the Al Rashid, I could hear the call to prayer filling the air over the city. It echoed in every corner of town except some areas of the Green Zone that were too distant from the old network of speakers that sang the words of the Koran to millions. The sound was eerily beautiful as it blasted cracked and distorted through speakers that long ago had blown out and were now failing. The call to prayer was an ever-present reminder that I was in a place like none I'd ever been before. It was also unnerving to have that constant reminder that, while we were fighting a war against radical Islamic terrorists, we were living in their part of the world. It was a reminder of the critical debate constantly swirling in the country and in the press. The separation of mosque and state would be one of the most significant decisions the Iraqis would have to make about the future of their country.

Religion was all around us, from the call to prayer wafting through the heavy air to the mosques that dotted the landscape like so many castles in this ancient kingdom. Far out on the Baghdad horizon, visible from the Green Zone and pretty much everywhere else, was what the locals called the Mother of all Mosques. Saddam, apparently tired of building palaces, decided to commission this mammoth project, designed to be the largest in the world when completed, to help cement his image as a leader of the Islamic world. The sand-colored dome sat incomplete, its construction cranes hanging over the exposed beams and girders during my time there. Millions of presumably UN Oil for Food dollars were wasted, while Iraqis suffered through decades of substandard medical care and essential services.

Clearly, the politics of religion might have been everywhere, but for many civilians and soldiers on the ground, we looked to matters of faith for more practical purposes. My relationship with God has been an important part of my life. I was a Catholic school kid, and faith was certainly a significant aspect of growing up in my house. We were a family that said grace at the dinner table and went to church on Sunday. I spent eight years at Saint Anthony's School in Nanuet, New York, running to the bus in my red sweater, plaid tie, and grey pants. The pastor of our parish would often come by for dinner on Sundays, while Saturday afternoon was often reserved for making a few bucks as an altar boy at weddings. The parish was an important part of my life and upbringing. The importance of my faith grew during my father's illness and later, when I was an adolescent dealing with his death. I could have become an angry, jealous, and resentful kid who turned away from God because life had dealt him a crushing blow. Though it wasn't easy, I turned to my faith then, two decades prior to my deployment, to help get me through difficult days when I felt alone and uncertain. In Corinthians 12, Saint Paul said essentially that we are stronger when we are weakest because God is most fully with us during such difficult times.

I think it's important to have faith—faith in yourself, in your nation, and in others. Although having faith can lead to the pain of disappointment and certainly to times when you question your beliefs, I'd rather live a life of faith in something than spend my days in the solitude that comes with unbending cynicism and distrust. I can say with certainty that nothing can make you cling fast to faith like being deployed to a forward area. Soldiers must have faith in each other to complete their mission and to survive. Government officials must have faith that they are making decisions with the best intentions of promoting freedom, justice, and assistance to those in need.

It is said that people find religion during times of war. Certainly, the church pews across America were fuller in the days after 9/11. In the palace, the busy throngs of soldiers and civilian personnel also came together in prayer to help them face the challenges of their work. It was a wonderful thing to see people from different religions worshipping together in a part of the world where true religious freedom is as rare as a torrential downpour, but in the palace, things were different. It was free exercise of religion not only in the midst of all the trappings of the Saddam's regime but also in the midst of a battle with Islamic terrorists.

For the first six months following the end of major combat operations, the south wing of the palace was quite possibly home to the most unique combination of church, mosque, and synagogue on the planet. Although the north wing of the building became a makeshift home for hundreds of military and civilian personnel sleeping in every nook and cranny of space, the south wing's dominant feature was the room we called the Chapel. True, we spent a lot more time in the chow hall, but the Chapel was a special place for those of us who were there in those early days. The significance and the symbolism went largely unnoticed by the media who traipsed in and out of the building. The room, which measured about sixty feet by ninety feet, was the most impressive in the palace and would be the scene of many emotional and spiritual moments throughout its time as the CPA's spiritual center. Visitors to the Chapel entered through one of three sets of double doors on the north wall. Above each white marble entryway were engraved quotes from Saddam in green Arabic letters. The heavy doors were inlaid with hand-tooled brass sheets imbedded in the frames and behind protective glass. It was a bright and airy room with large panels of ornate masonry reaching from the marble floors to the ceiling's carved wood panels. On the far left-hand side of the room sat a gold throne that was six feet high, carved by hand, and layered in twenty-four-karat gold leaf. The arms were the heads of griffins and the back was adorned with a crown and other elaborate designs. The green- and cream-colored fabric had patches of discoloration, no doubt from the hordes of perspiring servicemen who took turns having their picture taken sitting in Saddam's throne.

The Chapel was the throne room in the palace. It was a place where Saddam would receive visitors and hold formal receptions. It was a striking space not only for its size and flamboyant style but also because of the symbolism embedded at Saddam's direction in the room's design. Above the throne was a large mural, commissioned by Saddam in 1996, of missiles bearing Iraqi flags rocketing through the clouds. On the other end of the room, the side of the room at which he would be looking if he were sitting in the throne, was an equally large painting of the Dome of the Rock and the skyline of Jerusalem. In the center of the ceiling, he placed a dome that was painted with the images of seven horsemen. The number seven is significant in Islam and represents the seven transcendent Divine Powers. Saddam ordered the artist to add an additional horseman, representing himself. The inscription around the rim of the dome told the story of Jerusalem's long-awaited liberation. Saddam came to view himself as a modern day Nebuchadnezzar who would play a lead role in that liberation and the removal of the "infidels" from the holy city.

Anyone who doubted Saddam's desire to destroy Israel and expand his authority need only spend a moment in the Chapel to think differently. It was a similar yet more subtle evidence of his worldview than the mural found ringing the convention center's cavernous lobby. There, Saddam had placed a mosaic that depicts a soldier holding the power of the atom, preparing to hurl it at an advancing army. The United States is depicted in the mural as an American flag morphing into a band of black demons.

The palace was a home. It was an office. It was a place of worship. It was a place where the mission's most important and controversial decisions would be made. It was where significant social, political, and economic change would take shape or collapse on itself. It was our White House, our capitol, our Pentagon, our Downing Street, but more than that—it was our refuge. The palace was the one place that I felt safe most of the time, though that sense of security would also wane as summer turned to fall.

LEARNING CURVE

Even when everything seemed to be going south, these people were able to reach back into their storied history for the strength to carry on.

Working for the coalition ran the gamut—from having a repetitive Groundhog Day quality to being exhilarating and historic. What made it difficult was the fact that there were actually periods of relative normalcy. That normalcy would then be broken by unpredictable events like a rocket attack or terrorist bombing. Of course, I use the term normalcy loosely, but there were times throughout the latter half of 2003 and the beginning of 2004 when life settled into a strange routine, even despite the escalating violence. For many of us in the Strategic Communications Office, routine meant getting up, coaxing the shower at the Al Rashid to spit out some water, climbing into your Suburban or shuttle bus, driving past the bombed-out ministry buildings, and parking in the "dust bowl" parking lot across from the palace. You would walk through the palace security, grab a bite for breakfast, and attend the 8:30 a.m. planning meeting with Dan and Charles. After that, you'd get on with your day of meetings in the building or outside of the Green Zone, planning events, writing press releases, and talking to reporters who almost always thought you were full of crap.

Every few days you would take a trip out into the Red Zone for a meeting or event. You got used to running around in the heat between the checkpoints and the palace. You got used to your flak vest weighing you down, if you wore one. You'd jump in a car or Humvee. You would scramble from meeting to meeting.

Invariably, by midafternoon I and a few others ended up making the trip over to the convention center for the daily wrestling match with the press where either Dan or Charles were the main event. At night, at least back when the Al Rashid Hotel was still operating, you'd try, often unsuccessfully, to actually make it back to the hotel in time to take a quick swim before the pool closed. Then off to bed.

Looking back, those were truly special days. Many were grueling. Some of them were momentous. Some were historic. Some were seen by the world. Others were meaningful for me personally. Strangely, many days during my seven months in Iraq were not chaotic or filled with crisis. They were days when, for a brief moment, time stood still. Many were memorable, but three of them during those formative first couple of weeks stand out.

Everyone starting a new job has a learning curve. Working in Iraq was certainly no different. My first trip outside the walls of the Green Zone came just two days after my arrival. It was a short jaunt over to the Foreign Ministry Building that was not far beyond the gate of the zone. Bremer was holding a press conference to rededicate and officially reopen the building for business. It was a very symbolic moment for the coalition and Iraq. The Foreign Ministry represented the new Iraq's participation on the world stage as a peaceful contributor to the discourse of regional affairs. Put simply, Iraq would now be reaching out to the world in a way that had not been contemplated or possible for decades. Members of the press would be on hand, hopefully grasping the significance of the event and what it meant for Iraq's future. No, I'm not kidding. Remember, I was new. Iraqi Governing Council member and Shiite cleric Mohammad Bahr al-Ulum would also be on hand to address the audience of ministry workers, CPA personnel, and media.

I donned my helmet and flak vest and jumped into a Chevy Suburban, two cars behind Bremer's vehicle. Bremer's taupe-colored Suburban was heavily armored and contained so much additional steel plating it required an enhanced suspension system. The rear of this behemoth had been retrofitted with four wheels instead of two making it more difficult to immobilize by shooting out the tires. Security personnel scrambled into every car, sticking their long guns out the open windows. Armored personnel carriers led the way down the palace driveway and out onto the street past the M1-A1 tank that was standing watch nearby. Past the barbed wire, sandbags, and army sentries, we rolled. Past the gate, we swerved around the concrete barriers near the checkpoint and were on the streets of Baghdad. Security personnel, their weapons in plain view, feverishly warded off lesser vehicles that might try to disrupt our speeding path. It was a rough ride. Bremer's security detail often used their vehicles to push cars off the road and out of the motorcade's route, keeping the ambassador in a constant state of motion. Almost as quickly as we departed, we arrived, zipping through the gate at the Foreign Ministry. As we disembarked, I stood for a moment in the driveway of the building and looked up at its charred façade. Windows were broken, the masonry was cracked, and it looked like a good percentage of the building was uninhabitable. As I moved up the sidewalk, a low hum that I had noticed piercing the quiet when I got out of the car turned into a roar as we neared the main entrance. After passing through the glass doors, I stood along the side of the lobby, watching my colleague, Christopher Harvin, make sure that the press and podium were ready for the event to begin. I offered my assistance but mostly stayed out of everyone's way. The lobby was an atrium with a dormant, dirt-filled fountain at its center and an unobstructed view straight up to each floor where the offices overlooked the large open space. Looking up, black scarring from the fires lit by looters after the war streaked the walls, along with a jumble of broken windows, hanging wires, and dangling metal.

We are dedicating this? I thought to myself, as the imam said a prayer from the Koran in Arabic, another strange new sound for my ears to assimilate. As it turned out, there were only a few offices on the first floor that were beginning daily operations again. As I said, this was a symbolic event that was meant as a jumping-off point for new relationships between Iraq and its neighbors and the world. Bahr al-Ulum, then serving as the Iraqi Governing Council president, approached the rickety podium for his remarks. Small in stature, he sported a thick, white beard and thicker dark-rimmed glasses. A Shiite cleric, he was wearing his black turban and flowing black robe as he began what appeared to be an impassioned speech in front of a new, brightly colored banner that read "Ministry of Foreign Affairs" in Arabic.

With the exception of the building looking as if it would collapse at any moment and the loud whirring noise out front, it was going well, I guessed. About three minutes into the remarks, the electricity went out and the microphones went off. That roaring noise outside had stopped as well. It was the building's generator, now sitting quietly out front. Harvin and a couple of Iraqis rushed outside to make a diagnosis and fix the problem. I couldn't figure out which was worse, not having the ability to use the microphone or dealing with the incredibly loud noise from the generator polluting the area where the event was taking place. Either way, I thought it was terribly embarrassing. Strangely, nobody seemed to care much. Bahr al-Ulum kept on talking, not missing a beat. Bremer, while having dashed a quizzical look in the staff's direction, delivered his remarks eloquently, and the reporters jotted down their notes. The generator showed signs of life and cranked back up, but only for a moment before conking out for the remainder of the event. If you had done a press conference like this in the United States, you would have been beaten with a stick by your boss, or just fired. In fact, we would never contemplate doing an event like this back home. The lesson of the day spoke loud and clear: I wasn't in Washington any longer. Harvin convinced me to get out of there as the event was wrapping up. He was heading back to the palace, but his car wasn't in the motorcade. I wasn't entirely comfortable with the idea, but I threw my helmet and flak vest back on and made my way out to the car. He laughed at seeing me playing the part of the overly cautious newcomer, as he darted about out in the open with no protection.

First trip out of the Green Zone, now first trip back in without an escort. Harvin jumped into the driver's seat and slung his backpack between us. I turned to my right to fasten my seatbelt and when I looked back over, he was handing me a gun. "Take this," he said nonchalantly, as if people handed me loaded weapons every day and this was somehow normal. "You want me to do what?" I responded. Harvin cackled, saying, "Come on, Basile, you better get used to having these things around." He was right. It was a dangerous environment and it was only prudent that I do what I needed to protect myself in the event security was not available. Let me be clear here. I don't have any problem with guns. I'm a big supporter of the Second Amendment and always have been. It was just one of those things that for many civilians took some getting used to. I took the gun and spent the ride back into the Green

Zone far more concerned that an errant finger might slip and fire the thing than anything going on out on the street.

Over time, I and many other civilians became more comfortable with the idea of having guns around and in some cases actually carrying one. Several weeks later, when it became obvious to me that I would be going downtown quite often—and given that unlike the British government, the United States would not be providing dedicated security for the Americans in our office—I finally took it upon myself to get weapons training. I went along with a guy named Loki, a seemingly ten-foot-tall South African security contractor to the Baghdad Police Academy, where I spent time learning how to handle pistols, M-16s, and AK-47s. Eventually, for a time, I carried a French-made 9 mm pistol confiscated from a weapons cache uncovered near Uday's palace, or so I was told. It came with me whenever I left the Green Zone.

Given the seriousness of the issue, many civilians working in theater felt that although contract security was costly, it was necessary. As the insurgency grew in strength and the streets became more dangerous, it was imperative that the CPA do something about providing security to civilians who were taking great risks traveling in the open, potentially under surveillance, in doing their jobs. The Strategic Communications Office didn't even receive Kevlar vests with metal plates until the beginning of 2004. I didn't want to carry the gun, but I needed to be out downtown to work. I needed to *feel* secure as well as *be* secure. Having the gun meant feeling more comfortable and that meant doing a better job. Let's face it, if I ever actually needed to fire my weapon, it meant that I and those around me were completely screwed. You learned that you did what you had to do to get the job done. Contrary to what was portrayed in news reports, civilians weren't hanging out at the palace pool all day. We took risks and placed ourselves in harm's way on a daily basis.

Those first few weeks were critical to breaking me in and preparing me for the hard months ahead. About a week after my quick trip to the Foreign Ministry, I was working on the Ministry of Justice beat in the Strategic Communications Office and was trying to craft some news out of what was happening with the reform of the Iraqi justice system. The Judicial Review Committee that had been established by the CPA was a panel comprised of both coalition and Iraqi members charged with evaluating Iraqi judges and their ability to continue serving in the judiciary under the new government. It was remarkable that, in such a short time, a commission had been established to review members of the bench and bar in an effort to get the system moving again. They had made marked progress, though it was a hard to get the media to care about the workings of a justice system that they believed never existed in the first place. What complicated the telling of the story was that most Western journalists had little or no experience with the procedural differences between an American-style court system and the French system, used by the Iraqis for decades.

As a lawyer, I understand how tough it is sometimes to explain certain concepts to people who are not members of the profession. This problem was only amplified by the fact that the reporters who might cover a positive news story about the Iraqi justice system had little to no procedural information or historical perspective on the courts. They weren't terribly interested in learning either. Many in the media didn't know that Saddam created an extrajudicial structure to suit his own needs and how the regular Ministry of Justice's courts operated during the time of the regime. It was a lot to go through to sell the story.

Progress was being made toward developing a judiciary that provided modern due process and human rights protections to the accused, but the courts weren't functioning, jails were overflowing, and the U.S. military was trying to move people in and out of the system. Reengaging the Iraqi judiciary would demand a slow ramp-up to do it correctly. The press seemed content to rehash the existence of the current set of problems rather than focus on the redevelopment and reform efforts. Then again, many Western journalists thought that Saddam's kangaroo courts represented the only judicial tradition Iraq had ever known.

The opportunity finally came to push out a story that was simple enough and dramatic enough that I felt optimistic about the prospect of reporters recognizing its value. It was a real and unmistakable sign of change for the better in Iraq. Eight Supreme Court justices whom the Judicial Review Committee had determined were wrongfully removed from the bench by the former regime were about to be reappointed.

There was some discussion about how to roll this out. My vote was to do a press conference downtown at the Ministry of Justice Building where the justices could be sworn in and speak to the press. That's precisely what we set about doing. This was really the first project I could sink my teeth into. I developed talking points for the CPA officials, materials to help the media understand the significance of the event, and visuals with the message "An Independent Judiciary" in Arabic. With a couple of days of planning and some time to permit the judges to travel to Baghdad, we were ready.

Into downtown we went, to the Ministry of Justice Building near King Faisel Square. We pulled up next to the green iron gates of the hulking structure. The building was imposing in a Soviet sort of way with its simple, brutish design. What made it more unwelcoming was the visible damage caused by the looters who had burned the upper floors of the building, much of which was still unusable. About two dozen Iraqis were milling about as we walked under the archway at the main entrance toward the core of the building and into the courtyard that led to the interim justice minister's office. Not far from where we entered stood a large stone cartouche. It was a replica of the great tablets on which Hammurabi carved the first written law. It was a poignant symbol. I was about to learn just how long these people had been wrestling with the challenges of the law.

Justice minister Medhat Mahmood received us in his cavernous, sparsely furnished office just off the courtyard on the ground floor near where the ceremony was to take place. The air conditioner blew warm air throughout the room from large round white ducts near the windows. There was a conference table, a desk, and a couple of chairs. The walls were bare and freshly painted a stark white. The floor was a gray cracked terrazzo tile. It was as bare as bare could get while still being functional. This was the office of the man who ostensibly was the attorney general of Iraq at the time. Medhat was welcoming and warm. We talked about the ceremony and the activities of the Ministry of Justice. He liked the fact that I was a young lawyer. He sat leaning on his desk and talking to me, as if I was somebody. He wanted to have a dialogue. We talked about the judicial system under Saddam and the rich history of Iraqi jurisprudence prior to Ba'ath Party rule.

He talked about the rewriting of laws to remove torture provisions, the development of due process for criminals, and tolerance for political dissenters. We discussed the progress of de-Ba'athification in the courts and the ongoing work to bring the courthouses back on line. We even joked about the need for traffic courts above all else to deal with the wild drivers around town.

I told him that I appreciated that he had truly daunting tasks before him. Then, looking through his glasses across his desk at this young American, he said, "We have done this before." It was a not-so-subtle reference to the fact that people in what is now Iraq were writing laws and developing legal systems long before the perfection of the mechanical clock. There was a pride and a confidence in his voice that struck me and stayed with me on those days in Iraq when it seemed like the mission was doomed to failure. That pride, hope, and confidence was not uncommon, as I would find during my time there. Even when everything seemed to be going south, these people were able to reach back into their storied history for the strength to carry on.

A few minutes later, the justices arrived and took their seats at the conference table for a briefing with Medhat. I ran outside to check on the preparations and distribute materials to the media who had assembled. Saddam had stripped these eight men of their positions back in 1993, after they refused to bow to pressure to uphold the death penalty ruling of a lower court in a case involving a man accused of murdering an associate of Qusay Hussein. Nine justices at the time found that the killing lacked the element of premeditation required for the death penalty and they voted to instruct the lower court to investigate the matter further. For their exercise of judicial independence, Saddam Hussein had them removed from the bench and denied them their retirement benefits. They were lucky that they all didn't just disappear. The eight surviving justices petitioned the Judicial Review Committee for reinstatement. The committee, composed of two Iraqi and two coalition members, issued an order of reinstatement, stating that "the facts overwhelmingly support the conclusion that these judges were improperly removed from office. Their removal was wrongful and a severe interference with the independence of the judiciary." Medhat told me, "This was a true day of justice for them." One newly reinstated justice said to me, "I lost my position, my career, and my retirement rights. But at least I could sleep at night. I had my conscience and I never regretted my decision." In addition to retaking their places on the bench, the justices regained access to retirement benefits and received some back pay.

The men, now senior citizens, lined up in the courtyard in front of a small crowd and took their oaths of office. After a prayer from the Koran, they chose among themselves one man to represent them. He approached the podium and began to speak with confidence and passion about the law of Iraq. A translator nearby did his best to keep up with the justice's soaring words. He talked about history. He also talked about the future. He said, "We're not going to cut ears off anymore! We're not going to brand people anymore! We're not going to cut tongues out anymore!" He spoke of a justice system that all Iraqis could be proud of again. "No more fear," he triumphantly said. It was very moving and proved to me that with souls like these committed to the cause, there was real hope that Iraqis would work through the difficult times ahead to make it happen. That hope, that desire to be a pariah no longer wasn't created by the Bush administration spin machine. It was real. It may not always have been obvious, but it was there. The media coverage of the announcement was meager, but those few minutes in Medhat's near-empty office will stay with me for a lifetime. Medhat Mahmood went on to serve as Iraq's chief justice.

Not long after that inspiring announcement about the reappointment of the former judges, I awoke one morning to my first real professionally and emotionally challenging experience. That was the way life worked at the CPA. You'd have a day of inspiration followed by a day of gut-wrenching emotion and uncertainty. They were both special and instructive in their own way. There were many days when I'd say to myself, *Everything is going to be alright over here.* And then there were days when the cracks in the mission were very visible, particularly as the need for more troops became apparent to those of us on the ground, even as early as the summer of 2003. There were many times when I thought that it was just too high a mountain to climb. I suppose that is the case with most challenging ventures, but it was part of the unsettling nature of being in the middle of the occupation. We had good days. We had many good days, but they were often pierced by an attack, a close call, or some occurrence that reminded you just how perilous the mission remained. You also constantly analyzed the functionality of the operation, while reading or watching almost exclusively negative press coverage of the mission.

In the early morning hours of August 16, 2003, the infamous Abu Ghraib Prison on the outskirts of Baghdad was hit by a volley of mortars launched by insurgents. The attacks killed at least five prisoners and wounded more than sixty others living in tents at the U.S. military-run Camp Vigilant. The inmates were living in tents because the prison was undergoing extensive renovations to bring it up to international standards and repair it from looting and damage following the fall of the regime. Essentially, it was being rebuilt. As was the case with many government buildings and facilities (in particular military installations), what remained after the fall of Saddam was virtually unusable.

One of the other facts about the situation on the ground that was underreported in the mainstream media is that, just prior to the war, Saddam offered amnesty to all prisoners and flung open the doors of his detention centers across the country. That's right—full amnesty for thousands of criminals. Of course, Saddam did this to make things as difficult as possible for the coalition, and some suggest that it was yet another reason why a larger troop deployment for the postwar period was necessary. The presence of thousands of criminals on the streets while the coalition was trying to stabilize the country was contributing to the difficulty in winning the peace. Although it is believed that many of the prisoners were political, the Iraqi justice system was indeed functioning during the regime and actively putting legitimate criminals behind bars. As I mentioned earlier, there was a system that functioned separate and apart from the extrajudicial proceedings of Saddam's "personal courts." Those regular courts were dealing with murderers, rapists, thieves, and other dangerous people when the regime didn't want to chop them to bits for fun. Once the amnesty was issued, these legitimate criminals wreaked havoc in the prisons and throughout the country, until they were later caught or killed. Neither the Iraqis nor the coalition ever had any hope of finding all of them. In any case, the prison system was in a shambles after the war and required a massive and expedited reconstruction of its major facilities. Abu Ghraib was foremost among them.

In CPA-speak, Abu Ghraib was termed Baghdad Central Prison, as it was the main maximum-security facility in and around the capital city. Today, most people know it as a place where U.S. military personnel abused and humiliated Iraqi prisoners, but this wretched place had a former life that chills the souls of Iraqis by the mere mention of its name. Built in the 1960s, it was a mammoth facility, occupying more than 250 acres, with a security perimeter stretching more than four kilometers. By some estimates, fifteen thousand inmates were kept there at the height of its operation. We've all seen movies that featured dank, crowded prisons, dark torture chambers, and places where people prayed for death. This was such a place. Cells no larger than four by four meters were filled with as many as forty prisoners. Prisoners were subjected to mental and physical torture. This wasn't sleep deprivation or water-boarding mind you. It was sustained physical and psychological torment, including chemical and biological experimentation as part of Saddam's weapons programs. As an aside, there is also little dispute that prisoners were used as guinea pigs in support of Saddam's chemical weapons program. Yet critics of the war who sought to convince the American public that there was never any evidence of ongoing weapons of mass destruction (WMD) development by the regime conveniently forget this.

Abu Ghraib was also home to Saddam's notorious "red rooms," where the color of the rooms and lighting damaged the eyesight of inmates while creating a neurological effect that ultimately led to insanity. Over the years, thousands upon thousands of prisoners—many of whom were incarcerated for their religious or political beliefs—were tortured and killed within the walls of Abu Ghraib. One Iraqi journalist named Fareed, whom my colleagues and I had the pleasure of working with at the CPA, was incarcerated there for making a movie about great leaders of the Middle East. His crime? Not including Saddam Hussein in the film. He soon found himself dragged from his home, stripped naked, and placed in a cell with a dozen other men. He saw the light of day only through a small hole in the wall of the cramped compartment. Fareed maintained his sanity by living wholly in his imagination and counting the days and weeks by listening to the executions outside. Sounds like a strange method, but it actually made sense. For instance, they only hung people on a certain day, say, Thursday. When he heard the distinctive clang of the door beneath the gallows as it swung open, he knew it was Thursday. He endured this hellish life for years before being released.

The prison was divided into two sections during Saddam's time. The first section was the "closed" section, which mostly housed Shi-ites. Inmates in the closed section never received visitors and had no access to the outside world. Many of the torture chambers were in this area. The second section was the "open" section and home to a wider variety of criminals and activists who opposed the government. There were tunnels and chambers and, of course, the infamous death house, which the coalition and the Iraqi Governing Council sealed in late 2003.

It should be noted that Iraq did reinstitute the death penalty in 2004, but as part of a reformed justice system that included due process rights and a new judicial code. The subsequent American withdrawal from the country has led to significant political and military instability that continues to affect the administration of justice in accordance with that new code.

Inmates at Saddam's Abu Ghraib also lived in some of the most unsanitary conditions imaginable. Cockroaches and other vermin infested every dark corner of this foul-smelling hell on earth. Inmates drank contaminated water and when they ate, they ate rancid food. There were virtually no health care facilities. Prisoners would die in their cells and be left for days rotting in the heat. I could go on, but you get the point. It was a modern-day concentration camp. The actions of American soldiers at Abu Ghraib were in contravention to our values as a nation. They were unfortunate for a variety of reasons, not the least of which is that the incident overtook all other news about the mission for weeks. It is worth noting the conditions as they existed before the invasion to remind people that, although the management of the prison under American control helped create an environment where the abuse depicted in the *60 Minutes* exposé could happen, the actions of our military were not remotely in the same league as the brutality of Saddam's regime or others whom we continue to fight in the Middle East today.

From the outset, the coalition intended on doing something about the facilities that made up the Iraqi prison system. It had to do it from a practical standpoint. They needed a place to put insurgents and criminals. They also needed to send a message to the Iraqi population that prison and criminal justice reform was going to be a part of the new Iraq. Due process and human rights are the cornerstones of any free society and needed to take shape in various forms throughout the country. This by itself was a daunting task, let alone trying to do it while ministering to countless other needs, including political reform and reconstruction, and dealing with a terrorist onslaught that was trying to throw the whole operation in reverse. At the time of the mortar attack, the prison was just weeks away from opening a new cell block, hurriedly built by the coalition with new cells, beds, latrines, lighting, and other facilities.

I learned of the attack as I walked into the Green Room that morning, and discussions were already underway about what to do from a public affairs standpoint. The press corps was certainly frothing at the mouth for this story, but putting together a pool of journalists to visit the prison was not practical, preferable, or—for that matter—safe. Those of us in the office knew that having reporters visiting the prison would create more of a negative story than the incident warranted. I remember feeling dead certain that the sight of hundreds of prisoners living in tents would do two things, given the attitude of the media. First, it would make it look like the coalition was at fault for not protecting the inmates, and second, the damage from the first story would overtake the important story of the rebuilding of the prison with new facilities. I knew, as did everyone else in the office, that the media couldn't care less about why the inmates were in tents or the ongoing effort to rebuild a more humane prison system. The "blame America" movement in the press corps would fail to deliver the message accurately.

Consequently, we moved in another direction. We didn't want the reporters using the mortar attack to write stories on prison conditions.

The conditions weren't great, but other than rebuilding or refurbishing the facility, there was little to be done about them in such a short time after the war. It had nothing to do with the disgraceful nighttime activities of the MPs (military police) that would come to light at the Pentagon that fall and hit the papers in the spring of '04.

Ultimately the decision was made midafternoon to take a pool of reporters out to the 28th Combat Support Hospital, some thirty miles outside of town, to give reporters the opportunity to see that the injured prisoners were being given good treatment. The message was ostensibly, "They may be prisoners, but they are human beings who deserve quality care." It was also decided that Iraqi Governing Council member Samir Sumaidaie would accompany the group to give interviews and to visit with the wounded. Here again, the message was that, in the new Iraq, even prisoners would be afforded rights that Saddam had refused them. After all, Saddam would have left them to die. I would go to supervise this little field trip.

I remember very clearly feeling that we were trying to do too much with this. Not that I was in favor of bringing reporters to the prison either. The military advised us against permitting folks to come to the scene or the area around the prison. The vicinity of Abu Ghraib was a hot spot for insurgents who were operating in the area with mortars, rockets, and sniper rifles. The U.S. Army was also concerned that the mortar attack was part of an effort to perpetrate a jailbreak. It just wasn't a safe place to be. The U.S. Army and the civilians who were advising the prison system operations made that very clear to us, and I believed them. That of course didn't stop the reporters from complaining. They wanted to go to the scene. I really couldn't blame them for asking, but we were offering a legitimate alternative and they could take it or leave it.

I received a phone call from a Reuters producer who was particularly adamant that they be allowed to go to the prison. I informed them that on the advice of the military nobody should approach the area. That was the official CPA position, though I understood Reuters' reasons for wanting to send someone. My message was simple: reporters who wanted to go somewhere could come with me to the 28th Combat Support Hospital or not, but should not go near Abu Ghraib. The producer relented and agreed to take a seat in the bus that would depart from the convention center an hour later.

I gathered my helmet, flak vest, and notepad and set out for the convention center a mile away, unsure whether what I was about to do was the right thing, but I wasn't going to argue the point. I admit that one of the reasons I didn't question the efficacy of this plan was that senior leadership in the front office and the strategic communications operation were in agreement. They were considering this a serious situation and I needed to shut up and get the job done. I was nervous more than anything else. I was getting on a bus with an Iraqi Governing Council member, his security guard, one army major from the Coalition Press Center who didn't want to be there, and a bunch of cranky media to drive in heavy traffic into the middle of nowhere to see wounded prisoners. *I could get killed doing this*, I thought. The other complicating factor was that we were losing daylight—fast. We were to depart around 5:00 p.m. that afternoon and ideally needed to be back by sundown for security reasons. As soon as I boarded the sweltering KBR bus, the army major, sitting there in full battle gear, made it very clear to me that he was not going to be on the road after sundown. I understood his concerns, but didn't appreciate the attitude. He was clearly acting as if this was one big bother to him.

As we got under way, I said the prayer to Saint Michael, as was my usual practice when I was traveling around the country. My donning my helmet again brought a chuckle, this time from the USA *Today* reporter sitting behind me. She and the rest of the crews wore little to no protective gear. I might have looked a little silly to them, but we were in a thin-skinned vehicle and were hitting significant traffic along the route. A half hour passed and we had made little progress. An hour came and went and the reporters were getting restless. It was now 6:00 p.m. and, while we were now outside of town, we continued to wind our way through increasingly desolate areas. My tension rose. If we were attacked out here, there would be nobody to help us. We'd be sitting ducks. Let's face it, if we were in Baghdad walled in with traffic, we would also be a prime target, but at least there would be cover and the possibility of assistance.

By 6:25 p.m., with the sun descending in the desert, we arrived at the 28th Combat Support Hospital. It was a real live MASH outfit. I'd been a fan of the television show M*A*S*H my whole life and, along with most TV buffs, consider it one of the best shows ever produced. The movie is also one of my favorites. Now, I was visiting the real thing. It was a tent city in the middle of barren land where they cared for our soldiers and anyone else who needed treatment under less-than-ideal conditions. These guys were heroes. As we drove over the dusty landscape, I noticed two attractive young nurses, jogging along the roadside. Hawkeye Pierce would have appreciated the view, but I was far from being one of the "pros from Dover," there to save the day.

We pulled up outside the intensive care facility. I greeted the doctor who ran the unit and asked that I be permitted to do a walkthrough of the ward before the media were allowed in. Just as I was about to leave the bus for the tent, the army major, still pissed off that he was there and still concerned about the approach of nightfall, informed me in a very stern voice that this bus would be leaving in ten minutes. "Ten minutes!" he said, his voice rising over a passing vehicle. I pulled him aside and asked him to divide the press into two groups. One would rotate inside, while the other would wait outside and have an opportunity to talk with the doctors. He repeated again, that he would be on the bus in ten minutes and we were getting out of here. As I said, I understood his concern, but we had driven all the way out there. I owed these guys an opportunity to get something for their producers and editors. We were all sharing the same risk. I informed him, within earshot of the reporters, that we would leave when we were finished and we will move as fast as possible to accomplish what we came to do. I then again asked him to divide the group in two. He made a face. At which point I said, "Either help me out here to get this done, or go sit on the bus, but either way we are not leaving in ten minutes." While he didn't re-board the bus, he was useless for the rest of the trip.

Life is one big learning experience. You should never stop learning. If you stop learning, you stop growing. Well, I learned something that day—never take reporters to an intensive care unit at a combat hospital at nightfall. I suspected that this was a bad idea but had originally taken some comfort in the fact that we were assured that the hospital staff would separate the more seriously wounded prisoners from those with less life-threatening injuries. It didn't happen. I don't blame them. They either never got the message or it was just not feasible. Either way we shouldn't have expected that these doctors and nurses should alter their operation for the sake of this visit.

This was going to be bad. Lying in the ward together, within reach of each other, were an injured American soldier, an Iraqi child who had been hurt during an unrelated attack, and several Iraqi prisoners from Abu Ghraib in varying conditions.

The beige tents were climate-controlled and had air conditioning. The cold air circulated through a series of large exposed ducts that ran along the ceilings. The ward was actually a series of tents connected together, separated by pass-through walls that hung in strips of plastic like those one might see in a kitchen or a meat locker. The outer room was clearly meant for storage and to separate those who came and went from the patients inside. The tents were tight spaces cluttered with equipment and supplies. There were wires, cables, and air ducts that formed a small labyrinth under the canvas.

I hate hospitals and I hate what is commonly referred to as "hospital smell," the antiseptic aroma that is all-pervading in hospitals. The odor in the tents was overpowering, at least to me. It was a hospital smell, but more potent by an order of magnitude. It was probably caused by a combination of sterilization chemicals and plastics or vinyl used in the equipment. Though I was already feeling uneasy, I kept my composure and led the first group of reporters through the outer tent into the second. There were about six beds in the room; the first two near the door were critical patients, with the less-injured toward the back. The Iraqi child was on the left next to a prisoner who was able to communicate. The critical patient on the right looked to be burned over most of his body. I'd never seen a burn victim before and have to say that this was one of the most gruesome sights I'd ever seen. Samir moved toward the rear of the room and talked with the prisoner there. The journalists of course gravitated to the child and instantly became less concerned about the prisoners. He was a cute kid who had a relatively minor injury. Getting the kid to say that the U.S. military injured him would make great ink for many of them.

The reporters spent a minute or two with the other prisoner who was conscious and willing to talk. Even with the small group, it was cramped. I kept on trying to move the cameramen into locations where they wouldn't be in danger of hitting a patient. Between the beds, the medical equipment, the translators, the medical personnel, and the reporters, it was wall-to-wall people. People were bumping into beds and IV bags. After a couple of minutes, I tried valiantly, but not entirely successfully, to rotate the group out. I did my best, but some of the cameramen and writers just wouldn't leave. They weren't finished trying to get the patients to say something negative about the U.S. military. I pushed out as many as I could and grabbed the remaining group, hurrying them into the tent. After they were inside, I ran back out to make sure that folks hadn't wandered off. After all, as soon as we were done, we were getting out of there. I came back into the tent and it was again wall-to-wall people. Samir was doing his best to speak to the reporters and the patients, playing the role of local politician very well under the circumstances.

I wasn't doing as well. During the visit, I kept walking past that critical patient on the right and must have done so several times, being sure not to look at him. He was in bad shape, and I feared that I couldn't deal with what I might see. However, a minute or two into the second group's time in the ward, I caught a glance and became fixed on a face that I can still see when I close my eyes, his eyes fixed and his mouth gaping open as if frozen from unspeakable anguish. The burns had melted the flesh on his face and head. The wounds were oozing what looked like white puss, and blood covered the bed sheets around his head. There was a yellow fluid that also stained the bed. His hair had been burned off and his skin was a thin red veil over his bones. He wouldn't make it, the nurse told me. Suddenly the walls appeared to be getting closer. I was lightheaded and my breathing became heavier. I needed to get out. I didn't want to leave the reporters behind, but I needed air and I scrambled out of the ward into the first tent.

I took a minute to collect myself and then decided enough was enough. Although it took a few minutes, I managed to push everyone out of there. We left that poor prisoner and everyone else in peace.

Outside the tent, Samir and the doctors answered a few questions. Samir enjoyed holding court, and he said the right things about the effort to provide good care to the prisoners. He told them that what the opponents to the coalition wanted was mere chaos. Earlier that day, the insurgents had also attacked a major water main in Baghdad. With the pensive army major still standing idle, his arms folded in disgust, I called last question and moved everyone onto the bus. I thanked the head nurse for all the trouble, wished her luck, and boarded the bus. We had been there just under a half hour. As we drove from the camp, the sun was dipping under the horizon and night began to fall over the barren landscape. We headed back to the relative security of the Green Zone. While the drive would be shorter, we did manage to hit traffic once we were back in Baghdad. To be sure, this day wasn't over by a long shot.

About halfway home, the Reuters producer who was sitting a couple of rows behind me came up front with a look of panic on his face and asked to use my phone.

When I asked him why, he explained that he had received an urgent message from his bureau but couldn't raise anyone on the satellite phone system. Of course, I gave him the phone, but he again had no success. I promised him that I would ask the folks at the palace to contact the bureau. At that point, I called into the office to find out what I missed while out of cell phone range and to update Charles on the trip. Charles got on the phone, sounding what I thought was fatigued. That would have been normal. It was after 7:00 p.m., and Charles had hit the thirteen-hour point in his usually frantic day, with several more to go. He wasn't tired. He was upset and frustrated. It was then that he told me that the U.S. military had accidentally shot and killed Reuters cameraman Mazen Dana outside of Abu Ghraib. The soldiers mistook his camera and microphone for a rocket propelled grenade launcher and fired a volley at him at about one hundred yards. The bullet passed through his body and he died at the scene. Although Reuters was told directly not to send a crew to cover the prison in the aftermath of the attack, one was sent anyway. I asked Charles what I should do about the guys on the bus. He told me to tell them and bring them up to the Coalition Press Information Center (CPIC) to talk to the military. I hung up the phone and sat silently in that front seat thinking about what I knew and how I was going to tell those guys back there that their friend and colleague was dead. Once we made it through a crowded traffic circle, the bus, capably driven by one of KBR's finest, moved quickly over the bridge and back through the security perimeter of the Green Zone.

When we arrived at the convention center, the bus stopped outside the main gate. The reporters departed—off to write their pieces about the whirlwind trip. I asked the Reuters producer and his team to stay behind. There on the sidewalk, between the concertina wire and the wall, across the gate from the guardhouse, he asked me whether I had heard anything about Mazen. I knew as I looked at his face that I had specifically told him not to send anyone to the area. I knew that it was possible that it had been his decision to send Mazen to get the footage. I didn't know for sure and still don't, but this guy was going to feel in part responsible for what had happened.

I told them. I told them he was dead. The producer clutched his black hair and his wiry frame fell under him on the cement. I watched as these grown men collapsed onto the ground sobbing, holding their heads, and repeatedly shouting the word "No!" as they wept. They literally hit the pavement, dropping their gear on the ground unable to control themselves. I stood there silently, choking back some emotion of my own, until a young soldier at the guardhouse saw the commotion and came over, demanding that they leave. I have a great deal of respect and admiration for our troops, but in this instance, it was clear that this teenage army specialist either was on a power trip or wasn't observant enough to see that these men were devastated and needed a minute. I tried to explain the situation to the soldier, who would hear none of it. It was embarrassing that this soldier was standing there, threatening me and the crew, holding his M-16 while they mourned their loss at the hands of the U.S. military. I was furious but kept my anger in check. I told the crew they would have to move inside the convention center. I asked what I could do, and the producer requested that his bureau chief be called. They were able to call him and were asked to wait outside the CPIC until he could arrive. The U.S. military needed information about next of kin and the preferred disposition of Mazen's body.

I waited with them and, ultimately, Charles came by as well. I asked whether there were any special considerations that should be made for him. I really didn't know what else to do. I figured if Mazen was Muslim (he was Palestinian) and needed certain arrangements, then perhaps that information was important for someone to know. I had never been in this situation before and was just trying to be sensitive.

The producer glared at me as if he wished to take his anger over the situation out on some American—perhaps the one standing in front of him. He didn't. I think he realized that I was trying to help. I think that sometimes journalists believe that, when a mistake like this is made, the military doesn't care. Nonsense. Colonel Guy Shields, the coalition military spokesperson at the time, said of the incident, "Almost no one feels worse about this than the kid who pulled the trigger." He was probably right. Mistakes are made in complicated and dangerous situations. They can have deadly consequences.

We sat there on the benches on the second floor, overlooking the atrium, for an hour, until the bureau chief arrived to take them home. Charles and I headed back to the palace. In the Green Room I leaned with both elbows on my dusty desk and took stock of the day. My helmet was upside down to my right, and my computer with a hundred unopened emails in front of me. I just stared at the screen and concluded that this was a tough one; but, as I often did, I acknowledged that it could have been worse. After all, you learn more from your mistakes than from anything else.

Mazen Dana shouldn't have been there. It was a very dangerous location. I do however give him credit for the risks he took to do a job that he did well. In a way, we were all doing the same thing: taking great risks to do a job. I tried to remember that when dealing with an increasingly activist media; but, for God's sake, B-roll footage is never worth dying for. In the end, the journalists knew the prison was the better story, as we would all learn in the spring of 2004 one Sunday night watching *60 Minutes*. At that point during the occupation, the prison system, still undergoing reconstruction, was clearly overburdened. Unbeknownst to most people at the time, it was being grossly mismanaged by some number of officers and a few unsupervised and degenerate enlisted soldiers.

As anticipated, the injured Iraqi child and Dana's death dominated the news stories. We were damned if we did and damned if we didn't when it came to the story. Ultimately, the United States was even blamed for the deaths and injuries associated with the mortar attack. An understanding of the rationale for the conditions and the work being done still isn't appreciated to this day.

THE FACE OF EVIL

Genuine progress on a wide range of issues was hampered by a variety of complicating developments. Underlying those was the culture of uncertainly, distrust, and fear created by the former regime and ingrained in the soul of much of the population.

Americans and most Westerners alive today simply have no concept of the kind of environment that the Iraqi people were forced to endure over the three decades of Saddam's reign. Thirty years. That's nearly three times longer than Adolf Hitler ruled Nazi Germany. Such an extended period of brutal, authoritarian rule had a tremendous effect on the country and its people. Saddam's brutality struck to the very heart and soul of the Iraqi population. At the CPA, we often pelted journalists with statistics and figures about infrastructure and reconstruction. There was physical neglect to be sure, the extent of which few in Washington fully understood prior to the coalition invasion. Those were compounded by the looting in the immediate aftermath of the collapse of the regime. Even the most vital components of the country's infrastructure, such as water systems and oil production facilities, were hopelessly dilapidated. In fact, much of the oil infrastructure in the country was more than forty years old. Iraq was a nation that didn't have a funded school maintenance program for more than a decade prior to the coalition invasion. In some areas, schools were in such poor shape that enrollment had decreased to less than 50 percent of eligible students.

Roads and transportation infrastructure were poorly planned to meet the needs of the growing population, and all government facilities suffered from decay. The health care system was in a shambles before the liberation. Saddam spent less than one dollar per person per year on health care. Medical students and doctors used textbooks that were decades behind the times and then treated patients using equipment just as ancient. Buildings, including hospitals and schools, were flooded with sewage that backed up into the basements and onto the floors. The water and electricity were unreliable and dangerous.

Although it became popular and not inaccurate to blame the condition of Iraq's infrastructure on sanctions, it cannot be ignored that much of the fault lies with Saddam's total disregard for much of the population. CPA advisor Bob Goodwin and Senior Advisor for Health Jim Haveman worked tirelessly to build a health-care system from scratch because most of the population lacked even basic care. Saddam built two health care systems. One was modern and well-equipped, and it served only Saddam's family and senior Ba'ath Party leadership. The other was for the rest of the population and left to rot while he built his palaces and lined his pockets. Bob would tell me about Saddam's practice of not burying the bodies of dead children from the Al-Iskan Children's Hospital. He'd parade them out as propaganda for the press against the UN sanctions. Yet, while those children lay dying in a decrepit facility, down the block, he had built a new hospital with foreign doctors and the latest equipment. Virtually no one could seek care there.

Jim and Bob worked to ensure that the coalition engaged thousands of people in the strategic planning process for the new health care system. People who had never been asked their opinion before helped guide the reformation of the system to better serve the needs of all Iraqis. A CPA initiative brought in about two million dollars' worth of new textbooks and medical journals from the American Medical Association and distributed them across the country. A new drug formulary was established to give doctors confidence in the medicines that they were using. Nurses, who also lacked adequate training under the former regime, were given new curricula and increased levels of training.

As when it came to the Ministry of Justice and reform there, Iraqis in the health care field understood what needed to be done to make the system better, fairer, and more effective. Goodwin would often note that, when they engaged doctors in a discussion about reforms, the Iraqis typically had all the answers.

They weren't the way the media had presented to audiences back home. They had knowledge and ideas, but the centralization of all the systems of government meant that no one asked for their opinion. Of course, you didn't offer it if you wanted to keep your job. In less than a year, the collaborative process with the Iraqis helped to ensure tremendous strides toward providing better-quality care.

In 2003, I had assisted in planning President Bush's visit to Poland. While there, I was privileged to visit a small town outside of Krakow. It was hard to imagine, as we drove through the quaint village in the lush countryside, that it was home to one of the darkest crimes in the history of humankind. The town was home to the Auschwitz death camp. My colleagues and I spent an entire day touring both Auschwitz and Birkenau in preparation for Bush's visit to both camps. As our White House team walked in silence along the rows of brick buildings, we listened to the museum director, who described in detail the evolution of Nazi extermination techniques. Hitler developed a science around killing. It was a craft that took research, experimentation, and resources. We passed through the gas chambers. We touched the cold steel of the ovens made to burn flesh. We saw the mounds of human hair, shaved from the heads of thousands of Jews and people of other faiths, now preserved to remind the world of Hitler's madness. We walked the train tracks on that wet, overcast day and stood at the place where a million people learned whether they would live in a hell on earth or die a horrible death.

Everyone should come here, I thought. Each of us that day saw the face of evil. It was emotionally draining, yet I considered myself fortunate to have had the opportunity to visit such a shrine.

Only by confronting evil can we help prevent its recurrence in the future. There is real evil in this world. America saw it on September 11, 2001. We see it today in the unchecked advance of ISIS. Other nations have faced worse calamities. Many people saw real evil long before it touched American shores. In Iraq, I considered myself fortunate to have seen the face of evil. Saddam Hussein's barbarism is etched into the landscape of the nation he once ruled. By some estimates, Iraq before the war was a nation of 1.3 million missing people. Mass graves dot the landscape, and shattered lives litter the towns and villages from border to border. Saddam's acts of evil were of varying scope and method. All of the most infamous of history's dictators had their ways of committing democide, or in other words exterminating their own people. Hitler had his "Final Solution." Stalin used much simpler methods to murder on a scale that would have made even the Nazis envious. Saddam too, had his methods of extermination.

WMDs or no WMDs, what drove so many involved in the Iraq effort—both military and civilian—was the chance that we could rescue people in some respect from this past by giving them the opportunity to live free from evil in their midst. The withdrawal of American forces to the degree insisted upon by the Obama administration robbed the people of Iraq of that chance by forcing the Iraqi government to look elsewhere for guidance and support. It led to further instability that enabled ISIS to gain a foothold in the country and to continue to commit the kind of systematic atrocities that the Iraqi people had feared from the Hussein regime.

One morning in September, Dan, Charles, and I were discussing Secretary Powell's upcoming trip to Iraq when they suggested that, rather than handle the traveling press corps, I should travel in advance of the secretary to set up the various meetings and events for him and Bremer. Brian McCormack was already up in the Kurdish region, laying the groundwork for the trip with the leadership there. What Dan, Charles, and the ambassador's office wanted was for someone to pay close attention to the details and media logistics. I was excited about the trip. It was an opportunity to get out of town and see a new part of the country. It was also generally safer up in the Kurdish area. Our staff in the region could walk freely in the streets and shop in the markets. They were always quick to say that caution was still necessary, but it definitely wasn't Baghdad. The regional government was also more organized and had control over more financial resources than those in the central and southern parts of the country. The Kurds had been shielded to a certain degree by the UN "no fly zone" and benefited from their close ties and cooperation with the United States and other Western nations who were opposed to Saddam. They had their own currency and government as well as an army that was trained to fight Saddam's forces. The Peshmerga Army, translated literally, "one who faces death," helped the Kurds maintain their territorial integrity and stability. By 2015, they were fighting ISIS more effectively and fervently than any force in the region despite limited support from the Obama administration.

These were our truest allies in country. They weren't opportunistic expatriates or shaky coalition partners. The Kurds wanted a new future—out from under the shadow of Saddam. They knew from their own experience that a peaceful nation with an active economy was possible. This wasn't to say that they were anxious or willing to give up a lot of autonomy or resources to Baghdad, but they were at least at the table and participating in the new government.

I was happy to be heading out on the trip. We would be flying up in two Blackhawk helicopters that would pass through the Sunni Triangle on the way. The trip had the potential to be dangerous and quite long. I recruited two army AV (audiovisual) personnel working for the CPIC to install the mult-box (multiport audio box) for the press and the sound system. They also brought with them the new bulletproof podiums that had been recently shipped from the presidential retreat at Camp David and were now being used for Bremer's public events. Army staff sergeant J. J. Johnson and marine corporal David Bailey were the best of the AV group. It took a little extra coaxing, but their O-6 level (colonel) commanding officer agreed to let them come along. I was also going to need assistance in moving media and someone I could trust to help. I immediately thought of army sergeant Aaron Gibson. Gibson and I had become good friends, and his purpose on the trip was threefold. First, as a member of the psychological operations team he could use the time in Kurdistan to get interviews, footage, and photos for products being developed by him and his colleagues. Secondly, he was a capable person who could be trusted to do what needed to be done during the secretary's visit. If I asked him to do something, I knew he'd do it. Third, well, I thought it would be a good time for both of us. Gibson had a way of making me laugh and keeping me calm, much the same way buddies of mine did back home. It was a good old-fashioned road trip, with one exception: We weren't heading for Vegas. We were heading for Halabja, the town where Saddam Hussein gassed five thousand of his own people in 1986.

We loaded up the Blackhawks with part of Powell's security detail and lifted off from the Green Zone, heading for northern Iraq. Thankfully, it was an uneventful trip through the Sunni Triangle and northeast to Kurdistan. I learned that if I leaned my headphones on the raised collar of my flak jacket I could relax my neck and take short catnaps. About an hour and a half into the flight, we landed outside Kirkuk to refuel. As we jumped out of the helicopters into the blistering heat, we found ourselves in utter desolation. There was virtually no vegetation, and the blinding sun had baked everything to a crisp. After ten minutes, we were back on board and in the air. As we entered the northern part of the country, I was surprised to see mountains and lakes. The rock formations were beautiful and the terrain came to life. The pilots decided to have some fun, dipping close to the water and then bounding over the hills. Turning sharply, they rose and fell through the air, showing off for each other and their passengers.

We finally touched down on the freshly laid blacktop of the helicopter landing pad at the new Halabja Museum, which Secretary Powell would help dedicate in two days' time. Brian McCormack and Alex Zemek were waiting for us upon our arrival. We entered the museum building and met with the security team about the schedule of events and press coverage anticipated. Workers were frantically finishing the construction of the building. Windows were still missing, and scaffolding rose in the lobby to the top of the cone-shaped atrium. Tile was being laid, exhibits were being installed, furniture still bore plastic coverings, light bulbs needed installation, and, not surprisingly, everything was covered with a thin layer of dirt. It seemed that there would be no way that the building would be ready for the dedication. We were assured by our local liaison, Dildar Kittani, that it would be.

To the Kurds, this was their great monument. This was their Holocaust Museum. It was their tribute to all of those who had suffered at the hands of Saddam, not only at Halabja but also throughout the region. They were determined to get it finished in time for the secretary's visit. They considered it a great privilege to have the American secretary of state present at the dedication. The Kurds wanted the world to bear witness to their suffering and their strength.

Our group then set out to the local cemetery, where many of the more than five thousand who were killed by the gas attacks lay buried in a mass grave. We drove through town on the way there and saw the statues erected as an ever-present reminder to the people of Halabja of their collective tragedy. In the town square, there is a statue of a man and boy lying on top of each other; the father trying in vain to shield his son from the gas that would ultimately kill them both. There were simple homes and businesses on the route. Children played in the same streets where other kids their age had lain dead and disfigured back in 1986. It was life in a small town in northeastern Iraq: a frustrated and stilted normalcy in the aftermath of tragedy.

We came to the cemetery and, passing through the gates, I was immediately struck by how different a resting place it is from those I was used to back in the United States. The rocky terrain created uneven burial plots, with headstones of many shapes and colors haphazardly placed throughout the site. A dirt road led us to the new memorial, also to be dedicated by Powell, Bremer, and Kurdish leaders Talibani and Barzani. The memorial was in better shape than the museum but was also being readied in a frenzy of activity. The monument at its center was not yet installed and its base was still under construction. Local townspeople, all survivors or relatives of those lost in the attacks, worked feverishly to plant flowers and complete the project.

The memorial was essentially a large, raised area on the edge of the cemetery. Its backdrop was the dusty mountains of northern Iraq that form the border with Iran. Visitors to the memorial ascended several tile steps to a path that divided what appeared to be a burial ground. Rows of headstones stretched out for fifty feet on either side of the path, each marked with black Arabic writing. They weren't graves but rather markers. Each of the more than twelve hundred headstones represented a family that lost members in the attacks. Some families lost more than a dozen people.

In the middle of the memorial was a bone-white statue on a base of small smooth gray stones. The statue was designed and crafted by the Kurds and it depicted a woman clutching her chest and looking up to the heavens. It was a simple modern expressionist figure, virtually devoid of physical detail. It didn't need to be detailed to have impact. I was struck by its brilliance in the hot sun. It shone like a beacon of hope in the face of death and uncertainty. *Was she praying?* I thought. *Was it a cry for help?* I wondered. *Was she asking why this heartbreak should have happened? Was she thankful for the salvation of those spared? Was she wondering whether God had abandoned his obedient people?* Questions bounced through my head as I stood for a moment, captivated by the figure.

The people working on the monument all wanted to meet us. Brian showed me and the State Department security personnel around the site, while I began to think about what this event would look like. After an hour or so, we left the cemetery and headed to Sulaymaniyah, about ninety minutes northwest, for the remainder of the night. Brian and Alex were staying at the Sulaymaniyah Palace Hotel and we were hoping to do the same. Sulaymaniyah was a radical departure from Baghdad. The electricity, while spotty, was far more reliable. The Kurdish area was somewhat shielded from the economic sanctions imposed after the first Gulf War. The result was a functional city where the rule of law was enforced and people had a better quality of life than their countrymen to the south. Iraqis living in Sulaymaniyah had access to products not available in other parts of the country. There was even a McDonald's. Well, maybe. I know I saw the "Golden Arches" and some variation on the name but never quite found out whether it was part of the chain. I doubted it. It didn't matter. It was an outside commercial influence coming through in Iraq and it felt great seeing it. It showed that the people in northern Iraq wanted to reach out to the world and were willing to let the world reach in to them.

The hotel was very nice by Iraqi standards. Smaller than the Al Rashid, the Sulaymaniyah Palace looked to have been recently updated. There was a business center on the second floor and several restaurants, one of which was on the top floor overlooking the city. I remember the elevators played the same song over and over. Gibson and I strained our ears to recognize the lost eighties classic instrumental that was being piped through for our riding pleasure. We laughed about it for months, though neither of us ever named that tune. I truly felt at ease sitting in the lobby or walking out in the parking lot without protection. We had been assured by the Kurdish leadership that we were safe, and I believed them. Unfortunately, the hotel couldn't accommodate those of us who came up that day, and we had to find another place to lay our heads.

In the evening, as Gibson, Bailey, and Johnson went up to the hotel restaurant, Brian, Alex, and I were asked to attend a meeting with Barham Salah, the prime minister of the Patriotic Union of Kurdistan and one of the most powerful Kurdish leaders. We left the hotel in our small motorcade and headed into one of the nearby neighborhoods to Barham's house.

We drove through the streets, turning down various roads in one of the residential districts until we came upon a gated compound. The guards at the gate were not uniformed but rather wore dark collared shirts and slacks with AK-47s as their only accessory. We pulled up out back of a fairly large home with a walled backyard. More guards stood watch at the gate to the backyard. They all looked alike. We walked through the gate into Barham's backyard. A cement patio ran from the gate to the door of the house. To the right there was perhaps a twenty-by-thirty-foot patch of lush green grass, the likes of which I hadn't seen in months. Adirondack-style chairs and coffee tables formed a semicircle along the stucco walls and modest plantings hugged the perimeter. Fluorescent lights attached to the walls illuminated the yard. The scene reminded me of the small yards and gardens my relatives in Brooklyn used to keep. It was a postage stamp–sized yard, simply furnished but truly a center of activity. Guards stood ready to provide protection, tea, a bowl of fruit, or just about anything that the master of the house needed for himself or his guests. Like the guards at the gate, they were visibly armed and wore dark open-collared shirts, slacks, and black shoes.

At the far end of the yard sat Barham, holding court with some other Western guests discussing human rights issues. Barham added to the Francis Ford Coppola quality of the whole scene. He was a charismatic figure, and in many ways a looming presence. He too wore a dark open-collared shirt and gray slacks. On his feet were black socks and slippers. A cigar protruded from his mouth, jutting out from beneath his round, steel-framed glasses and thick, black moustache. I really felt like I was back in Brooklyn with the older members of my family, especially after noticing the black socks and slippers.

We waited our turn. After a few moments, he noticed the time and stood up, signaling the end to one meeting and the beginning of another. He showed his guests to the gate and then invited us to sit down. Brian sat to Barham's right and I next to Brian, who was taking the lead in the meeting as the ambassador's representative and because he had been in town working the details of the trip for several days. Barham immediately sent for tea and fruit. Moments later, one of the staff came out of the house with our drinks, a sugar bowl, and an assortment of fruit. The tea was hot and sweet, as Iraqi tea usually is, and while Alex ate what seemed like half the fruit on the table, I chose just to nibble. I was typically very cautious about what I ate, especially when it came to raw fruit or vegetables, as I couldn't afford to get sick with so much work to be done.

Several times during the meeting, our host was interrupted by guards who handed him a cell phone to address some burning issue. Barham would bark in Kurdish into the phone, presumably solving a pressing problem, and then return to the discussion of Secretary Powell's schedule without missing a beat. At one point he asked us whether the road leading to the memorial in the cemetery had been paved. When we responded that it had not, he immediately asked for a phone, placed a call, and again barked some orders at some unknown worker. Needless to say, when we arrived at the site at 10:00 a.m. the next morning, the road was finished. Watching him work, one definitely got the impression that he wasn't someone to screw with.

One of the aspects not only of the meeting but also of the entire visit was the sense of deep appreciation on the part of the Kurds for the liberation. Barham and his people made it clear that they would provide anything we needed. I'd often talk with reporters about the tremendous feelings of gratitude expressed by the Kurds, but it was almost always considered unimportant by the media. Members of the press would openly dismiss Kurdish support as inconsequential, naturally preferring to focus on the difficulties of bringing together the Shiites and the Sunnis. It is true that prior to the liberation, the Kurds maintained close relationships with the West and were protected in many ways. They were indeed staunch supporters of military action to depose the regime, but there were reasons for that support. The Kurds suffered greatly under Saddam. It is believed that Saddam killed more than eight thousand members of the Barzani family alone. He killed thousands more Kurdish men, women, and children. Their bodies fill many a mass grave in Iraq. All this was in addition to the chemical weapons attacks that we were there to commemorate.

Although the Kurds were working closely with the coalition, the media seemed to perpetuate the notion that the Kurds were not part of Iraq in the first place. They might not have had some of the security and resource challenges that those in the south faced, but they nonetheless were abused, neglected, and murdered en masse by the regime. The coalition liberated them as well. Most of the time that I was in Iraq, 95 percent of the attacks and violence were in only 5 percent of the country. Although the media was painting a picture of a nation in total chaos, the people in the north—more than five million strong—were welcoming of the CPA's efforts to rebuild and create a democracy that protected their rights.

A decade later, as they faced being overrun by ISIS, the United States would dither for months in giving them the support that they needed and never fully equipped or assisted them to the extent that they deserved. President Obama's strategy left the Kurds fighting for their lives.

The meeting with Barham lasted about thirty-five minutes. At the end, he walked us to the gate and gave each of us a Romeo and Juliette cigar in a silver tube. He was all business, but his excitement over Powell's visit to dedicate the memorial and museum could not be hidden. Although the international press would have the world believe that all Iraqis would rather pelt American and coalition forces with rocks, this large chunk of the country was warm and welcoming. Before we walked out of the gate, Barham told us that he had arranged for me and the other latecomers to stay under guard at one of his houses in Sulaymaniyah. We took our leave of Barham Salih about 10:00 p.m. and went back to the hotel.

We gathered our duffle bags and piled into the cars. I could tell, as we drove through the city, that the security detail was nervous about staying in a residential neighborhood and not in a more secure area. I was a little nervous as well but had confidence that Barham would do everything he could to make sure we were safe. We pulled up to a small two-story house that looked hurriedly vacated and cleaned in anticipation of our arrival. There was a plainly furnished living room with a tiny television and a kitchen near the back of the house. On the second floor, there were three bedrooms, each with its own bathroom. Oddly, there were green armchairs in the hallway outside the bedrooms, perhaps for security or for some sort of waiting area in the passageway. The beds were dressed with clean linens, and most important the air conditioning was working. There were guards carrying AKs milling about the first floor and outside the house. Despite my confidence in Barham, looking at these guys hanging out down there, I was a little uneasy about the security. Corporal Bailey, the marine, slept with his M16 on his chest. Gibson roomed with me and kept his 9 mm under his pillow.

Early the next morning, we set back out for Halabja. As we drove through the countryside shortly after dawn, I was struck by the beauty of the landscape. It was comparable in many ways to Arizona and parts of the western United States. We drove through villages where women in traditional Kurdish dress made their way to the market and children played in the dirt. Sheep and goat herders tended their flocks and shopkeepers stacked their produce in rickety carts along the road. The rising sunlight danced low over the mountains and began its daily cooking of the landscape.

More striking than the landscape were the Kurdish children. For some reason, the children in northern Iraq dressed in bright colors. Clad in pinks, greens, and blues they provided a sharp contrast to their drab surroundings. Gibson remarked that they were like crayons running in the dirt. It was the perfect description. The children would run alongside our cars and wave as we drove through the villages. Crumbling homes and infrastructure did not seem to erase the smiles of these young people. It was comforting to think that perhaps some degree of innocence still existed for these children, despite the horrors Saddam unleashed on their families in this quiet countryside.

In one of the villages, I peered through my dusty window and saw a young girl. She was perhaps ten years old standing on the side of the road near a crumbling cinderblock wall. She was wearing a bright pink dress and held a lace scarf over her head. The adults in Iraq wear earth tones; blacks, dark blues, and browns. It almost seemed symbolic of their struggle. As we drove past the girl in pink, I hoped and prayed that one day that would change—that the hope that springs from freedom would bring more color to a nation all too often draped in mourning black.

Along the road, we also noticed the security that Barham had promised. For more than fifty miles between Sulaymaniyah and Halabja, at each electrical pole was stationed a Peshmerga soldier. There were hundreds of them, and thousands more we never saw in the mountains around us. In the morning sun, these soldiers along the road toweled off their faces and made ready for a day keeping faithful watch.

We drove into the cemetery and the villagers were again working on the memorial. In fact, they had had been working all night. As I previously mentioned, they had paved the road leading to the memorial following Barham's curt phone call to the project manager. The workers had installed the statue and finished its base. Children were washing each of the headstones and planting flowers along the rows of little monuments that bore witness to tragedy. In the hot sun, we enjoyed working side by side with the townspeople. We took pictures with them and talked with them about their experiences. Everyone was doing their level best, as advance folks say, to "build-out" a site for a major event. We moved in flatbed trucks to serve as press platforms and built a barrier between the memorial and the audience for security purposes.

The memorial had four flagpoles, positioned to the right front of the statue. The gentleman in charge of the construction brought me an American flag and pointed to the first flagpole. He motioned with his hand that he intended to raise it first in line with respect to the others, which would have been a huge breach of protocol and, certainly, something the media would jump all over. Regardless of the media fallout, it was simply inappropriate. The Iraqis explained that they wished to raise the Stars and Stripes and the British flag first and second, as an expression of thanks for our work to liberate Iraq. They wanted to show their respect and appreciation for Secretary Powell's visit. I relayed that, while we appreciated the gesture, this was their country and that the Iraqi flag should be raised first in line, the Kurdish flag second, and the American and British flags last. The great flag debate eventually made its way back to Barham, who after some coaxing on our part agreed that the Iraqi flag should be first in line.

The Iraqis in Halabja eventually did agree to our request and, after another discussion about the position of the Kurdish flag, it was settled that the Iraqi flag would be raised first and the Kurdish flag second, and neither the American nor British flags would be flown. No American present that day will ever forget the applause heard from the workers at the memorial as they watched the American flag make its way temporarily to the top of its pole *before the official ceremony*. The hair stood up on the back of my neck. Although I wished the press corps could have witnessed this simple expression of gratitude, they likely wouldn't have reported it anyway.

While Corporal Bailey and Staff Sergeant Johnson were busy laying the groundwork for the sound system, I was looking at the camera shots and negotiating with the diplomatic security agents about logistics. Sergeant Gibson was busy doing what he did best—learning about the people. As a psychological operations guy, it was important for him to connect with the people for whom he was charged with developing communications products. Throughout the afternoon, he took photos of the survivors and talked with folks about the experience of living through the attacks. At one point, a man pulled from his pockets a stack of photos and began showing them to him. I walked over and we looked at the pictures together as the gentleman described that fateful day in 1986 and its aftermath. The pictures were of the dead. Men, women, children, burned alive and horribly disfigured by the gas that rained down on the town. Many of the corpses in the photos were the friends and family of this man. "This was my brother," he said. "This was my cousin." It was moving and more than a little disturbing. I can still see clearly the face of one particular child frozen with the expression of terror, burned and melted by the gas.

In our culture, we might carry pictures of loved ones lost, but those mementos are meant to remind us of the person before the event or illness that took them from us. The cause of death is often less important than the memories of the life once lived. These people, however, carried the gruesome images with them to remind them of the tragedy. *Why did they choose to do this?* I thought. *Perhaps they had they seen too much death to avoid the images. Perhaps their pain was a source of strength and determination.* One thing was certain, they will never forget. Nor will we who walked that hallowed ground. Working together, we believed we could ensure it would never happen again.

After two days of planning, Powell and Bremer were on their way. The workers at the museum had hung a cone-shaped Kurdish flag from the top of the atrium covering the windows. The flag was three stories in height and gave the room a warm glow. The red, green, and yellow stripes of the flag reflected in the shiny, black granite walls of the atrium where the names of the dead were etched in the slabs that encircled the room. Talibani and Barzani, the two Kurdish leaders, arrived with their entourages and took seats on newly unwrapped furniture in the meeting room off the atrium. We waited for the helicopters to arrive. As I stood out on the helipad in the beating sun, my boots began to sink into the newly poured asphalt. Finally, in a whirlwind of dust and dirt the helicopters landed one by one to deposit their precious cargo. Bremer was in his boots, as usual, and Powell looked relaxed and confident, typical of his character.

Of course, there was also a load of press in tow. Alex, Elisa, and I hurried the media into waiting buses and readied the motorcade for departure. Bremer and Powell entered the memorial and were greeted by Talibani, Barzani, and Barham, who was beaming with pride on what was a bright, beautiful, and historic day in Kurdistan.

I was in the second press bus, and I asked Alex to handle the first. We set out ahead of the principals, much to the chagrin of the press corps, who firmly believe that it is their God-given right to be at the side of their subjects at all times. We wanted to move them to the cemetery early to stage them in time for the arrival of the secretary and others. As we made our way through town, hundreds of people turned out to welcome Powell, Bremer, and the Kurdish leaders. They had erected signs along the motorcade route that read, "Thank you President Bush for Our Freedom" and "Thank you America and Great Britain." I made it a point to watch the reaction of the media as we drove down the narrow streets. Most seemed unimpressed by the outpouring of gratitude. One wondered aloud whether the CPA had produced the signs.

At one point, the bus in front of us stopped. Two men from the crowd jumped on the bus, with one of them hanging out the front door. Concerned, I radioed to Alex to ask about the situation. All of us were naturally concerned about security and this looked to me like a potential situation. No response from Alex. I tried again and again, no response. I began to get seriously concerned but could not outwardly show my trepidation because of the media presence on the bus. A State Department press officer made her best attempt to continue a press briefing, while I tried in vain to reach my colleague and discern what was going on up ahead. Finally, after a few tense minutes, the motorcade stopped again and the two men jumped off. When I reached Alex on the radio, the explanation was simple. We had taken the wrong route and the driver got lost. The two men were just giving directions. It was clear: Alex needed to pay more attention to his radio. Either that or I needed to relax.

When we arrived at the cemetery, more than five hundred people, mostly women, dressed in black, traditional Kurdish garments and headscarves were already waiting in the blistering sun for the ceremony to begin. Nearly all of them carried framed photographs of their loved ones lost in the gas attacks. The townspeople had come that morning and placed banners around the site, thanking America and Britain for their freedom. Several large banners said, "I am a victim of Saddam's WMD." Another stated firmly, "Halabja Never Again." I was moved by the banners and signs but nervous as well. We were always walking on eggshells with the media. We never wanted to be accused of over-engineering an event, especially when it involved public expressions or support. The CPA did not take steps to hide Iraqi discontent from the press nor did it pump up Iraqi appreciation for the liberation. I feared that the journalists would speculate that the CPA had asked Kurdish officials to produce the banners or worse yet actually placed the banners along the route and at the memorial. To my knowledge, none of the published reports speculated about their origins, but more than a couple of journalists skeptically asked me where the banners came from.

Four Kurdish children waited at the steps of the memorial in brightly colored traditional clothing, bearing flowers for the dignitaries who were yet to arrive. The scene was stunning. It was full of stark contrasts. The sky was blue, the mountains a sandy beige, and the monument at the memorial's center gleamed in the sun. Yet on the ground was this swath of black, where the women of Halabja stood waiting among the headstones clutching pictures of the dead.

The Kurdish leadership arrived first, followed several minutes later by Powell and Bremer. The crowd surged forward against the improvised security barrier. The children presented their flowers and the men ascended the steps to pay their respects. Each one of them placed flowers on the smooth stones at the statue's base that two days before had not yet been set in place. Each man spoke. They spoke of a new era free from fear. They each assured the crowd that the tragedy of Halabja would never happen again. Then Powell came down to greet the assembled crowd. The women cried as they reached out to touch him, pointing to the photos that for many were all that remained of their families. The press swarmed the secretary trying to catch a glimpse of his reaction. Powell held their hands and looked at the photos as he made his way along the rope line. They spoke to him in Kurdish. He didn't understand much that was said and he didn't need to. Powell knew what they were saying without speaking the language. The women of Halabja were still searching for answers. They were perhaps still searching for the hope and happiness that once graced this quiet mountain town.

We made our way back to the memorial museum, where the secretary, Bremer, and the Kurdish leadership stood in the atrium with two survivors of the attack. Surrounded by the names of the dead, they lit candles in the center of the room, officially opening the new building. They then toured the exhibits that encircled the atrium. The museum's galleries contained photos of Halabja before the attacks. Mannequins depicted scenes of the normal life of the town's people. In another series of rooms, the displays turned to graphic photos of victims lying in the street, their skin melting off their bones and their bodies lying in heaps, waiting to be transported to the mass graves. The mannequins also dramatically depicted street scenes during the attack. It was difficult to view.

Following a brief outdoor press conference, it was time to take our leave of Halabja. I was able to board the press helicopter and lift off with the rest of the official party. As I looked down at the museum, with its blue glass tower reaching towards heaven, I was more grateful for my Iraq experience than I had ever been. I was more certain that I had made the right decision and more certain that I would carry the lessons I learned with me for the rest of my life. The people of Iraq were, I thought, making me a better person, a braver person, and a better American.

On the flight home, I sat next to Brian, who was sitting next to Bremer. All of us heading back to Baghdad were stuffed into a C-130 plane, along with two bomb-sniffing dogs, one of which had a bad case of diarrhea. The smell was terrible, especially as we sat on the runway in the midday heat. Once we were airborne, I drifted off to sleep along with most everyone on the plane. Brian had been sick with a stomach virus and was out like a light by the time we took off. It took me a little longer, but at least I had acquired the ability to doze amid the noise of a cargo plane. Everyone was sweaty, exhausted, and content to spend the flight napping or otherwise idle. That was everyone except Paul Bremer.

I awoke to find the ambassador hunched over paperwork piled high on his lap. He was reading and writing notes. While his staff slept, he was intently focused on what looked like memos, reports, and undoubtedly observations for his book. I watched him for quite some time, wondering how he had the stamina to bear the pressure placed on his shoulders. A while later, after he had come to the bottom of the pile on his lap, instead of leaning his head back against the red mesh jump seats to get some rest, he put away his papers, reached into his back pocket and pulled out a stack of index cards. They were his Arabic flashcards. He flipped through them feverishly. I couldn't believe what I was seeing. The man kept on going. There is a reason we all got through those days as the bombings became more frequent and the death toll began to rise. It was because the man at the top led by example. The CPA staff constantly marveled at Bremer's acumen, his energy, and his confidence. Rajiv Chandrasekaran with the *Washington Post* was sitting across from me. He too was watching Bremer intently. I made eye contact with him and he smiled, shaking his head as if to say, "Wow, how does his do it?" Despite the access he was given, the briefings, and the work he saw firsthand, Rajiv would ultimately write a scathing critique of Bremer and the CPA, naturally to much critical acclaim. It ignored virtually all of the good work being done by the military and civilians during that period.

Bremer became a figure much like President Bush for many of us. In Washington, Bush's confidence, clarity, and values at that time served as an inspiration for those who served the administration. In Iraq, Bremer's tenacity, passion, and poise in the face of mounting odds served much the same purpose.

Extermination by WMD was not the only way that Saddam sought to destroy the lives of large numbers of his people. In the southern part of Iraq, the method was more indirect and perhaps less gruesome but no less damaging to hundreds of thousands in that area of the country. The southern part of Iraq was once one of the most fertile places on the face of the earth. We've all heard the term "cradle of civilization." Southern Iraq, in the areas between the Tigris and Euphrates Rivers, was indeed one of the most vibrant, fruitful places in the world. It *was* the cradle of civilization. The culture that developed there around the marshes of the floodplain can date its origins back more than five thousand years. Its residents, called Marsh Arabs, lived off the fertile land and waters teeming with fish and vegetation in an area the size of Southern California. It would be fair to compare the Marsh Arabs to the American Indians. The cultural similarities and connection with the natural environment were quite similar.

I use the past tense to describe the environment deliberately. In the early 1990s, Saddam built a series of dams and dykes that diverted the water from the Tigris and Euphrates Rivers, having the catastrophic effect of drying out the land. He did this in part to punish the Marsh Arabs, who are Shiite Muslim, and (some speculate) to provide more stable land on which to mobilize ground troops and heavy artillery.

The diversion of the water destroyed everything. It killed virtually everything. Today, where the marshes once teemed with life, only desert exists. The fish died, the plant life died, and the livestock died. Saddam even built the dams high enough and steep enough to prevent animals from accessing the remaining water.

Those who opposed the Iraq operation conveniently overlook the gross human rights violations of Saddam's regime but also ignore the environmental devastation that was caused by its intentional acts. The same people who would block midday traffic in Washington DC to raise awareness about human rights issues and the perpetually impending environmental disaster somehow think that the abuses of the Hussein regime would have been best left for others to deal with. It remains striking to me that people can be so blatantly hypocritical. These issues were additionally often glossed over by the media, who focused mainly on the insurgency and propping up their opinion that the United States botched the peace.

Having spent my first two years in the Bush administration at the Environmental Protection Agency, the story of the Marsh Arabs appealed to me. It was a story that needed to be told. The press and the Western public needed to see for themselves not only the devastation but also how the coalition was working with the remaining Marsh Arab population to begin the process of restoring the wetlands. The Iraqi Ministry of Water Resources was also involved in planning a gradual re-flooding of the area to restore the destroyed habitat. After some discussion at the palace, Bremer decided that it was time to pay the region a visit.

I put together a group of media of mostly Middle Eastern journalists to travel with us to the south. Of the Western reporters, I asked Dr. Bob Arnot of MSNBC to come along. I knew that he would give the story a fair shake. Arnot was one of my favorite reporters in Iraq. He was a walking whirlwind and full of energy. Most of the Baghdad press corps approached their assignment to cover Iraq as if they'd lost a bet. Most of them stayed a short time and couldn't wait to get out of the country. Many just wanted to check the box with their news organization that they had done their duty in the war zone and could then be given a far better and safer assignment. The reporting clearly showed that mindset. Dr. Bob was an exception. He kept on coming back. Although most reporters were too cynical and skeptical to report about Iraqi-American relationship-building and other progress, Arnot believed that the American people deserved to see what their fellow citizens were doing to improve the quality of life for the Iraqi people. Oddly enough, he believed that in some places it was actually happening. Arnot used to call the small army of young CPA staff "true believers" and "young Turks." He would come bounding into the Green Room, asking about a variety of subjects and locations that he wished to cover. It didn't matter where we suggested that he go. Arnot traveled widely and was one of the few major American network correspondents who in the postwar period had the balls to touch every corner of the country. He didn't mind sleeping in the dirt. Arnot was also embedded with a variety of military units during and after the war. Those of us in the communications operation at the CPA had come to trust him. I knew he would be perfect for the visit to the Marsh Arabs. On the day of the trip, he was one of only two American journalists who actually showed up to go with us.

It bears mentioning that Bob Arnot was eventually let go from NBC. According to the network, his contract was simply not renewed. It was widely reported by other outlets, and speculated within the industry, that NBC brass apparently felt that his reporting was too positive and lacked the hard edge that the network favored. Arnot constantly pitched stories to NBC *Nightly News* and the *Today Show*, receiving rejection after rejection. Not enough blood and bombs. Too many smiling children and stories of hope and potential.

Our first stop was the CPA South Headquarters in Basra, where the Iraqi interim minister of water resources briefed Bremer about efforts to restore the marshes and the habitat they once supported. The press covered the first portion of the meeting and we then took lunch at—you guessed it—the small KBR dining facility on site. We then headed for the motorcade, and our first site visit was a look at one of Basra's many canals. Basra was once known as the Venice of the Middle East. A series of canals once played a vital role in moving goods throughout the city and flushing the sewage system out to the Persian Gulf. After Saddam diverted the water from the rivers to dry out the Marsh Arabs, one of the consequences was a sharp reduction in water flow to the city. Eventually, the canals became nothing more than stagnant, green, sewage-filled waterways. Children played in the sewage as there were no fences, barriers, or signs warning of the dangers posed from the water. The British Army, which was in control of the area, had begun erecting signage, but as we drove to the site, we still saw children knee deep in the sludge.

The smell was almost intolerable. It was more than 100 degrees outside and the contents of the canals simmered in the sun. Bremer emerged from his armored vehicle and I asked whether we could let Arnot be present when the minister's briefing took place. Bremer, Arnot, and the minister stood on a bridge over the Al Ashar Canal with a swarm of nervous security guards in tow, discussing plans to get the water flowing again. It would take an estimated forty million dollars to build a series of gates that would permit the flow of water to flush out the sewage and debris. CPA and Iraqi engineers were working on placing gates at the ends of each canal that could be opened and closed as the tide rose and fell, thus facilitating the water flow. It is a good story, one that in my opinion was never given proper attention by the major media outlets.

We then took a twenty-minute helicopter ride to the Hawizeh Marsh outside Basra. On our approach from the air, all of us were moved by what we saw outside the windows of our CH-56 twin prop helicopters. The damage that Saddam had caused to the environment was striking and clear. As we flew over the dams, we could see the Euphrates River and its floodplain with its lush green waters and dense vegetation. I didn't think that such a scene existed in Iraq. The terrain was abruptly interrupted by manmade structures that, like a razor's edge, cut through the landscape leaving beyond nothing but desert. The dams literally formed a line in the sand separating life from utter desolation. The marshes once covered an area of more than seven thousand square miles. By the time of the liberation, they had shrunk to less than 5 percent their original size.

We landed on one of the dikes and exited the helicopter while its rotors were still moving so that it could quickly lift off again, making room for Bremer's arrival. We were engulfed by a small dust storm caused by the aircraft as it took off. For a few minutes the press, other staff, and I had the opportunity to stand along the dam and view the landscape. The hot midday sun was scorching the cracked, dry earth beneath us. There was simply nothing left save a few dried trees and some brush. The once fertile marsh was like the surface of the moon.

After Bremer landed, he again received a short briefing on the plans to help the Iraqis restore a portion of the habitat. The plan was to open the dams at certain points and install control regulators that would allow for the management of water outflow and water levels in the remaining marsh areas. It would also permit regulated water flow to areas targeted for restoration. The problem was, you couldn't simply tear down the dams and re-flood the area. Much of the water would dry up and it would place a burden on the water sources used for the restoration. The engineers hoped that the regulated introduction of water back into the area would help with restoration. Progress would be slow, but it would happen.

We then took an aerial tour of the Central Marshlands and once again saw the devastation from the air. The reporters on board were astonished by what they saw as we made our way to the last stop. Unfortunately, much of the reporting following the trip would be defeatist in its character. One journalist muttered aloud within earshot of one of the Iraqi government officials, "They'll never fix this." Arnot naturally couldn't wait to get back on the ground and meet more people.

Again, we landed on one of the dikes ahead of Bremer. Our group ran through yet another dust storm caused by the twin rotors to find large numbers of children who had come from the nearby village to greet us. They lived in the remnants of the marsh. They were dirty little kids with sand and mud on their ripped clothes and faces and under their fingernails. They had so little, yet they smiled as they ran to us. It was like a scene out of a movie. The experience was surreal. The children wanted to talk to us, touch us, and walk with us. "Mister! Mister!" they would yell. "You American?" they would ask. They'd grab your arm and ask to see your watch. I never quite figured out why. "What time is it, Mister?" one child would say to me over and over, perhaps it was the only English he knew. "Dollar, Mister?" another asked. And of course, they all wanted their pictures taken. They climbed over each other to get in the photos, making faces and jumping up and down. I would show them the photos on the screen of my digital camera after I took them. They loved it.

In the middle of all of this, as we waited for Bremer, the children with us did something utterly incredible. For the rest of my life I will hear their voices shouting in unison, "No more Saddam! No more Saddam!" I and my colleagues from the CPA grinned from ear to ear. It was like a generation of Iraqis was saying thank you to America and the coalition. Arnot stood there, all 6'2" of him with his shaggy, wind-blown blond hair, as moved as we were. Children were on all sides attracted to his camera. To be fair, so were they to some of the other reporters. However, other than in Arnot's report, I don't recall ever seeing the chants of the children reported by any of the news organizations present.

Bremer landed and got right to business, meeting with the local leadership and discussing the coalition's efforts to restore the marshes. We walked with him several hundred yards to one of the villages located near the dike. In the village stood one of the remaining large reed huts traditionally used by the Marsh Arabs. It could be rightly compared to a longhouse used by the Native Americans. About thirteen feet high and fifty feet long, it was a monument to the culture Saddam tried to destroy. The townspeople gathered at the front door to the hut, while Bremer went inside to meet with the tribal leaders. A few minutes later, I followed, pushing my way through the throng in front of the building and quietly entering. The floor was covered with a patchwork of handmade wool rugs. Poles down the center of the room supported its barrel-shaped roof. On the rugs to my right when I entered were the boots and shoes of the meeting participants who were already engaged in discussions at the far end of the room. I took off my desert boots and walked slowly and quietly toward the meeting. There was no conference table, no comfortable chairs. Bremer and the others were sitting legs folded on the floor discussing the future of the marshes and the new Iraq. Bremer was very cognizant of when he should speak and when he should listen. He spent most of this meeting listening. The Iraqis had concerns and ideas. They were excited about the possibilities.

Contrary to the impression often given by commentators about the Iraqi people, Iraqis are eager to work to improve their society. After the liberation, they were able to speak more freely about the problems that existed in their communities and could plan to correct them. They often did. Whether it is in the marshes or in the heart of Baghdad, Iraqis across the country began planning for improvements almost from the moment that the statue fell. They often talked about their grand designs for Iraq's future. As members of the coalition, we were there to help them build the capacity to achieve their goals on their own. The marshes were no different.

At the conclusion of the meeting, Bremer, the tribal leaders, and the rest of our group headed for the helicopters, and the villagers followed to send us off. Once onboard, we lifted off. As we looked out the open back of the Chinook, the villagers waved goodbye, their dark clothes, hair, and skin made them look like a shadow on the ground as dust swirled around them and we headed back to Baghdad.

Westerners living and working in Iraq were thrust into a world where the face of evil could be seen virtually every day. It could be seen in a mass grave, in the scarred flesh of a torture victim, the black dress of a widow, the face of a rape room victim, or even a neglected hospital or neighborhood deliberately barred from essential services. It took getting used to, as it was so foreign to most of us. Sometimes, it made you just plain hurt and ask yourself, *How can such evil exist?*

Nevertheless, through it all, the brutality was a constant reminder of the potential of our mission, despite the increasingly damaging efforts of foreign fighters and other terrorists to prevent it. For the Iraqis, each grave found by a wife or mother and each scar seen in a mirror served as a painful reminder of the past. Civilian and military alike, we hoped to help turn their pain into strength. Iraq was not about absolutes. It was about potentials. Halabja's residents will never truly recover, but the American presence brought some confidence that stability could be achieved. Today the marshes are nearly 50 percent restored, but only a few thousand of the more than five hundred thousand people who once lived there have returned. Progress on health care continued steadily despite a massive flight from the country of physicians because of escalating violence. Access to more modern methods and facilities increased long after the CPA transferred power to the Iraqis. Infant mortality rates have steadily declined, while life expectancy is up. Iraq's health care budget went from thirty million dollars to more than five billion dollars annually.

In Iraq, trying to make progress was like renovating an old house. Often, you drew up plans and plotted a construction timeline and then opened the walls to find mold and termites. The task did not then become insurmountable, but it required more time, more money, and a willingness to suffer setbacks. For the Iraq mission to succeed that situation needed to be articulated effectively and accepted broadly among all components of the mission including the political folks back in Washington, the military, the State Department, opinion leaders, and the media. From the outset, the breaks in that broad acceptance were not just between the Bush administration and the press but also within the apparatus. Genuine progress on a wide range of issues was hampered by a variety of complicating developments, but underlying those developments was the culture of uncertainly, distrust, and fear created by the former regime that was ingrained in the soul of much of the population. Sectarian violence, an adolescent and divisive political establishment, the American withdrawal timeline, and later the presence of ISIS, blunted perhaps the most important contribution of the CPA—our constant drive to help Iraqis believe that they could freely participate in crafting a better destiny for themselves, their families, and their nation.

THE CIVILIAN AND THE SOLDIER

As the media were pushing the perception that we had "botched the peace," they were also stoking the opinion that we civilians were on some sort of working vacation.

Ci-vil-ian?" Sergeant Gibson said to me one morning not long after I met him with an intentionally perplexed look on his face. He then burst out laughing. Understanding the communications challenges surrounding the Iraq mission, particularly in those first fourteen months after the end of what the military called "major combat operations," requires an understanding of the organizational dynamics of the CPA. The Iraq mission, during the time of the CPA, was a unique blend of people and talents. The relationships between the civilians and the soldiers in those early days made for a remarkable education. They also made for some remarkable results under very difficult circumstances. Those who worked in the Pentagon were used to the melding of the two very different cultures that comprise a civilian-run military. Not so for the military folks deployed to Iraq from posts around the world or the State Department personnel not used to sharing influence and responsibility with others.

In that first year, under the umbrella of the CPA, the two worlds clashed in an awkward partnership that certainly had strengths and weaknesses. Civilians and soldiers worked more closely in Iraq than they had previously and that made for enormous potential.

Gibson would say he envied us civilians. He envied us because he could still remember what civilian life was like. He was after all a reservist, deployed to Iraq just days after his wedding by way of Ohio and Fort Bragg. Reservists were part-timers. They were different. They participated in civilian American life, sacrificed to serve their country when called, and returned to their livelihood when the mission was over. These guys were close enough to civilian life to bask in the memories of what it was like to be a civilian. They were not active duty. They were called to active duty. One of the things you learn when working with and observing soldiers is that there is distinct class delineation in the military. Reservists were treated differently by the career military folks. I saw it and heard about it. Gibson was lucky in the sense that he had been on active duty so long now that even the active-duty soldiers thought that he was active duty. Got that? Active-duty soldiers, usually the career senior enlisted and officers, would attribute the active-reserve distinction to what they privately called the "stink" of civilian. Gibson and other reservists whom I knew longed for that smell. He liked being a civilian more than he had liked being a soldier. He had acquired an allergy to bullets being propelled at him. Personally, I think that his outlook on the military dropped a few notches after the army sent him across the border from Kuwait into Iraq during the war with only one clip of ammo and no plates in his flak vest—but I could be wrong.

The words "civilian" and "individual" were words and ideas to career military men akin to what "cooties" were to third graders. Active-duty soldiers were the full-timers, usually lifers, and career-oriented. They were the ones who have truly committed their professional lives to serving our nation and protecting our freedom. They do what they're told and make a living making sure others do what they're told. They do whatever it takes to hold the military operation together.

These enlisted soldiers, noncoms, and officers signed a series of agreements with the government and kept careful track of their accumulated retirement points. This was an important calculation, because when they reached their End Time Service, the acquired points meant receiving their twenty-year service letter and retirement. It was a discussion often heard in the hallways and chow halls. Many soldiers and marines seemed to talk more about getting out of the military than what they were doing in the military. I always guessed it was just a way of passing the time, but after several deployments real fatigue must set in.

In May and June of 2003, the Iraq mission made a critical transition from a military operation to a civilian one. When the civilians began trickling into Saddam's massive Presidential Palace, many soldiers were anxiously waiting. Some of them were dreading it. A military's primary role is to wage and win war. "It breaks and destroys things. Civilians on the other hand fix and build them," one non-commissioned officer (NCO) once told me. When the CPA arrived at the palace, Gibson and his team were pushed out of the rooms they were occupying to make room for office space. What had largely been a gigantic barracks with chandeliers was beginning its transformation into a government office building. His unit moved into an upstairs hallway for a time where the marble floor tiles made for better, cooler, sleeping. It would not matter for long. After all, civilians have a tendency to bring with them particular luxuries like air conditioning.

When the CPA showed up, many soldiers were assimilated into a civilian organization. It brought a certain normalcy in the Green Zone. Powdered food and MREs (meals ready-to-eat) became KBR Chicken Kiev, mountains of potato concoctions, and pasta at every meal. People went from using MRE toilet paper and having to fill garbage cans with water from the Tigris River to flush the latrines to shower trailers and functioning restrooms. Office equipment sprouted everywhere, as did computers and phones. The floors were cleaned and the windows were washed. More than anything else, though, the mission spawned these frenzied and ambitious people who didn't wear uniforms.

Sometimes soldiers would explain that civilians brought some logic to their work and their world. They didn't have to "stop the war," as they'd often put it, to make sure that all of the soldiers were wearing black issue socks. We didn't have to go to formation. Formation, for those who are unfamiliar, is when all the enlisted soldiers are called to line up according to rank and file. Soldiers are then addressed by their senior ranking NCO or their senior ranking commissioned officer. This can vary depending on doctrine of the individual military unit. Formations were called in the morning and afternoon. Mail was handed out, information was provided, and exercise and ass-chewings took place, several occurrences of which I had occasion to witness over time.

Civilians did not have formations or have to worry about the "group" mind as much. We could exist as more autonomous individuals. As civilians we could call a hat a hat and did not have to call it a "cap," "patrol cap," or "p.c." or by some other military designation. We could even walk outdoors without a hat if we wanted.

Civilians didn't have to take shifts on guard duty. They could call dinner "dinner" and not get looks for calling it something other than "chow." Many soldiers would ask that I call them by their first names rather than their rank. One enlisted guy told me that it was nice not having his first name be "Sergeant" sometimes. We weren't regular army or another bunch of marines. After all, there was nothing regular about many of us civilians in this setting. Perhaps that was refreshing in a way for the folks in uniform. We looked at things differently. We approached a crisis differently. We approached being there differently. The collaboration worked best when the civilian allowed himself to learn from the soldier and the soldier himself to learn from the civilian.

One the biggest differences between the classes that lower enlisted soldiers in particular would mention was that civilians were allowed to purchase and drink alcohol. We didn't have to sneak downtown or out to the airport to buy it. Of course, just because the military made drinking punishable under the United Code of Military Justice didn't mean that soldiers did not want to drink, need to drink, obtain a drink, and drink a drink—or two. After his vehicle hit an IED (improvised explosive device), Major J. R. Reiling, who was one of the senior officers in the psychological operations unit in the Green Room, wanted nothing more than a stiff drink. You could see it on his face. One day Sergeant John Lutz found a forgotten beer that had been left in the office refrigerator. He and Gibson were going to split it, but they ended up trading it to a 3rd Army supply clerk for two magazines of ammunition to issue to one of their soldiers who was departing for Kirkuk. It got to the point that I just went out to the airport with some folks and bought some of the enlisted guys a couple of cases. Nobody got drunk. There were simply too many of them to split up the beer, but I thought they had earned at least a taste.

Civilians had to be productive. That was the priority. We were directly accountable to the civilian leadership and needed to get results. On top of that, if you were a political civilian, you were also accountable to the political leadership. You didn't want the White House finding out that you were slacking on the job. You'd find yourself not only heading home but also unemployed. The military had to be disciplined and orderly. The members of the military whom I dealt with felt that the civilians added a new way of thinking and a new way of attacking problems. To be sure, I think they felt like we were in over our heads, but we got a lot of credit for coming over there, working in the environment, and trying to make this a success. We were all neck deep in this. In many ways, they were unprepared to fight an urban guerilla war compounded by Al-Qaeda terrorists, and the CPA civilians were unprepared for the utter neglect they found throughout Iraq's civil infrastructure and the impact of the looting on literally everything.

The military is obviously more group-minded and group-focused. Civilian staffers had more individual tasks and roles that made for a more normal working environment for the soldiers attached to the CPA. The military is based on rank. Whoever has the highest rank wins. The respect for rank is ingrained in the military mindset. It has to be. The chain of command must be respected for a unit, battalion, brigade, or division to move as one large organism. Sometimes, folks on the civilian side didn't understand that when a soldier is given an order, regardless of what it is, he or she has to follow through. In the absence of leadership, soldiers will lead themselves. It can be dangerous. We saw that most clearly at Abu Ghraib. The structure and discipline is important to the efficient and effective operation of a fighting force.

That doesn't mean that the system or the orders always made sense. Soldiers, both officer and enlisted, liked to gripe about the nonsense. One day the military decided to do a physical training (PT) exercise test in Baghdad. The guys in my office complained that PT had nothing to do with psychological operations and took a whole day away from their actual duties putting together communications products for the Iraqis. The officers made them run along the edge of the Green Zone. Never without a clever remark, Sergeant Gibson came back into the office frustrated saying, "Sometimes, I think the army is more concerned with killing me than the insurgents are."

A lot more listening went on within the civilian ranks. If you had something to say, you could say it. Civilians have more of an opportunity to give opinions and share ideas to the benefit of the operation. Sometimes, I would ask the opinion of some enlisted soldier or junior officer, who would feel awkward about engaging with a civilian if he or she wasn't the highest-ranking person in the room, whereas I could walk up to Bremer or Kennedy and express my opinion without fear of paying some price for it.

There was a genuine camaraderie that formed in some offices. Strategic communications was one of them. After all, the soldiers were taking care of us.

When the rubber met the road, these guys saw it as their job to make sure that we could do our job. Members of the military also had generally good relationships with the folks working with the CPA ministry offices. There was an understanding of the nature of what we were trying to do. It was important for the military to understand what the civilian organization was trying to accomplish, and we appreciated their sacrifice. Complex operations work best when people come together.

However, the active-duty officers and senior NCOs sometimes seemed a little less thrilled about having the civilians around. After all, they were the ones whose careers depended on soldiers retaining the characteristics of good soldiers. They often must have felt as if they were competing with civilian influences that were natural consequences of the unique CPA organizational structure. Sometimes the sheer number of career majors, lieutenant colonels, colonels, and generals running around the palace affected productivity and collaboration. Of course, you had to understand where they were coming from. They were fish out of water much in the same way that we were. Being attached to or having to work within the CPA, they were also in a foreign working environment. Ordinarily a lieutenant colonel in the field or back on post would have command of an entire battalion of soldiers. In the palace, they were tasked with important responsibilities but clearly were not granted the authority that they were used to wielding or the pomp that comes with command. They were also interacting with civilian FSOs, who in the eyes of the military had questionable commitment to the mission and were in direct competition for control of the mission. Of course, they were additionally dealing with a cadre of young, ambitious, eager personnel attached to the Bush administration. My point is that collaboration and efficiency was hindered sometimes by the very cultural differences that made each component of the organization effective as separate entities. Personally, I think the military and civilian worlds would have benefitted from the existence of fewer colonels and the presence of more lieutenants and captains. Certainly, the mission as a whole would have benefitted from everyone having some degree more experience in this type and scope of enterprise.

The CPA wasn't your typical military operation. It wasn't an embassy or diplomatic mission either. It was a bureaucracy, and agencies within a bureaucracy compete with one another. Individuals compete with each other. It is the nature of government structures. They compete for resources, attention, and most of all control. Bureaucracies build walls that inhibit cooperation. Pulling the military and civilian worlds together during the year that the CPA managed the Iraq mission was a bold premise intended to break down barriers that would have stifled our ability to coordinate. It had its problems. There still was duplication of effort. People still butted heads. But the complex relationship worked in a way that made it possible to address the hugely diverse number of tasks and issues that we faced every day.

The press loved to make the point that we were greeted as liberators but were quickly viewed as occupiers. Again, it is true that the Iraqi people didn't want to have foreign troops in their country. Who would? Ever hear of the Alamo? Even U.S. history has its share of examples of soldiers stationed in contested territory facing great risks. That however didn't mean that the Iraqis didn't understand the utility of our troops being there. It sounds cliché, but it's true. There really were a thousand unseen acts of compassion and heroism every day. There also were countless special relationships forged between our soldiers and ordinary Iraqis. While photojournalists and reporters jumped on every situation to present the impression of a heavy-handed American military that was invading people's homes and violating their rights, relationships built on mutual respect were the goals of commanders in the field. It would be nonsensical to suggest otherwise. The kind of relationships the media loved to suggest, even in those early days, would have made life far more dangerous for our military.

The military needed cooperation and information from residents to protect themselves and the local population. Sometimes of course, things got ugly. Audiences back home heard many examples of such situations. In many cases, though, battalion commanders and their soldiers in the field became part of the communities they protected. They became more than just finders of terrorists and defusers of bombs. They were like the local beat cops back home who knew the shopkeepers, restaurateurs, and residents. Ultimately, as the surge brought more troops and more robust strategy to find, capture, and kill foreign fighters, the military was able to build and leverage relationships to gather better human intelligence for the fight.

While combing reports from army civil affairs, a colleague and I stumbled upon a story that serves as an example of what it was like when things went right. An Iraqi woman named Sarahiah ran a school for children with Down's syndrome from her home in Baghdad. Under Saddam's regime, child services were virtually nonexistent. In fact, children with disabilities were considered more property than people. Any child with a mental or physical disability would be segregated from other children and often placed in institutions. Iraqi institutions didn't provide for special needs, depending on a child's disability. Early on, a child would be classified as either educable, trainable, or neither. If a child were classified as trainable, he or she would not be afforded a traditional education. Sarahiah wanted to change all that. Her school was believed to be the first of its kind in Iraq. The school served more than one hundred students at the time that I visited there. The children were grouped according to ability rather than age, and each of them was educated in reading, writing, and arithmetic, in addition to being given occupational training and speech therapy. Some of the more advanced students even learned English.

As it happened, the area commander, Lieutenant Colonel Bowyer of the Fourth Battalion First FA of the U.S. Army First Armored Division, also had a son with Down syndrome. He and his unit took the school under their wing. The unit helped organize groups in Kansas, Kentucky, West Virginia, and Tennessee to raise funds for improvements to the school. They helped provide teachers' salaries, clothes, dental supplies, fans, school supplies, and a television set. On the back wall of the main classroom, Sarahiah had the kids make a collage of photos of themselves. One photo stood out. It was a picture of Lieutenant Colonel Bowyer's son Samuel, whom the kids made an honorary member of their class. Sarahiah called Lieutenant Colonel Bowyer "our first friend and our best friend."

We got word about the work of the unit back to Washington. Elisa Pruett and I sat with Bowyer and his unit to watch President Bush talk about their work during a televised speech back home. He stared at the TV with a certain degree of disbelief as the commander in chief praised his unit for helping those kids. The American military is the best trained and best equipped in the world. Militaries destroy. They break things. They're good at it. Yet the Americans and other coalition forces in Iraq were "makers" as well. A critical transition was made, not just by the civil affairs personnel who were helping with reconstruction but also by regular units. They were helping build a society. They were bringing pieces of themselves and the homes that they left behind to a nation that was starving for peace and even the most basic of necessities.

We were so different; but despite the difficulties of melding the world of the civilian with the world of the soldier, those who were working at the CPA gained strength from the work of the other. As I indicated earlier, with respect to Bremer's position on how best to handle looters, the larger conflicts that did arise between the civilian and military leadership were more of an inside-versus outside-the-palace nature. I'll discuss some additional examples later on, but the biggest strategic disconnects were seen among field commanders, Pentagon brass, and the CPA's civilian leadership.

When it came to the military members who were attached to the CPA, there was less friction. We were always more alike than unlike, though sometimes it was difficult to see. Sometimes, you felt like they didn't respect you because you didn't wear the uniform. Other times, you believed that they would do anything for you precisely because you didn't wear the uniform—or because you worked for Bremer or the president or Donald Rumsfeld. At the end of the day, we all had the mission in common. It went beyond that though. I liked to think that working with civilians made it seem to the military a little more as if they were back at home. Each brought radically different qualities to the mission, but there were certain commonalities that were inescapable.

This was never more evident than on one particular two-hour trip to Kuwait in December 2003. Boarding the flight Elisa, Matt Fuller, and I found ourselves traveling with some very special cargo. We entered the C-130 aircraft from the side front hatch and took seats on the left side of the plane. It became a tight fit as two long metal cases were carefully placed end to end in the middle of the cargo area between us and the jump seats along the opposite wall. Toward the front of the plane were two soldiers sitting alone across from us. Along with us were members of a congressional delegation on their way back to the United States. Once we were on board and before the engine noise made communication between us difficult, one of the soldiers rose from his red mesh seat. He was a casualty assistance officer charged with escorting two brave young men back home to their families. The heroes were contained in the silver transfer cases at our feet. He instructed us that no photographs would be permitted of the caskets and to refrain from touching the cases in flight. Elisa's eyes filled up with tears. Matt and I looked at each other and the congressmen fell silent. Flying out of BIAP was always a nerve-racking experience. This time it would be emotional as well. Throughout the flight, I stared at the cases, not more than twelve inches from the tips of my boots. I wondered about the men inside, about their families, about how they lived, and about how they died. They fought for a vision of a safer world and to stem the tide of terrorism. When we landed, we were instructed to remain in our positions until the cases were removed from the plane. The back of the aircraft opened, revealing a waiting honor guard who boarded the plane. The honor guard removed the cases, one at a time, marching carefully in step off the ramp. Once removed from the plane, the cases were draped with American flags and taken to a nearby vehicle. We stood. I noticed some of the civilians making the sign of the cross as the bodies passed before us. I did as well. Others took the time for silent prayer. The plane's National Guard crew stood at attention and saluted. The silence of that moving moment was pierced only by the sound of a camera snapping a photo. One of the Democrat congressmen, against the instructions of the casualty assistance officer, had taken a picture. To the casualty escort's credit, he demanded that the photo be erased from the man's camera. The congressman retorted indignantly that he was member of the U.S. Congress. The soldier essentially responded that he didn't care. The congressman handed over his camera and the escort officer left the plane.

It was a sobering moment that I will never forget. For a civilian like myself, it made me more focused and determined to help tell their story—to ensure that their sacrifice was not in vain. It made me more frustrated at the rhetoric back home and the perceptions of failure that were becoming a false reality. That flight was also a reminder that all of us were sharing this risk in some way.

The bond that we shared as civilians and soldiers extended to another simple fact of deployed life. Everyone missed home. This is not to say that everyone wanted to go home, but everyone missed to a certain degree being back in whatever corner of the country or the world from which they had come. There were simple things you missed like good Chinese takeout or sleeping in on a Sunday. There were also more fundamental freedoms that were absent from life in a forward area. They weren't freedoms that are codified in laws or constitutions but freedoms that are just a normal part of life back home. Walking down a street without much thought to your safety and certainly without body armor, sitting in a restaurant, going shopping, and eating with real silverware. Whether you were a civilian or a soldier, you had to keep up your situational awareness regardless of where you were or what you were doing. Relaxation came in fleeting spurts. It was an hour at the pool or some time at the new CPA gym. The old gym literally consisted of two-liter soda bottles filled with sand duct-taped to a broomstick. I'm not making that up. It was a late night movie watched on your computer, or a little get-together out near the trailers. You could take a DVD to the palace theater and watch your favorite flick. Achieving some semblance of normalcy when you needed it was tough all the way around. The place was so radically different from a lifestyle point of view. That made the experience immensely interesting and extremely difficult at the same time. You learned to live in a bubble like the Green Zone, or out in the field at an operating post, or a combination of both.

By far, most of us were mission focused. As the media were pushing the perception that we had "botched the peace," they were also stoking the opinion that we civilians were on some sort of working vacation. We remained focused and determined. People worked to the point of utter exhaustion. That prevented you from dwelling on all those things that you missed back home, whether it be the sight of the American flag flying above a building on a cool fall night, the embrace of your spouse or child, a night out with friends, a baseball game, the leaves changing color, your favorite restaurant, the clergyman who was always there to encourage you, the feel of a long, hot shower, or the sound of rain on a roof.

Sometimes the press would make a big deal of the fact that they'd interview members of the military who would tell them that they were looking forward to getting home. A senior officer once said to me, "The only time you really worry about a soldier is when he quits bitching." Makes sense if you think about it. Of course, the cynical media would interpret any indication of homesickness to mean or at least hope the viewer would perceive it as, "George Bush took me away from my family. I don't know why I'm here. Get me the hell out of this place!" Most everyone wanted to go home at some point during his or her deployment. That shouldn't shock anyone. The vast majority of soldiers in all wars since the beginning of time would probably rather have been home than at war. This is not a news flash.

I'm sure the Peloponnesian navies were frustrated at eating dried fish for months at a time in their fifth-century BC war with Athens. The point often neglected by the reporting was that the vast majority of military personnel and nearly all of the civilians in Iraq understood what the mission was about and why they were there. This was especially true of the civilians attached to the president's administration. Remember, none of us were told to go. We were asked. We made a choice that servicemen and women did not have the ability to make. I have never been with a group of people so focused on a mission, so focused on doing what often seemed like the impossible and risking life and limb to do it. It was one of the most exhilarating aspects of the whole experience. We looked forward to going home, but make no mistake: we understood why we were there.

Mission focus helped us to deal with some of the material things that we missed. It cast them into the recesses of your mind. What it couldn't do is overpower just how much you missed the people in your life who were worrying about you back home. Those emotional attachments don't fade. You miss your wife, your husband, your kids, your friends, and your relatives. I was lucky in some respect, as I was unmarried and didn't have any children during my time in Iraq. Tens of thousands of others left families behind. We would let the marines who guarded the palace come into the office at night and use our phones to call home. After 9:00 p.m. most nights, there were usually three or four of them in the office checking in with family. For those of us working in the office, we couldn't help but overhear the father talking to his son about the little league game he missed that day or about the math homework his daughter was struggling to complete. We'd hear the strongest of the strong lower their voices to say "I love you" to a tired wife, now serving on the home front as a single parent. Sometimes we'd hear the problems at home, the frustrated spouse and the pleas of a soldier hoping that she would still be there when he got back. More than once, I and my colleagues choked back tears at what we heard from the cubicle or desk nearby in our cavernous workspace.

Being away from the people you care about is more difficult than dealing with the bullets, the mortars, the bombings, and certainly the lack of the creature comforts of home. I often found myself worrying about people back home, perhaps as much as they were concerned about my well-being. "What if a friend needs me? What if someone got sick or died while I'm here?" I'd ask. I've always believed that we have a responsibility to be there to help one another. You have to take care of the people who take care of you. It's that simple. I work hard at it and it's an important aspect of who I am as a person. In the third month of my tour of duty, I felt the powerlessness of being so far away for the first time. One of my closest friends from my college days, David Berez, called one night to tell me that his mother was in the hospital. David is a cop and a cop's cop at that. He is a pillar of strength, focus, and determination. His father left when he and his sister were young and played virtually no role in their upbringing. David achieved his goals anyway. He is regimented and disciplined. He was the guy who ironed his jeans and boxer shorts in college. He was the fraternity pledge master. David has a softer side, but unless you know him well, it stays carefully hidden. As a cop, he often had to bury his emotions. Part of the difficulty for him in this situation would be learning to acknowledge those emotions and deal with them. I knew that because it took a while for me to do the same thing when I was a kid, coping with the death of a parent.

David's mom had inoperable brain cancer. During her hospitalization, he and his fiancée, Stephanie, stood at the foot of her bed and were blessed by the family rabbi. They knew, as she drifted in and out of consciousness, that she wouldn't live to see their wedding day.

Ordinarily, in a situation like this, I would have been there by his side, doing whatever I could to help him through the difficult time, the pain, and the process of moving on. I knew what it was like to go through this kind of loss. We had a chance to talk several times during his mom's brief illness. Whenever I saw his number come up on the phone, I took the call. I was fortunate to have the ability to communicate so easily. It didn't matter where I was or what I was doing. One morning, I was getting ready to walk into a press conference at city hall in downtown Baghdad when the phone rang. Cell service was poor in the building so I ran outside to take the call and stood behind a brick pillar near a staircase at the front of the building. I didn't want to stand out in the plaza, which was overlooked by several tall buildings. "My mom died," he said from eleven thousand miles away. It was early in the morning back on the East Coast of the United States. It had just happened. I tried to tell him that she was still with him. "You have to believe that," I said. After we hung up, I walked back into the lobby of the building. At that moment, I wished I were back home more at that moment than at any other time while I was in Iraq. It was interesting, I thought, that it wasn't the increase in the bombings, the mortar attacks, the assassinations, or the sleepless nights that made me long for home but a desire to be with a suffering friend.

Emotions ran high. It wasn't just what was happening on the ground but what was happening at home as well. Everything about this was challenging. You had to work every day to keep faith—faith in yourself, in your colleagues, in your government, in the mission, in the Iraqis, and in your Maker.

Every Sunday, the Chapel in the palace became a venue for the stark contrasts that made the Iraq experience and the CPA extraordinary. It also gave emphasis to the common ground that we shared as stewards of this mission. The Catholic mass would be held in the morning and the evening, with other Christian denominations holding services throughout the day. Attendees at mass would sit on green and gold couches that were some of the palace's original furnishings. Beneath the mural depicting Saddam's liberation of Jerusalem, we prayed together, civilian and soldier alike. Often a soldier or marine would come in from patrol in full battle gear, including their M-16 rifles. As discreetly as possible, they would remove their body armor, revealing a uniform stained with salt and saturated with sweat. They would set down their weapon and join in the service. You could be sitting next to a general or civilian senior advisor or a lower enlisted soldier. Everyone in the Chapel had a different job and took different risks. Everyone had a different role. The military's natural barriers broke down in the Chapel, as did civilian divides. They had distinct experiences and petitioned God for different things. We were different, but we were the same.

SOCIAL MECCA

The press liked to portray CPA civilians as living high on the hog, while people beyond the Green Zone were getting killed. I will always contend that, for civilians, the few social outlets that we created were vital to our ability to manage stress and ensure productivity.

For civilians, if the palace was the heart of our professional lives, then the Al Rashid Hotel was the center of our meager social lives. The hotel had been made famous during the 1991 Gulf War for being the location where CNN broadcast the first pictures of the war. I can still hear Bernard Shaw saying, "The skies over Baghdad have been illuminated" and seeing those riveting night-vision pictures of anti-aircraft fire streaking in vain toward American fighter planes. The Al Rashid was legendary and, for a few months in 2003, it was home to many of the CPA staffers who were risking their lives to rebuild Iraq.

One of the first things you learn when you arrive in Baghdad is that if you need something, the best way to work it out was by way of some sort of deal. Some people called them "drug deals." A drug deal was essentially getting what you needed or wanted under the table. That's how I came to live at the Al Rashid. In fact, that's how many people came to live there. The omnipresent KBR deity ran the hotel, managed the staff, and tended to the maintenance. They also had set up the system for billeting according to a number of criteria such as when you arrived in the country, your rank, whom you worked for, and so on. After a few days of living in the palace, I was telling Pearse that I was interested in perhaps moving into the hotel. Pearse's roommate had moved out a couple of weeks earlier and KBR had yet to place someone else in his room. Nearly everyone shared a room at the Al Rashid. I didn't care. At that point, I was sharing a room with 150 people. Pearse was the CPA webmaster and certainly an interesting personality. He was in his late twenties, a former marine who spoke something in the way of seven languages, including Hebrew, Arabic, and Latin. He also held a strong commitment to his Catholic faith—but happened to be dating one of the Iraqi translators in our office. As you might imagine, she wasn't terribly Catholic. Like I said, Pearse was an interesting personality. He also played a variety of instruments. Over time, the guitars and sheet music multiplied in our room like rabbits. It was like living with the Partridge Family.

Pearse was nice enough to offer me the space. This worked out for his benefit, too, as one never knew whom the management would place in your room. At the Al Rashid, civilians sometimes roomed with military personnel. No attempt was made for people who worked together or knew each other to share rooms. There was understandably no time for any of that. If there was a hole in the building roster, you filled it. One colleague of mine roomed with an army lieutenant colonel who slept with his 9 mm pistol in his right hand. Some nights, this guy would come home to find the colonel fast asleep with the gun pointed at his bed.

The day I moved in, Pearse gave me the hotel guest ID card belonging to his former roommate and told me to just move my stuff up to room 1003. He cautioned me not tell anyone, betting that by the time they figured it out we could explain the name change as an oversight in the billeting system. I threw my luggage into one of those dusty new American SUVs that may as well have had targets painted on them and drove through the gate. It was my first time on the grounds and, in so many ways, the Al Rashid is still with me.

The Al Rashid Hotel was Baghdad's finest large hotel. Saddam built it in the early 1980s to support regional conferences and other international events that the regime hoped to attract to Baghdad. The hotel was conveniently located across the street from the Baghdad Convention Center and was near the Tomb of the Unknown Soldier, the Parade Grounds, and the Baghdad Zoo. It was also in close proximity to the various palaces in the area and many of the ministry buildings. The Fourteenth of July Bridge that spans the Tigris River was also just down the road and served as a major artery to downtown.

The Al Rashid was in many ways a testament to the regime that created it. The building was, like many others in Baghdad, a fairly modern-looking structure in a very 1970s sort of way. It was built during a time when Saddam was trying to make visible improvements to the city, presumably in an effort consolidate power and garner stronger support from the population. Typical of the regime, little was done to upgrade or maintain the facility once it was constructed.

Moving through the now heavily guarded gates, one saw the centerpiece of the entryway, a twenty-foot-tall modern fountain depicting women standing on top of rocks, pouring water from jugs into a pool below. It looked almost sinister as it loomed there staring back at me, bone dry, covered in sand, and baking in the hot August sun. The driveway and sidewalks were pitted by the remnants of falling munitions and cluster bombs. The pockmarks in the asphalt were an ever-present reminder of the environment in which we lived.

The first thing any visitor to the Al Rashid who knows its history notices is what isn't there. Again, that's if you've done your homework. Passing through the automatic, sliding-glass doors into the lobby, it's obvious where a new slab of terrazzo flooring has just been laid. It replaced the mosaic of former President George H. W. Bush that Saddam had installed so visitors would walk over his face when they entered the hotel a not-so-subtle way of insulting the American president. On the bottom, the mosaic read, "War Criminal," not, interestingly, in Arabic but in English so the press and foreign dignitaries could read it.

Much as with Iraq as a whole, nothing had been done to the place in more than twenty years, except repairs after the first Gulf War. All of the furniture was original. It was dark wood and boxy in design, bearing years of water rings, scratches, nicks, and gunk. Many of the cracked and worn brown leather chairs in the lobby and guest rooms were covered in a thick black crud, also from a lack of cleaning.

Much of the carpeting looked to be original as well. Once beige, the carpet seemed to have never been shampooed—or vacuumed much for that matter—and had taken on a gray color accented by a variety of stains in all shapes, colors, and sizes. There were stains on the rugs in nearly every hallway and almost every room. Some people I knew didn't walk on the rugs with bare feet for fear of catching some fungus from what appeared to be years of dirt. Dark wood paneling covered the hallway walls, making the passages feel claustrophobic.

The Al Rashid was legendary for its listening devices, secret passageways, two-way mirrors, and other surveillance equipment that was snaked through the entire building. The systems were built into the hotel early on to facilitate intelligence-gathering from the foreign guests who frequented the hotel in its heyday. There were rooms located in the basement that contained video monitors and recording devices. In the movie, *Live from Baghdad*, recalling the CNN crew's stay at the Rashid during the 1991 Gulf War, they discovered small surveillance devices installed in their bathroom. They didn't make that up. The system was real. The secret passages between the rooms and the video equipment weren't used to spy on foreign guests only. Uday Hussein infamously used the equipment to identify women with whom he wanted to have sex. Once he found the woman he wanted, his bodyguards would simply take her from her room. If she were lucky, she'd only be raped. If she were lucky. I once met a gentleman whose daughter was raped by Uday after she was abducted from a Baghdad street. She apparently put up such a fight that, when he was finished with her, he sent the pieces of her body back to her family in a plastic bag.

As I walked the halls of the hotel day after day, I often wondered which of the panels led to the passageways. I wondered whether the devices attached to the ceiling in the bathroom still worked, or whether the staff could see through the mirrors. The video equipment and the other devices had in fact been destroyed following the fall of Baghdad, but the passages still remained. A friend of mine used to complain about prank calls that she and her roommate would receive at night after they came home. The person, who tried desperately to cover his unmistakably local accent, always seemed to know just the right moment to ring their room.

The Al Rashid was right out of the late seventies and early eighties. One fully expected to see a guy in a butterfly collar or leisure suit walking through the lobby at any moment. The outer lobby had a two-story entry hall and four modern Lucite chandeliers. Another permanent fixture was the rug dealer whose other wares included old Iraqi military uniforms, thirty-five-dollar Rolex watches, bundles of mostly counterfeit Saddam dinars, and of course hookahs of all shapes and sizes for smoking flavored tobacco. Above his shop was a modern sandstone frieze that ran the length of the outer lobby area. To the right were shops that sold various items, including paintings, antiques, more Iraqi knickknacks, and other merchandise that seemed specifically designed for the American clientele. A lot of the stuff was just outright crap. Anything with Saddam's face on it was like gold to the dealers. There were swords, Iraqi military ribbons and medals, flags, and "friendship" T-shirts. The Iraqis at the Al Rashid, as well as those on the streets of Baghdad, quickly figured out that Americans have money to spend and will buy virtually anything.

Past the shops on the far end of the first floor was the Rehanna Coffee Shop. The coffee shop served Iraqi food and was often just what an American who'd had his fill of KBR fare needed for variety. The Al Rashid had exceptional hummus and baba ghanoush. My strategic communications colleague Elisa Pruett and I would come back to the hotel at least four nights a week and stop in for a plate of each before we called it a day. It became almost ritualistic, especially as we grew more tired of the food at the palace. About 10:00 p.m., we'd wander in take a seat. She'd order a diet Coke, I a club soda, and we'd split a plate of hummus. The waiter knew us well and often brought the rolls and pita to the table warm from the oven. We'd spend a half hour or so, discussing the day's events, griping about the press, bitching about disconnects between Washington and Baghdad, strategizing how we could improve information flow, or just critiquing our own performances.

It was dimly lit and each table had its own stained glass light. I'm glamorizing this place unjustifiably, but it was a nice diversion. Ordinarily, we ate all our meals in the same place and in the same room. After a couple of weeks, you pretty much had tried everything and it just repeated. Truthfully, I probably fell victim to "Saddam's revenge" on a couple of occasions from the food at the hotel, but it was worth it. In the end, it was all about variety. "Saddam's revenge" incidentally is the Baghdad equivalent of "Montezuma's revenge," or in layman's terms, explosive diarrhea. You usually got it by drinking the water or eating some of the local food. It was unavoidable and happened to virtually everyone, although it took me a month to have my first case. I'm still pretty proud of that. The condition lasted from a day to a week, depending on the case.

The waiters at both restaurants in the hotel spoke English pretty well—some better than others though. On my birthday, a few folks from the office went out to the restaurant and, when the time came for dessert, one colleague inquired as to the flavors of ice cream that were available for the banana split. The waiter replied that they were chocolate, vanilla, and cheese. The menu, too, had the fuzzy English that folks in the States often find on Chinese food menus.

Also in that area of the building was the ballroom, with its stained turquoise upholstered chairs and soiled green carpeting. Along the hallway down from the ballroom was another KBR dining facility for the residents of the hotel that was also frequented by the workers across the street at the convention center. This cafeteria was different in that the food, while prepared in the same fashion, was somehow a lot worse than the food over at the palace. The manager played an odd selection of music for your dining pleasure. It seemed that, every time I went in there, "Who Let the Dogs Out?" was blaring on the overworked stereo system. We really had nothing to complain about when it came to food. After all, there were soldiers in the field eating MREs on their laps.

Moving through the outer lobby, one usually walked past at least one hotel staff member who was shining the marble floor with an upright buffing machine. He was always there. Of course, the custodian didn't use any cleaner and for that matter didn't even have a buffing pad but used an old towel to shine the dull white floor all day and night as if to show the new American management that he was performing a valuable service. The front desk was to the right and a lounge with a decrepit baby grand piano was to the left. There were cracked leather chairs and peaked, wilting potted palms. Pearse could often be found in this area with his guitar, serenading himself and a small group of regulars late into the night. At the far end of the reception area was another modern fountain with Lucite crystals that often wasn't working. When it functioned, it always seemed to be the days when I'd wake up and have no water in my room.

One of the little things that always added to the surreal nature of the hotel was the "elevator music" that was played in the lobby. Given the location, one might have expected Middle Eastern music, but the instrumentals wafting through the first floor were American movie themes. There were several songs played on perpetual repeat that greeted guests and residents all day and all night. My personal favorite was the theme from *Chariots of Fire*. Baghdad had a very *Groundhog Day* quality about it in many ways. At one point, every morning for a month, the *Chariots of Fire* theme was playing on the speakers as I came off the elevator and walked out to the parking lot.

Then there was the lobby bar, a favorite spot for hotel residents who needed watering after their usual fourteen- or sixteen-hour days. It was a small, loud, and smoky place where the bartenders learned quickly that Americans would pay four dollars for a beer they'd never heard of, even in Iraq. It was a great place to sit and relax after a long day. Not much of a drinker myself, on most nights I'd come in and make the rounds to see who was there, who was drunk, and who was well on their way. It was a good place for folks to unwind and socialize in a setting that, at first glance, could very well have been anywhere in the world.

I should mention at this point that Iraq is not a dry country. Back then, the news media, always hyping the drama, helped extend the myth that Iraq was always on the brink of becoming an Iranian-style theocracy. In fairness to the press, the separation of mosque and state was of course a central issue in the redevelopment of the country, but the real threat of theocracy wasn't truly felt until the onslaught of ISIS more than a decade later.

The prevalent secularism was high on the list of reasons why Iraq arguably made sense as a starting point in attempting to create a more pluralistic society in the heart of the Middle East. Separation of mosque and state for more than three decades of Ba'ath Party rule meant the culture was highly suspicious of religious fanaticism, especially as Saddam reframed himself in the last decade of his rule as an Islamic crusader. Saddam found religion only when it became politically expedient for him to do so. It became necessary after the first Gulf War for the regime to curry favor with the clerical or certainly more religious leadership within the larger Muslim world. He wanted to be seen as mainstream rather than some radical or secular figure. By connecting himself with the Islamists in the region, he further attempted to reinforce his own vision of himself as a liberator of the Middle East from the "infidels."

Essentially, Iraq wasn't Saudi Arabia. Most Iraqi women, particularly in the urban areas, did not wear burkas or *abayas*. Many wore makeup. The Iraqis are open to women having an active participation in government and business. Most strikingly, however, were the poll numbers that suggested that Iraqis attend mosque services on a weekly basis in similar numbers to those at which Americans attend church services. That fact is significant because it shows that religion, while important, was in many cases not a driving issue. Islamic law was less important to your average Iraqi than running a business, getting an education, having essential services, improving security, and maintaining freedom from onerous religious doctrine. People simply didn't want the clerics running their lives.

It was always understood that the Iraqi people would end up with a government that was influenced in some form by Islam. It may have made some officials in Washington nervous even to consider the possibility, but it was a fact. Remember, one of the knocks against the Iraq mission amplified by the media was that America was supposedly trying to build an American-style democracy in the Middle East. We weren't. What Iraq ended up with was going to look and function different. Those of us on the ground, working on the issues of sectarianism, understood that Iraqi culture is tied inextricably to Islam and that naturally it would influence the decision-making of those who were tasked with writing the Transitional Administrative Law and, later, the Iraqi Constitution. The trick was to maintain that separation of mosque and state. The challenge was to forge a balance between acknowledging the importance of religion and promoting women's rights, free speech, and the other tenets of pluralistic, participatory society.

The vast majority of Iraqis had grown accustomed to the separation of mosque and state and would have liked to keep it that way. The Iraqis have always been acutely aware of what the mullahs have done to Iran, and those Iraqis whom I worked with and met during my time in Iraq didn't want to suffer the same fate. They were adamant that they didn't want to become like Iran. Shiite leaders like the Grand Ayatollah Ali Al-Sistani appeared to understand the importance of secularism and voiced a desire to continue a separation of mosque and state in the months following the fall of Baghdad. The Iraqi political leadership realized that the success of the reconstruction effort, the expansion of the Iraqi economy, and the acceptance by the West of the new government were all predicated on Iraq not becoming a state that would be grounded on Sharia law. The media and the opinion leaders who were watching the Iraq mission, however, presented the impression that the emergence of a theocracy in Iraq was imminent. We were always trying to beat back the contention that any day now we would wake up and Iraq would be a theocracy. To the contrary, the external political and economic factors loomed large over the decision-making process of the Iraqi leaders during the writing of the Transitional Administrative Law and the Iraqi Constitution. Had the Iraqis not gotten that decision right, the whole process would have collapsed under the weight of public uproar overseas.

I say all of that for the sake of conveying that a bunch of CPA civilians who might be drinking at the Al Rashid bar wasn't an insult to the larger population. Baghdad had nightclubs and bars back in the day.

Following my stop at the bar, I'd make my way up to the tenth floor. If I found the electricity was out, I'd march up the stairs, using the glow of my cell phone to light my way, as even the emergency lights in the hotel didn't function. When I first arrived at the hotel, in the summer months of 2003, the electricity was unreliable. We lost power about three or four times a week, during the evening and nighttime hours when most people were in the building. You'd be sitting in the bar or the coffee shop and suddenly find yourself in the dark. At first, it was unnerving when the lights went out because of the loud rumble the air conditioning system would make when it suddenly shut down. It sounded very much like a bomb and would occur precisely at the time of the blackout. More than once, I jumped out of my skin or nearly hit the deck when we lost power. After a while, though, people got used to it and paid little attention to the outages. They simply went on with their conversations, drinks, and meals, just accepting that they would be climbing the stairs that night or sleeping in rooms that were ninety-five degrees.

The elevators were also unreliable. Out of five in the hotel, only two worked at any given time. They were slow and often skipped floors or suddenly changed direction. Once the CPA checked in, the hotel was well beyond its capacity and the lack of elevators made it an adventure to get from the upper floors to the lobby in time to catch your shuttle or make your car pool to the palace.

The Al Rashid's water was also erratic. Staff who lived on the palace grounds had far more reliable water. If you lived in a trailer, you shared your water with the other people in your immediate area. As long as the tanks were filled, you could turn on the faucet and get water. In the shower trailers, as I previously discussed, more often than not, the pressure was good and the water was warm to hot, unless you hit the shower during or just after a peak period. On the other hand, the Al Rashid's water system had a number of issues, stemming from general neglect and disrepair. The CPA contributed to the problems by overburdening the hotel with a double occupancy policy. I'm not faulting them. It was necessary for folks to double up in rooms, but the hotel simply couldn't handle it. Most mornings I'd wake up about 6:00 a.m. and turn on the shower to find one of several conditions: 1. No water; 2. A loud vibrating and gurgling noise and then no water; 3. Ice-cold water only; 4. Scalding hot water with no cold water; or 5. Trickling water of varying temperatures. It was enough to make you crazy. I wasn't going to wake up at 4:00 a.m. to shower every day, nor could I shower before bed, because I had to shave in the mornings.

At this point, I should mention that I was truly grateful for the opportunity to live in the hotel. Our soldiers in the field did not have the accommodations that most of the CPA civilians or military personnel were able to enjoy. Thousands of coalition troops ate MREs and showered only irregularly. Many of them were dug in or at facilities where the whole concept of air conditioning was as foreign as a cold, rainy day there. They roughed it. Our conditions presented mostly mere annoyances and modest challenges.

Outside sliding glass double doors, near the bar and down the sidewalk, was the pool and pool bar. This was by far the best feature of the Al Rashid, in my opinion. Beneath the palm trees, it was the perfect way to end a Baghdad day, spending an hour or so in the pool to beat the oppressive heat and having a cold drink at the bar. Circumstances beyond the walls melted away and my colleagues and I were able to relax. That was until you'd hear automatic machine gunfire. The funny thing about the pool was that it was located on the perimeter of the Green Zone. That was actually the funny thing about the hotel in general. All of us were living in a thirteen-story target on the edge of the Green Zone. We might as well have had a big bull's-eye painted on the side of the building. We tried our best to ignore the danger. The unprotected area was not far beyond the wall of the pool area. It was common to hear gunfights while poolside. The first time I heard the gunfire, I couldn't believe that nobody seemed to care. It was all so normal to them. They just went about their swimming, not paying any mind to the weapons discharging a few blocks away.

I thought they were nuts, but after a while I too became desensitized to the gun fights. We'd actually sit and listen to the small arms fire, trying to guess whether it was fire from an AK-47 (which would be Iraqi) or M-16 (which would be American). When coalition forces would fire back from the Bradley Fighting Vehicles, using their fifty-caliber machine guns, the sound was actually comforting. It meant that the "good guys" were on the scene.

The pool at the Al Rashid, like the pool at the palace, was also fun for people-watching. The pool at the palace was fun because of the energy of all those soldiers, happy to be in from the desert and enjoying themselves. They had a blast. It was contagious. The pool at the Al Rashid, on the other hand, brought out a much more diverse group. There were far more civilian CPA officials. There were Brits and Aussies, Italians, Poles, Spaniards, and Japanese personnel to name a few. The media fails to recognize that we had a coalition, so I guess we can call them all non-American vacationers. There were contractors, government civilians, ranking military officers, senior diplomats, and this rather obese Iraqi in a Speedo who would blow his whistle when it was time to close for the night.

Thanks to the lopsided press coverage, many Americans still think that we went into Iraq alone. The press and opponents of the war have continually tried to paint the effort as unilateralist. They never came to the palace during dinnertime or to the Al Rashid pool after dark.

In early September, KBR put on a "Jimmy Buffet in Baghdad" party out at the pool. People wore their Hawaiian shirts, which surprisingly a lot of people brought with them to the war zone, and KBR organized some food for the event. People were always having birthday parties, going-away parties, and other gatherings out at the pool. One night we managed to get the guys from the psychological operations unit over to the hotel for a going away party. Their leader, Lieutenant Colonel Chad Buehring, was famous in the palace and the hotel for his wide variety of Hawaiian shirts. In fact, all the members of his unit followed his lead and wore their own. Sergeant John Lutz, who styled himself a singer—a very amateur singer—entertained everyone with his renditions of various country tunes, in particular "You Never Even Called Me By My Name" by David Allen Coe.

It may not sound like much, but it was an escape. There were few real social outlets in the Green Zone, especially early on in the occupation. Critics might suggest that they were unnecessary or inappropriate. It is important to recognize that people were working under very stressful conditions and dealing with life-and-death situations every day, while placing themselves in harm's way. Most civilians in Baghdad had little to no experience or training to cope with this very unique set of pressures. I've learned the hard way in my life that stress is like a pressure valve. If you don't release some steam every once in a while, the result is very damaging. When you were in Iraq, that meant that your productivity went down, your relationships suffered, and your attitude became potentially contagious, ultimately affecting others who were trying to do their jobs. The press liked to portray CPA civilians as living high on the hog, while people beyond the Green Zone were getting killed. I will always contend that, for civilians, the few social outlets that we created were vital to our ability to manage stress and ensure productivity.

Which brings me to the social outlet that became the most storied and yet most mysterious of the Green Zone: The Al Rashid Disco. The disco was located on the second floor of the hotel, in the same wing as the restaurants and shops. This was a renowned place, and for all the wrong reasons. The disco was rumored to be a favorite hangout of Uday Hussein, who, as I mentioned before, frequented the hotel. By some accounts, he designed the club to his specifications. It was right out of *Saturday Night Fever*. John Travolta would have felt right at home in the confines of this nightspot.

The disco was open most nights of the week and played music of different genres depending on the evening. There was karaoke on Tuesdays, country on Wednesdays, pop Thursday and Friday nights, and R&B on Saturdays. One country music night in October 2003, U.S. secretary of commerce Don Evans, who was staying at the hotel during his visit to Baghdad, sat there with me and his staff, clapping along to some of his favorite tunes. Boy, was he was a long way from Texas. The uniqueness of it all wasn't lost on any of us.

The big night out for folks was Thursday night. The CPA was technically closed Friday mornings, as were the rest of Iraq and the Arab world in observance of the holy day. Friday mornings were the only time off each week for most of us. Government offices were closed and most businesses were closed at least part of the day. So Thursday night was the night of the week that most folks looked forward to for the opportunity to let their hair down at the disco—and they did.

Before I go further, I mentioned earlier that the disco was a mysterious place. It was mysterious in the sense that it was one of the few places in the Green Zone that was strictly off limits to members of the press. Of course, a couple managed to sneak their way in during those months, but it remained a forbidden realm for nearly all of the media. Press were allowed in the Al Rashid but were not permitted at the pool, in the bars, or in the disco. If they were in the building, the rule was that they had to be accompanied at all times and, under no circumstances, could they take pictures or video or conduct interviews with CPA or military personnel. This drove most of them crazy. The press, after all believe that they are somehow entitled to access every piece of information and location when and wherever they want.

The folks who came to the disco or lived at the hotel needed their privacy. They were working smack in the middle of the biggest story of the young century. Sixteen-hour days were the norm, working in a volatile and dangerous environment, trying to advance the most ambitious foreign policy initiative undertaken by the West in more than fifty years. No matter what ones' station was with the coalition forces, the scrutiny of an increasingly cynical news media was never far away. People needed a place where they could get away from the prying eyes of the press. They deserved it. There was nothing surreptitious about the policy. It made sense to help people enjoy those few precious moments a week when they could attempt to unwind.

Jim Crane from the Associated Press and other reporters were fascinated with our social lives. I never understood it. They always wanted to know what life was like at the Al Rashid and what we did for fun. Sure, I think they may have been a little envious, but to my mind it was really all about the story of primarily civilians living it up while Iraqis were dying in increasing numbers. One colleague of mine in the press office was once harshly reprimanded for sneaking a reporter into the disco. The reporter, according to several witnesses, began asking questions of soldiers having fun at the bar. The soldiers weren't supposed to be drinking. Eventually, no uniformed personnel were permitted in the disco and, while no story ultimately developed from the incident, a very ugly article could easily have been written. The media were looking for any way to expose alleged waste at the CPA and compare our Baghdad lifestyle with that of the average Iraqi.

This wasn't "CPA Gone Wild" or a tale of drunken debauchery. The CPA personnel whom I was privileged to work with were dedicated to their mission and to the goal of a free and democratic Iraq. Nearly all of them took tremendous personal risks to be in theater and made sacrifices to be part of something bigger than themselves. The fact that some of them had a few drinks or danced at the hotel bar should in no way detract from their commitment to Iraq or their respective countries and governments.

The disco was hot, smoky, loud, and invariably mobbed on those Thursday nights. It was a relatively small, dimly lit space over the main ballroom. Its dark red walls were decorated with small groupings of mirrors that were cut in the shape of Ba'athist stars and framed in wood moldings that matched the color of the walls. The elevated, circular dance floor was the centerpiece of the club. Yes, I said elevated circular dance floor. Above it hung a large disco ball reminiscent of the Studio 54 era. The dance floor had a light-up Ba'athist star at its center and the foot-high ridge around the edge of the surface contained multicolored lights that flashed as music played. At ground level, around the dance floor were tables and, on either end of the room, two raised platforms with seating. The bar was located in the rear of the room, also elevated with a seating area adjacent.

It was a feast for the senses and provided everyone in attendance with a variety of experiences, generally ranging from strange to bizarre. Only at the disco could one find soldiers, who had hoped to find the club bursting with women, forced to dance with each other to the rap and hip-hop that often blared from the speakers. Only at the disco could one find middle-aged men and women trying to dance the box step to Shaggy or attempting to move to the pounding beat of Eminem. If only their kids could see them, I often thought. These people didn't know who Eminem was nor had they ever heard most of the other music in the DJ's meager play list. They didn't care. It was a place to blow off steam. This is not to say that it was all clean fun. The club responded to the two overarching desires for people under stress: alcohol and sex.

In many respects, it bore resemblance to Washington's Capitol Hill social scene. Except in Washington, congressional staffers in their twenties and thirties can be found out at the bars virtually every night of the week. As with any group of primarily younger people, some would come out, get drunk, and try to make a connection. There were a lot of Baghdad romances among the staff, and many of them started right there in Uday's disco. I'm not suggesting that it was a bad thing. Most of the people getting together appeared to be young, single, responsible people. Of course, there were those who drank too much and spread themselves around enough to establish a reputation. There were the messy drunks, stupid drunks, and of course the emotional, homesick drunks. Naturally, there was the occasional scuffle.

At one point, a colleague of mine started dating a member of Bremer's security detail. He was one of these former Navy SEAL types who looked like he knew about a hundred ways to kill a man—and did. One night, she was out at the disco and hanging out with some of her boyfriend's fellow guns-for-hire when she caught the unwanted attention of a member of the Department of State's Criminal Investigation Division (CID), also in Iraq to provide security for U.S. government officials. The contract security guards had recently replaced the CID staff as the principal protection for the ambassador. Needless to say, there was tension between the two groups and a scuffle over her ensued. It wasn't an all-out brawl, but the two groups of meatheads came close to doing some serious damage.

As the security situation got worse, sexual activity increased as well. Of course, the military frowned heavily upon sexual relations between soldiers of the opposite and of course the same sex. There were no such regulations about civilian relationships. After the third consecutive night of Ramadan mortaring all bets were off. Tensions were running high. You began to hear the stories of soldiers getting together with soldiers. Civilians went with civilians. You get the idea. Every now and then, a lucky soldier would score a civilian and vice versa.

There were many Baghdad relationships, some of which outlasted the CPA, and at least a few resulted in marriage. As you might imagine, it was a challenge to date in the Green Zone. There may have been thousands of coalition staff in and around the zone, but everyone knew everyone else's business. It was like Peyton Place—with guns. If a couple wanted to be alone, it was necessary to coordinate schedules with roommates to facilitate some privacy. That led to rendezvous at odd times during the day. Sometimes, two people you knew were dating would simply disappear in the middle of the afternoon. That usually meant one thing. The seemingly ever-present roommate was at work. Back at home in a regular job, stealing an hour would be big deal, but most of these folks were barely taking breaks for food and were working at least twelve-hour shifts if not longer, six or seven days a week.

It more often though wasn't about sex. Although Pearse and I were friends and colleagues, I found myself time and again wishing that he'd be transferred to one of the provinces for a week or two, just so I could have a little alone time. It was like that for many people. In Baghdad, it was hard to get away and enjoy the sound of nothing but your own inner voice. Before I left, I kidded my brother that I had never been to summer camp and was now making up for it.

I went to the disco about once per week. Not a fan of most of the music played, smoke-filled rooms, or drinking to release stress, I wasn't one of the regulars. One night, I met someone. She was a little older than me, an army captain with long blond hair. She was available, or so she said, and for some reason wanted to spend time talking to me. In my modest opinion, she was one of the few women in the zone who could turn some heads. Eventually she pulled me out onto the dance floor and let's just say things went well. In case you need reminding at this point, for good measure, I'll repeat it—I was single. Later on, we took a walk at my suggestion to get a little privacy. On the side of the hotel, across from the pool, was an overgrown garden and what looked to be an abandoned outdoor bar. There was also a lawn that had once used for landing helicopters on the property. We sat on a bench near the far wall and talked about the war, the future, and our lives back home. That moment and the others that we would spend together over a couple of months were times when it all melted away. It wasn't Baghdad or the Al Rashid, it was just two people helping to make the time more bearable. It was a brief Baghdad relationship—or as Frank Sinatra once said, "a brief episode." One morning, after we were spotted together at the Al Rashid, Chris Harvin and Chad asked rather loudly in the office to the sound of muffled snickering whether the good captain had "broken all the furniture" in my room the night before. They really cracked themselves up. It wasn't like that. It was a nice distraction, a brief escape from the worsening tension—like the Al Rashid.

DRIVING THE MESSAGE

The failure of the Bush administration in Washington to manage expectations effectively or to broaden the strategy by the administration in Washington made our ability to counter the editorial filter all the more difficult. It made a tough sell even tougher.

One morning while working in the office, I noticed one of the Iraqi translators who was a regular part of our team glaring intently at one of the three televisions perched atop the rickety storage closets in the Green Room. He was watching Fox News or one of the American cable networks that were perpetually flickering on in the office. His arms folded, he was taking note of some coverage from the California recall election. It was the day that Governor Gray Davis lost his bid to remain in office. One of my colleagues, Shane Wolfe, was watching with him. The translator turned to him and asked, "So what happens to this man now? Does he go to jail? Is he exiled?" Shane, sporting a big grin on his face, responded that the governor simply left office. Our Iraqi friend asked again whether Davis would be punished in some way. Chiming in, I said something to the effect of, "No, he just leaves office. He is free to go on with his life as he chooses." This brought a smile and an expression of almost disbelief from the man. I admit that I got a real laugh from the whole exchange, but it underscored just how much learning about participatory government and Western society these Iraqis had to do—and were they learning! Perhaps in that moment, watching this unusual transfer of power, an extraordinary exercise of authority by ordinary people back in the United States, this one Iraqi believed in his heart just a little more fervently that government by the people was possible. I like to think that he believed a little more that democracy wasn't some untested theory. It was real. There was nothing like seeing the light bulb go off over someone's head when they came to that realization. We all had the opportunity to see it many times during our tours of duty in Iraq.

We were indeed having an impact on this nation, and it was the job of the Strategic Communications Office, the CPA, the White House, and the broader U.S. government to bring that message home to the Americans who were paying for the war with both blood and treasure. Although we were fighting the political and media wars, the coalition forces were combating the rising insurgency in the towns, villages, and cities of the country. When I say political battle, I don't mean as between Republicans and Democrats but the struggle to clearly articulate the strategy and results to the body politic.

Americans were starving for something more than the daily car bomb played over and over on their television screens. Poll after poll of the American people by a range of outlets showed that large percentages of the public believed that they weren't getting a balanced view of the operation. The job of the Strategic Communications Office was to do the tough day-to-day block and tackle with the press to achieve fair coverage of the work that the CPA and the coalition military were doing. We also needed, in creative ways, to break through the editorial filter to deliver a broader, more accurate view of the situation on the ground. Now, before you go sounding off about the government propaganda machine, let me just say that disseminating information is a vital and legitimate government function. In that first year, we had much to talk about. From day one, most of us in the office and in the palace knew full well that this was not going to be about rosy progress reports. This story wasn't going to be cut and dried. It also wasn't going to be reported fairly.

Today, many people truly believe that nothing of substance was accomplished in those first twelve months. In fact, the majority of folks you speak with know all about the mistakes and the problems that came into specific relief during the time of the CPA. We had to cobble together a communications operation that tried desperately to ensure that the good outshone the bad—at least every once in a while. It was a tough sell to be sure.

When I first arrived, we were terribly understaffed. On the day I showed up in Baghdad, there were more British press officers working for the CPA than there were Americans working for it. It was clear that, aside from Bremer, the Iraq message was being articulated to the Western and regional press principally by Charles and Naheed. I didn't have an issue with either of them, but as I'll discuss shortly, the American media needed to be handled by American communicators who understood the journalistic culture, the editorial mindset, and the American news business, which is far different from that of any other place in the world.

In addition to me, only three other people were handling the digesting of internal information and dealing with the media. Shortly thereafter, the Bush administration sent over two additional political appointees to augment the staff. Three others followed them by September. More people meant that more planning could be done or at least more focus could be given to each individual subject matter.

We were dealing with very complex issues reaching into every aspect of the Iraq mission. To be credible and aggressive, anyone handling the media needed to know the history behind an issue, the personalities, the cultural concerns, the facts, figures, timelines, and progress updates. That information needed to be distilled, monitored, and developed into some useable form for dissemination to the press and communications offices in Washington and Downing Street. The office and the operation began to grow rapidly and, with Gary Thatcher's long-awaited arrival at the end of August 2003, the operation finally had someone definitively at the top to provide an anchor. The strategy from an operational standpoint wasn't much different from a Washington public affairs or corporate communications operation. Grab information, distill it, write the release or briefing documents, push it out to media outlets, and follow up. Wash, rinse, repeat—for basically every issue under the hot sun.

Every communications operation relies heavily on the ability of the organization to harness information. This posed a significant challenge given the unique structure of the CPA. The first problem we faced was one of internal communication inside the CPA. It is imperative that any organization have good internal communications to facilitate information flow and, therefore, good external communications. The professional and personal interplay between the civilians and the military personnel was one of the most interesting dynamics of the Iraq mission. It also created communications challenges. Many of the civilians who found themselves in Iraq were deployed in much the same way as I was. Some were folks that, in some fashion, were connected with the Bush administration, although most were military and career government workers. In addition, subject matter experts from the private sector were recruited to serve. You also had contractors attached to KBR, Halliburton, or another private company and a wide range of nongovernmental organizations (NGOs) who also contributed to the effort. Most of the political civilians had virtually no training or experience working in an environment like Iraq. Although the military trains for months and years in anticipation of being deployed, the civilians who were sent to Iraq received little or no preparation from the government. In fact, the private companies and contractors spent more time and money preparing their people for deployment than the federal government had. The name of the game was just "get people over there," and when it came to civilians, they did just that—by the hundreds.

The government and, consequently, the CPA were following a standard management consulting formula for staffing. Grab a bunch of talented, young, enthusiastic, smart people, put them under the pressure of a steep learning curve, and throw them into the deep end of the pool. You had to trust that they would do the job. In strategic communications, more often than not, folks did the job as best as could be expected. Overall, the lack of preparation or experience didn't mean that people couldn't perform their assigned duties. It did mean that you had a bunch of folks who were used to wearing suits and going to Washington receptions who were suddenly dropped into the furthest thing from life as they knew it. Those people were then paired up to work alongside career FSOs and members of the military. The result was combination of M*A*S*H and the *Odd Couple*. In many circumstances, it worked, but it often produced serious friction.

This diversity was not a failing of the CPA structure. It was necessary to meld these different worlds and styles to accomplish such a broad mission. You needed the career diplomats to help with the building of democratic and government institutions. You needed the military not only to fight the insurgents but also to train Iraqi security forces and to assist with civil affairs and reconstruction. You needed the core of passionate, committed civilian political appointees to ensure that the interests of the administration and its policy would be furthered by people who were directly accountable to the civilian leadership. That would be the case regardless of which party controlled the White House or Downing Street. Of course, in a situation like this you would want the most experienced personnel possible in every seat. That simply wasn't feasible given the timetable for development of the operation and the nature of the environment.

When it came to the management of large-scale projects, ranging from infrastructure reconstruction to developing communications strategy, the military would plan the way military organizations often do. I discussed earlier the military's natural caste system and methods. Operationally, they plan and plan and then plan to plan. They have meetings to prepare for meetings to prepare for meetings. They can turn even the simplest strategy into a three-hour presentation complete with graphics, charts, photos, logos, and an invariably one monster of a PowerPoint deck. On the other hand, the political civilian types wanted everything done yesterday. That was our nature. As a political appointee to the Bush administration, we were expected to just work it out until we accomplished whatever task we'd been assigned. If it meant working overtime, so be it. If that meant changing directions several times, so be it. If that meant doing what seemed like the impossible, so be it. If it meant thinking outside the box, so be it. In Iraq, however, few situations presented themselves that provided the possibility of a lightning response. It was frustrating.

Then you had the FSOs who were pretty convinced that they were the real experts on the ground and had very clear ideas individually about what they would and wouldn't put up with in the way of assignments. There were also serious questions from military and civilian staffers, regarding whether many FSOs supported the mission in the first place.

The disparate and unique relationships that were created by the CPA bureaucracy had positive impacts, notably among them the capacity to accomplish a wide variety of tasks simultaneously. It also created certain challenges and negative repercussions, including maintaining disciplined internal and external communication. The key to good internal communication is the ability of the organization to break down walls that stifle information-sharing. In other words, the bureaucracy that the coalition had created made delivering the external message and promoting the progress of the mission more difficult. The bureaucracy in the palace and between the different stovepipes within the CPA created barriers to effective strategic communications.

A basic example of this was our constant attempt to ascertain an accurate number of the Iraqi security forces who were trained and on duty at any given time during the occupation. This was complicated by several factors, none of which the media cared to understand. Several Iraqi security services were established by the coalition, to assist with a variety of needs throughout the country of varying scope. They included the Iraqi Police, the Iraqi Army, the border guards, prison guards, and the Iraqi Civil Defense Corps (ICDC). Each of these had their own training program and each was run by different groups in different locations throughout the country. The border guards and the prison guards were relatively small in number and could be tracked more easily. The training of the new Iraqi Army was very tightly controlled by the coalition and the trainers involved. There was also only one primary basic training facility for the army during most of the CPA's tenure in the country.

The problem was more evident with respect to the ICDC and the Iraqi Police. The coalition forces recruited the ICDC members to assist the coalition directly on the ground in a particular area. Literally a dozen small training programs existed throughout the country. In addition, trainees were divided into several categories: recruits, recruits in-training, trained but not equipped, trained and equipped, and in service. To determine for public consumption exactly how many ICDC were on the street—and therefore the effectiveness of the program and return on investment—we had to rely on reports from coalition forces in the field who were conducting the training. Communication is tough in a forward area, and the form and frequency in which these reports came into the command was often different from one location to another.

In the case of the Iraqi Police, the situation was far more complicated. When a reporter would ask for a number of Iraqi police officers, it was a difficult question to answer. Many journalists would say that the coalition outright lied to them about the number of security forces it had trained. The reality was that the numbers that came out of the strategic communications operation were the result of a very real attempt to reconcile information from a variety of sources in an honest way. We needed to provide answers. The building of new, effective security forces was the foundation upon which the coalition's ultimate withdrawal would be built. That was understood early on. The insurgency was gaining in intensity, public support back home was cracking, political support was shaky, and people were getting killed in larger numbers by the week. Despite the media's suggestion that we were doing nearly nothing, a multibillion-dollar plan was being executed to develop these forces.

The Iraqi Police, however, were being recruited and trained under the direction of the Iraqi Ministry of the Interior, with the help of the coalition, not the other way around. One of the facts about the CPA that the press liked to ignore is that Bremer, very wisely, I might add, appointed ministers and turned the day-to-day operation of every Iraqi ministry over to the Iraqis by September of 2003. They were in charge of policy and budget. They worked in concert with a set of advisors from the CPA who assisted them in meeting the goals and objectives that were established after the war. Bremer had the ability to overrule the decision of a minister, but overall the Iraqis played major roles in operating their ministries.

With the Iraqi police force, this posed a problem when it came to determining exactly how many of these guys were on the street. It was a determination that we were naturally expected to make for public consumption. During the reign of Saddam, the police force had little enforcement power. They were little more than traffic cops. The police had no investigative duties, and any major crime or suspicion of criminal activity was handled by the secret police. So the CPA found itself not merely having to rebuild the force but actually having to build from

scratch a modern police force that was trained in contemporary policing skills. It would be an enormous task to accomplish in a medium-
sized city in the United States under the best conditions.

One must keep in mind that print and broadcast media in the United
States were complaining loudly about the supposed lack of progress in
creating a new police force as early as September 2003. The CPA and
the Iraqis were attempting this massive undertaking on a national scale
within a few short months of the war. When the Iraqis took over the
ministry and the payroll, they would submit numbers to the CPA that
included barbers, cooks, mechanics, and cleaning personnel. During
the regime, if you worked for the Iraqi police force, you were a member of the police force. It didn't matter what role you played. Even if
you never hit the streets, you were a police officer. Saddam didn't care.
The secret police were the real enforcers, and the police force was little more than a patronage den. The original numbers that we began
using also included officers who were not working because they were
retired. In addition, hundreds if not thousands of police were paid who
never showed up for work or who were not placed on duty. This was
further exacerbated by the national scope of the force. Although most
of the force was in Baghdad, naturally, other police were in cities and
towns throughout the country. The coalition forces who were operating in these areas were not about to begin calling roll in the morning
and spending time wondering whether some new cop was showing up
for work. Padding was also going on as a result of political favoritism
on the part of the Iraqis.

Understandably, it took time for the ministry to clean up its books,
and the CPA had to help them do it. I remember getting briefed by
folks in the CPA office that liaised with the Interior Ministry and not
being able to get any solid answers from them about equipment, uniforms, payroll, and delivery of new weapons and gear. It was terribly
frustrating for me and for them.

When it came to the police service, there were CPA personnel from
both the military and civilian worlds who often had two or more sets
of numbers for everything. The categories mentioned earlier were
often confused; therefore, the numbers would change constantly. On
one occasion, somebody back in Washington fed Secretary Rumsfeld

a number that was fully ten thousand more than the number he had used during a press briefing the previous week in response to a question. Something had to be done. I attempted to get a hold on all the reports from all the sources within the CPA who had some grasp of reality. I went to the Iraqi Ministry of the Interior's CPA office, which at the time had problems accounting for everything from equipment and ammunition to personnel. They gave me their report. A report came back from Washington to Baghdad that had its own set of numbers. Then the tally that the military maintained was for some reason classified. Although I was at first told that I couldn't see it because it was only for military use, after several weeks of protesting, I was allowed to get copies of the report each week.

The result was a situation in which no one was willing to bet the farm on any of the numbers. I'd sit there with my colleagues and try to reconcile the different reports to so that I could come up with a number. I tried to impress upon Dan and Charles that despite the desire for us to tell people we had one hundred thousand cops on the street, we needed to assess where we were and stick with it, according to the facts, such as they were. They agreed. Some might say that we weren't up front with people about these numbers. Quite to the contrary, an enormous amount of staff work went into trying to be as accurate as we could. We did our best, given the challenges of getting correct information through several organizational barriers and from different, often unreliable sources on a national scale. This was to say nothing of the effect that the internal problems at the ministry had on our ability to assess the situation accurately. We took our best guess and developed a series of talking points that permitted officials to explain why the numbers jumped one week and declined another. There was a guy in the JOC taking numerous reports on these forces, trying to make sense out of them and consolidating them into one report. Of course, he wasn't thinking about public perception. The numbers were supposed to go up. When they did, I assumed that he thought that was a good thing.

For our part in strategic communications, it was important to be up front about the challenges, manage expectations, and give a number that made sense. Then we had to be consistent. Bremer, the secretary, and the president were all using different numbers during the same week at one point. That hurt our credibility. Despite what some reporters have suggested, however, it was not an effort to dupe the American public into believing that the process was going faster than it was. The training of new security forces was an enormous undertaking complicated by internal challenges and a preexisting culture of Iraqi government corruption. The press grossly oversimplified it, and even the most astute observers of the mission never fully appreciated it.

Internal communication problems between the military and civilian arms of the CPA were a result of the complexity of the mission. From the CPA's standpoint, it was vital that external communication be tightly controlled to ensure message consistency. The press were constantly trying to poke holes in the operation. We were on trial every day. Every trial attorney will tell you that one of the tactics in your arsenal is finding inconsistent statements to call into question the credibility of a witness. Our problem was no different. I don't blame reporters for trying to do this, but it made our lives in strategic communications all the more difficult. It made winning the war at home nearly impossible. Reporters would attempt to circumvent the official CPA spokespersons and go directly to the CPA Ministry Office, the actual Iraqi ministry, or the military in attempt to get contradictory information.

The CPA eventually instituted a policy that was mostly effective in curbing this activity within the walls of the palace. No CPA ministry office or senior advisor was permitted to "do press" independently without the knowledge or permission of the strategic communications operation or the ambassador. Obviously, you had some folks, embattled former New York City police commissioner Bernie Kerik foremost among them, who often would end up in the newspaper or on television giving an interview before anyone in the press office or Bremer knew about it. As time went on, most of the advisors recognized that speaking to the media was likely not something they wanted to do on a freelance basis. It was like walking into a firefight with a knife. They preferred to spend most of their time doing their jobs, which were difficult enough without the media challenging their priorities and twisting their words.

A somewhat larger communications problem arose when it came to the media's interaction with the military. Although heroes who represented incredible dedication and courage, the coalition forces through-out the country had little discipline when it came to their exposure to the press. A military spokesperson and his staff were stationed in the Strategic Communications Office in the palace. They sat across from me. For most of my time in Iraq, army colonel Bill Darley and marine captain Mike Freil were the go-to guys in the office when we had to coordinate our message and ensure that we had accurate informa-tion. It was a good relationship. We respected the military's right and expectation that they would be the lead for issues such as ongoing operations or coalition forces' response to a bombing or other attack. The military public affairs staff whom I worked with were good, solid folks. The problem they and, as a consequence, we faced was the lack of control that the military had over their own people on the ground when it came to the media. I was shocked to learn that the U.S. mili-tary does not restrict members of the armed forces from speaking to the media. It didn't matter whether the person speaking was a private, a sergeant, a major, a colonel, or a general. If you were asked a ques-tion, you could answer it. That's right. We had potentially 125,000 spokespeople out there in the field. The reporters of course knew that, meaning that some random sergeant or army specialist who might not be an authority on anything or have accurate information would end up being asked for comment. Reporters asked and they got answers. It happened at least once a week. Somebody appeared on television or in print commenting on coalition operations, the security situation, reconstruction, or any number of topics. These folks didn't mislead the media, but they often gave incomplete information. They also sometimes helped to create bigger stories. Give a reporter a quote or footage of a soldier commenting on an incident and you have your news package half in the bag with little effort. Whatever that person said, regardless of its accuracy, was repeated fifty times a day or made it into the newspaper the following morning.

If reporters wanted to advance a negative angle, they could ask a leading question of some kid who wanted his mom to see him on television—and get an answer. Many of the questions had to do with assessments of the overall military situation. Some were about specific operations or incidents. The worst kind of this behavior on the part of the press consisted of questions like, "Do you miss your family?" and "Don't you want to go home?" So the soldier answered in some fashion that presented the impression that he didn't understand or support the mission. They all wanted to go home. They all missed their families. If they didn't, I think something would be seriously wrong with them. Soldiers also complain about conditions. You can always find people who are willing to say one thing or another about living conditions or the dangerous environment. It was understandable and a persistent characteristic of deployed personnel. It's been going on as long as nations have sent troops into battle. Half of Washington's army almost deserted over deplorable conditions and lack of pay. What was shameless was the way that reporters would use some of these statements to pull the heartstrings of Americans and coalition partners to advance an anti-Bush, antiwar agenda. The soldiers whom I was privileged to have met and worked with understood and supported President Bush's decision to liberate Iraq. From the youngest of them to the most seasoned, they appreciated the strategy to address the terror threat through a combination of active deterrence and the spread of the tolerance that comes from freedom and open societies. Of course, they didn't put it that way, but they got it. Most of the journalists didn't understand it, nor did they want to. The journalists more likely than not believed that we were on a fool's errand. It showed in the reporting.

I don't blame the soldiers, but the culture and practice of letting anyone speak to the press without consequences simply led at times to misinformation being disseminated. On one occasion, following a mortar attack on the Green Zone, a soldier who was not part of the public affairs operation told a reporter how many mortar rounds landed and where the impacts occurred. First of all, we had a policy of not disclosing the impact sites of mortars. Disclosure helped insurgents with their targeting. Second, the soldier could not have been more wrong as to the type of weapon and number of hits. That of course didn't stop every major network from reporting it. The press knew that we were in a brief media blackout, so they just went around us.

Military responsiveness to CPA civilian requests for information also presented a challenge. Military personnel live and work in their stovepipe. It is an essential element of a good military operation. You're given an area of responsibility and you stick to it to get the job done. The civilians in the press operation required the military to provide a continuous flow of information to plan effectively. Unfortunately, civilians were not in the stovepipe. Further, in a military environment, senior officers don't respond to lower-ranked personnel. There was a perception on the part of some officers—certainly not all, but some—that if you were to receive a request from some younger civilian, it could or should be ignored even if he or she were working for the ambassador. That required, even before my arrival, that civilians begin including their general schedule (GS) distinction on their emails and memos to give the military a sense of where that person resided in the CPA pecking order. The military technicians who set up the CPA's email system made the decision. It was a simple fact that some military personnel, especially generals, colonels, and lieutenant colonels, would pay more attention if your designation was Senior Executive Service (SES), a civilian designation that indicated the individual was a high-ranking official with the U.S. government. SES-designated individuals had a rank equivalency of a general officer in the military. The GS scale tops out at level 15, which is comparable, salary-wise, to a colonel in the army or a captain in the navy. Senior officers also viewed GS-14 civilians as more credible. As a GS-15, I found that my "rank" often helped me obtain information or get in contact with officers with command authority.

To have well-planned external communications you needed information. Reliable information is your ammunition in the media war. That information needed to be harnessed and funneled into an apparatus like the strategic communications operation that could think tactically and then leverage it into exposure. Constant preparation and analysis was central to the success of an offensive, outbound Baghdad communications operation much in the same way that it would be the key to any government or corporate public relations effort.

In September 2003, I actually had my chance to prove that it could be done. Lieutenant Colonel Joe Wunderlich was commanding an army civil affairs battalion in Baghdad that was working on road infrastructure improvements. He was a burly and boisterous guy who would bound into the office with news about his latest achievement scribbled on a piece of copy paper. Joe reminded me of a proud union guy.

He was committed, unpretentious, and down to earth. A regular old Joe you could say. He once grabbed me, put me in his Humvee, and took me on an excursion to visit an asphalt plant on the edge of Baghdad. The plant had been dormant for months but was now churning out blacktop for the countless number of roads being paved, some of which in the Shiite neighborhoods had never seen asphalt under the former regime. It was in a desolate area of town. The smell of the tar was thick in the air. The three asphalt mills were surrounded by brush-covered, undeveloped land.

Three other things were interesting about our little trip. First, Joe was very excited about this facility. I'd never seen anyone so proud of tar. Second, while at the plant, the manager pointed out to us an unexploded land mine that was endangering the workers. Joe would see to it that it was detonated and removed. I had never seen a land mine before and played tourist for a few minutes taking pictures of the tan, doughnut-shaped object half buried in the dirt. Third, about fifteen minutes into our visit, one of Joe's men came running over to give him a message. I wasn't paying much attention, still taking in my surroundings, when the colonel walked calmly over to me and said with shockingly little urgency in his voice, "Well, I guess we have to go. The guys say they heard on the radio two men with RPGs (rocket propelled grenades) were spotted in the area heading in our direction." I didn't need convincing. By the time Joe meandered back to the vehicles, his men were more than ready to get out of there. Leaving a cloud of dust behind us, the armored vehicles sped back to the main road into town.

I had met Joe while attending one of my regular meetings in the Baghdad Central Office in what was usually a vain effort to get a handle on what the heck was going on. I had mentioned to the group that our goal was to be able to lay out all of the major projects in a particular area and estimate when they would be completed. Each week, we would update the plan to announce the inception, new progress, or completion of the transportation projects for the next several months. From that information, the communications plan would be developed to allow the Strategic Communications Office to prepare announcements, events, ceremonies, and press releases, or just to provide the media with appropriate information. It would be a basic communications matrix with a series of potential news stories, each a moving target over the coming weeks. After all, at this point the name of the game in the office was offense. We needed to put out as much reconstruction information as possible to counter increases in attacks by former regime loyalists and foreign fighters.

Joe came forward at the end of the meeting excited about being able to help. Like most of the members of the military I encountered, he was anxious to help develop some good news. They knew what their families were seeing back home and wanted to try to change the narrative. Even if nobody from the Western press cared about some transportation project, it was likely that an Iraqi journalist would be interested in knowing about an improvement in his part of town. Gathering the information was necessary, regardless of the issue, and any coordination coming out of Baghdad was a step in the right direction. It was fortuitous that he was willing to help, because transportation was an issue that was often raised by members of the Western press as an example of Baghdad being a city in chaos.

In Baghdad, the roads, much like the water and sewage systems, were planned for a city of one million and were never upgraded as the population grew to more than three million. There were basic problems, like sinkholes and potholes in major thoroughfares, that created dangerous conditions. Other projects were more complicated, such as rebuilding damaged bridges. Basic safety features that we take for granted were virtually unheard of. Traffic accidents were common as medians were never installed on major roads. I hate Jersey barriers and guardrails when I'm driving, but in Baghdad there was usually only a faint yellow line separating you from speeding oncoming traffic. Roads had no shoulders and were often too narrow to accommodate the volume of traffic zooming across the city. Saddam had removed nearly all of the street signs before the invasion to confuse American troops, so new directional signage needed to be installed.

All of this was complicated by the fact that the traffic lights didn't work in most of Baghdad and the meager police force had much better things to do than administer traffic laws that no court was prepared to enforce. People sped around in unregistered cars, paying absolutely no attention to the rules of the road. Being out in a car on a Baghdad city street or highway was one of the most dangerous things one could do. New York City cabbies have nothing on your average Iraqi driver. The conditions were a real example of what happens when you have a breakdown of the legal and other government systems. Anyway, the Western press, often caught in the gridlock, used it as an example of how Baghdad was a lawless, chaotic city.

Joe provided me with a list of all the major projects he and his team were working on along with estimates of the completion dates. The communications plan then developed key messages about the coalition's efforts to improve, in this case, roads and bridges. Those key messages were then expanded to specifics about each project. In addition, recommendations were also laid out in advance for specific tactics and strategies to drive out the story. Details about each project were also then given to Dan, Charles, or anyone who needed the specifics for the daily press briefings and reporting to other agencies. Key messages would be general, short sound bites. For instance, "The coalition is working closely with Baghdad city officials to address traffic congestion and improve road conditions in the city" or "Improving the infrastructure will prepare Baghdad to again begin attracting investment and economic growth" or "Emergency repairs identified by the City are nearing completion." Expanded or more tactical messages would look more in line with these:

Designation of 12 gridlock areas that will be given special attention by the City and Coalition to alleviate congestion. The Amanat Baghdad, the Company for Private Transport and Public Transport under the Ministry of Transport and Communications, the Traffic Police, the Ministry of the Interior and 1AD 519th MPs now meet weekly to identify areas of major congestion and find solutions to the traffic problems.

Twelve sites have been identified as critical problem areas and are receiving special consideration from the above entities. The Al-Teheran Sq., Al-Rashid Street, al-Jamhoria Street in the section opposite al-Sorja, al-Kifah Street (money exchange location) and al-Shaikh Omer Street are being addressed first.

Operations are continuing periodically at Al-Teheran Sq and future operations between now and 15 September will be conducted. The major problems are the illegally parked busses and private transport vans as well as vendors blocking traffic lanes.

Plans are currently being developed to place more parking enforcement police on the streets and move vendors to designated open-air markets to alleviate congestion.

New road signage, directional and public service oriented to be erected. The military is currently working with the City to replace road signage damaged or removed during the conflict or neglected by the former regime.

Just prior to the conflict, Saddam Hussein instructed the military to remove most of the road signage in the Baghdad area. We are working to replace signs throughout the city. The signage is being produced by a local Baghdad vendor.

Tactical recommendations would then be made for action by the Strategic Communications Office in preparation of a project's completion. Of course, it was Iraq, so timetables slipped and priorities changed, and some projects were canceled in favor of others. The matrix developed was constantly updated and shifted. It didn't matter. The important thing was the ability to be organized and ahead of the game.

Around the middle of October, Charles had had about enough. This guy was a machine and had been working like one for months. He slept little and ate less. We in the office truly believed that if he did one more press conference or had one more argument with Al Jazeera, he'd snap. Charles needed a vacation. Much to my surprise, he actually recognized that he needed a break and, after hemming and hawing about it a bit, left for what the Brits call "holiday." Dan was with Bremer in the United States and Thatcher was shouldering the load of the operation.

Before Charles left he asked me to handle a communications planning project with the folks in governance and CJTF7. A couple of days later, I attended a meeting in Ambassador Greenstock's office with

Lieutenant Colonel Krivo, the CJTF7 spokesperson, a representative from the CPA Governance Office, and a couple of others. The discussion related to the possibility that coalition and Iraqi forces might, in very short order, conduct an operation to capture rebel Shiite leader Muqtada al Sadr.

Sadr, the son of a respected Shiite cleric, Sadiq Muhammad al Sadr, had been instigating violent protest within the Shiite neighborhoods in Baghdad for several months. His father was murdered by Saddam's regime in 1999 and, consequently, the elder Sadr became one of the great martyrs for the Shiite community in Iraq. After the war, the members of the neighborhood council in the poor Shiite area of Saddam City voted to rename their section of town Sadr City. The younger Sadr was forming his own army and looked to bring his own brand of theocratic dominance to the new Iraq. He was thirty at the time and, although he held himself out as a holy man, had no formal training and was described by some clerics as an apostate. Sadr was a thug with a gang, but he was becoming much more than that. It was believed that he had ordered the killing of Grand Ayatollah Majid al-Khoie in Najaf in April 2003, and he was suspected of stealing more than two million Iraqi dinars from a mosque. An Iraqi court had even issued an arrest warrant for Sadr in connection with the al-Khoie murder. He and his followers were also suspected of being behind several attacks on coalition forces.

His influence was growing, and his ability to incite violence and anti-coalition demonstrations among poor Shiite populations was also on the rise. He shrewdly established a newspaper that became his mouthpiece throughout the country, while his Mahdi Army was growing in strength. Sadr's forces were young, unemployed, downtrodden Shiites whose years of desperation and abuse had turned them into pieces of clay, ready to be molded. In that way, they were not much different from the terrorists and Sunni fighters. *What was different*, I thought, *was that, in their case, they had someone to follow. They had a leader and a public face who was building a platform to influence the direction of the country. That made Sadr more powerful than the former regime loyalists.* What added to the urgent need to deal with this threat, to my senses, was the fact that it seemed to be generally accepted in the palace that Sadr had connections to Iran and was being assisted financially by the Iranians.

I had not been part of the discussions that had been going on for months about Sadr among Bremer, Horan, the CIA, and senior Defense Department officials, but in the Green Room, we were certainly watching his power base develop. His handiwork was making it onto television and into the papers. It provided the latest evidence in the eyes of the press that the mission was falling apart. Nothing made an editor giddier than ethnic strife in Iraq. The fact of the matter was that Sadr's forces, even at their height during those days, represented only a small fraction of the population of Sadr City, or Karbala, or wherever he happened to be holed up at the time.

Although the media were reporting that Sadr City was rioting, the reality was that even the largest protest was only a couple of thousand men in a section of Baghdad that was home to more than one million people. The press presented the impression, as they often did, that tens of thousands of people were rioting in the streets. Many of the few who did protest the coalition were raising hell about the lack of essential services like electricity or water. Some wanted jobs. Some just begged for help.

Sadr City was a slum. It was clearly the poorest area of town and with clear reason. The Shiite population had been oppressed by Saddam and the largely Sunni members of the Ba'ath Party for decades. The streets were filled with mud and sewage. Many streets weren't even paved. Whole portions of this section of Baghdad were denied the most basic services. Residents tapped into waterlines that had been deliberately designed to bypass their homes. The sewage system backed up and was nonfunctional. Electricity was also pirated from the system, for lines were not dedicated for their use. The population density was as staggering as the smell of rotting garbage was revolting. The air was often thick with the stench of burning refuse and human waste. These were not new conditions that arose from the coalition invasion. This was largely the way these folks had lived for years. Sadr City was divided into nearly one hundred small sections no larger than a block or two. Saddam's agents in the area, called *mukthars*, acted as the eyes and ears of the neighborhood. They informed on residents, who would often disappear in the night at the hands of the secret police.

After the fall of the regime, the area was primed for the emergence of some ambitious religious leader who could promise all things to all men. Who better than the son of a martyr? In those early months after the war, while the media was busy blowing Sadr's influence out of proportion and telling the world that America faced a "Shiite uprising," they did have one thing right—the young Sadr was a problem. Bremer and the CPA hierarchy agreed early on that he had to be stopped. To their minds, once he started inciting real violence it was time for him to go. It was clear to many in the palace that, left unchecked, Sadr's militia would soon be a real army. One Shiite militia would embolden others and those forces would be a direct impediment to stability.

The activities of the Mahdi Army were a harbinger of the sectarian violence that would grip portions of the country as the mission wore on. Sadr needed to be out of the way. The question was how to do it. There were several complications. At the time of our meeting, Sadr was holed up in Karbala, where he had been taking refuge with a number of his followers for some time. He was located in an area that was surrounded by homes and presumably families and other innocent people who would potentially become collateral damage in the event of a military operation. Such damage, it was thought, might create more enemies of the coalition and possibly incite a real Shiite uprising. The other major roadblock was, I believe, the correct notion that any operation against Sadr to enforce an Iraqi arrest warrant for crimes against Iraqis should be conducted, in large part, with the participation of Iraqi forces. It would have sent a much better message to the Shiites if this renegade were to be taken down by his own than just coalition forces. The problem with that concept was there were no Iraqi forces truly prepared to carry on a mission of this kind without serious, significant side-by-side support from American troops. The military wasn't about to conduct an operation that could potentially be a bloodbath all the way around. An evaluation had to be done as to whether this made sense.

We had to prepare strategy for talking to the press about the potential of some form of operation again Sadr. From what we discussed, it could have happened within days. It would have to be a multifaceted communications plan that would encompass Iraqi and coalition officials as well as religious and community leaders with messages tailored toward audiences as disparate as American network television news viewers and Karbala residents. Over the next couple of days, the group of us came up with a time-released approach to how we would deal with the outcome of an effort to capture Sadr. It was going to be an Iraqi-led approach with messaging focused on Sadr's crimes against fellow Muslims and the Iraqi people. The plan would also rely heavily for the first time on the Iraqi Media Network (IMN), the new Iraqi television network, to mobilize and assist the Iraqi government in delivering strategic messages to the people. Our group developed a strategy that would have Nouri Badran, the Iraqi minister of the interior, broadcast a statement on the operation on IMN immediately following the operation, supported by footage of Sadr in Iraqi custody taken with pre-positioned cameras in Karbala. The CPA and coalition forces would provide only a brief statement after the outcome of the operation had been assessed. Messages for that statement and for Iraqi officials speaking for the record would highlight that no one is above the law in the new Iraq and that Sadr's capture or killing was in response to his suspected involvement in the murder of Grand Ayatollah al-Khoic.

The most important message though would be the urging of calm, particularly in Sadr City. The morning following the operation would see a flurry of activity. Badran would again give a statement in support of the action and welcoming the coalition's support of what was, we hoped, a largely Iraqi operation.

In addition, the CPA Governance Office would contact and engage a host of religious, community, and tribal leaders throughout the country to encourage them to speak out in favor of the capture. This would be the critical surrogate operation in support of the effort. Specific staff members were assigned to liaise with leaders ranging from Grand Ayatollah Al-Sistani and Supreme Council for the Islamic Revolution in Iraq (SCIRI political party) to the leaders of the Dawa Party, Dr. al-Ibrahim Jaafari and Abdul Mhedi. It was a long list, again underscoring the differences in the way Sadr was portrayed in the press and the way he was viewed by leaders on the ground. Most saw him as a threat and would have been happy to get him out of the way. Once these parties and others were engaged in assisting in disseminating a message of calm and understanding, the Iraqi and coalition forces would circulate leaflets in Sadr City, urging cooperation with authorities to forestall any violence. Later in the afternoon, the CPA and CJTF7 would brief more fully, but not until after another statement from Iraqi government officials.

It was a solid crisis communications plan not dissimilar to the kind of planning that happens routinely here in the States in government agencies and corporations. There was going to be public blowback, but most of those I spoke with in the palace agreed that the outcry would fade within days or weeks. From a communications standpoint, we were prepared to do what we could in an organized way in the event that we had to go in and get him. A notable tactic would be the video footage showing that he was in custody to put to rest any rumors of his avoiding capture. It would also send a message to the Mahdi Army that their leadership was no more. This approach was used very effectively earlier in the year when the bodies of Uday and Qusay Hussein were permitted to be filmed by reporters. Two months after our discussions about Sadr, the tactic was used again after the capture of Saddam.

Today, we all remember the footage released at Bremer's press conference that proved without a doubt that we had Saddam in custody. It was a good way to cut off rumors and prove to a frightened—and skeptical—population that what they were hearing was the truth.

I never thought that Sadr would allow himself to be taken alive—neither did the military. That belief goes back to the original set of difficulties in conducting the operation in the first place. After we had the strategy in place, we waited. One day turned to two and then into a week. As it happened, despite the urging of CPA personnel, intelligence officials and military leadership began to oppose taking the very real risks involved with the operation. It was apparently common knowledge in the South Central region that certain coalition commanders in Najaf opposed the operation because the division responsible would have had to delay its rotation out of the country to execute the plan and to deal with the aftermath. The CIA and some Pentagon officials are also believed to have made enough inroads within the administration over time to soften the overall will to go get him. We faced similar blowback when the CPA urged coalition forces to execute a policy of disarmament when it came to Iraq's growing number of militias. The military simply wasn't prepared or willing to take on the mission of disarmament. Consequently, it didn't happen. This was that disconnect over strategy between the CPA and the commanders beyond the walls of the palace (discussed earlier) on full display.

Ultimately, Sadr remained at large. It was a difficult decision for senior leadership to make, and I am certainly no military tactician. I believe it was a mistake. Our cautious posture in this instance cost lives and endangered all that we hoped to accomplish. I would also have been in favor of coalition forces leading the operation with the Iraqis playing only a minor supporting role. Although I understood the desire to put an Iraqi face on the operation, the longer Sadr stayed free, the more trouble he could cause for the mission, especially because there was wide speculation in the palace that Sadr was being propped up by the Iranians. This guy had a famous name and spoke to a disaffected public yearning for leadership.

More broadly, the militias throughout Iraq needed to be sent a message. Their existence had been and would continue to be a destabilizing force that would cost thousands of lives, mostly Iraqi, and continued to provoke confrontation between Sunni and Shiite. Sadr would remain a thorn in the side of the goal of a more tolerant, pluralistic Iraq. In November 2003, Sadr's associates took over a district council building in Sadr City. He later appointed his own set of cabinet ministers and threatened to bomb Iraqi ministries. In April of 2004, his Mahdi Army fought several pitched battles with coalition and Iraqi forces, all of which they lost.

In September and October of 2003, we were working to paint him as a renegade, a thug, a lawless apostate. We were in many ways successful with the American and other Western media outlets in labeling him as a radical. By the end of 2005, however, his followers had won several seats in Iraq's new parliament. Sadr went from being the leader of a street gang to a potentially genuine political force. The relative legitimacy provided by the democratic elections had come to cement the threat he posed to the new Iraq. We never used the communications plan. In 2006, I heard him referenced several times on American networks not as a "radical cleric" but as "influential cleric" Muqtada al Sadr. In 2007 the *Washington Post* story extolled his ability to provide "aid and hope."

After President Obama called for the removal of virtually all American forces and the subsequent rise of the ISIS, Sadr was able to maintain his relevance through the creation of new militias intended to fight the new Islamic State. By 2015, and in the face of the ISIS threat, he had further solidified his relationship with Iran's Qods Force and again threatened to attack American interests in and outside of Iraq if the United States officially recognized and directed aid to Sunnis and Kurds threatened by ISIS.

One of the biggest triumphs of the coalition's efforts in 2003 also produced one of the best examples of planning, coordination, and communication of the entire effort. Like so many other achievements that had a lasting impact, it unfortunately remains an overlooked CPA accomplishment. Karen Triggs, a British government employee and press advisor in the office, was tasked with helping to coordinate both the media and public awareness campaigns for the Iraqi Currency Exchange (ICE). ICE was a massive undertaking aimed at stabilizing and increasing the value of the Iraqi currency. It would require the removal from circulation of all of the Saddam dinars in the country and replacing them with one unified currency. There was no in-between with a project of this scale, especially one involving the life savings of every Iraqi citizen. It was either going to be a disaster of gargantuan proportions or a logistical triumph. The key was developing a solid plan to communicate to the Iraqi population all of the details and benefits of the exchange well in advance of the start of the program. Then that plan needed to be overlaid with a media strategy that reached Iraqi media, regional media, and Western press. Like any good communications strategy, it also needed to anticipate the questions and concerns of the target audience and prepare for any contingency.

Beyond merely standard media relations, the plan included billboards and posters, leaflets, and meetings with residents, clerics, and other influencers throughout the country. Karen and the folks in the

ICE office were ably assisted by members of the army's psychological operations forces in Iraq, who helped develop the communications products for the Iraqi population. Karen would often provide me with handouts to distribute at the city hall press conferences and talking points to answer the inevitable and heated questions.

The most critical part was the outreach that Iraqis conducted themselves to communities across the country. Iraqis at the local and national level were heavily involved in grassroots outreach and discussion. The Iraqi Governing Council and new political establishment fostered by the work of the CPA were able to support the exchange and convince Iraqis to support it.

The complexity of the undertaking cannot be overestimated. Imagine taking all the money out of circulation in a country and exchanging it in a nation where paper money is still the measure of wealth. People didn't trust or use the state-owned and -controlled banks during the regime. The closest thing I can compare it to would be Depression-era America, where people kept their life savings under the mattress. Take all of those people and place them in an environment where crime was rampant and no permanent government existed to instill confidence in the process and you can begin to appreciate the task at hand. Every Iraqi was going to have to bring all of their money to an exchange point where it would be checked for counterfeits and then traded in for new currency. More troubling still was the fact that, if someone brought in counterfeit dinars, they would receive nothing for the bills, even if they had acquired them through what they thought was a legitimate transaction.

The first time I heard the plan, only one word came to mind—bedlam—but it had to be done. Currency is the foundation upon which trade and investment are built. Iraq's currency was flooded with counterfeits, by some estimates comprising one-third of the all bills. As a result, it had been devalued to the point of worthlessness. Additionally, Iraq had two currencies: one for the Kurdish area and one for the rest of the country. The coalition felt strongly that a unified nation with one government and economy would need one currency.

Over the course of just four months, while the media were pushing their story of complete dysfunction and incompetence, the ICE system was established to reach every last Saddam dinar in the country. New paper money was designed without Saddam's image and multiple counterfeit protections were imbedded in the bills for the first time. The new money was printed and flown into a secure area at BIAP on twenty-eight Boeing 747 aircraft carrying ninety tons of dinars per load. Stop and think about that for a second. It was then transported by coalition forces to the exchange points. The public information campaign in September and October 2003 saw the nationwide distribution of more than 375,000 posters in two designs and 4.5 million handbills. The information "road show" visited cities and towns in thirteen Iraqi provinces, where representatives of the Central Bank of Iraq and coalition met with hundreds of community leaders to discuss the exchange process and answer questions.

The planning paid off. What the coalition had done in four months had taken post–World War II Germany three years to accomplish. During the three months of the currency exchange, the value of the dinar rose more than 25 percent. We actually received some positive press from the Western media on the orderly and virtually incident-free process across the country. Very few of the convoys of cash and exchange points were attacked and the riots in the streets that I had envisioned fortunately never materialized. The Western media had no choice but to pick up on it.

Today, it's hardly mentioned in the public discourse about Iraq's progress. It is clear that the economic growth that Iraq experienced in the years following would not have been possible without this stunning achievement. By the end of the Bush administration, the economy of Iraq had increased in size several times over from its time under Hussein. Per capita income had also increased between four and six times what it was before the war. Billions in foreign economic investment flowed into the country and Iraq was on its way to having a thriving private sector. The power vacuum created by the American withdrawal helped to provide ISIS with a foothold in the country and, therefore, created additional political and economic instability. That instability along with the decline in oil prices has led to negative economic growth in recent years.

For all the frustration, there were times when the press, in the absence of car bombs, spent the time to cover some feel-good stories. There was the Iraqi Olympic soccer team's return to competition, now playing without the fear of being tortured by Uday Hussein. In the southern town of Hilla, my friend and colleague Hilary White was working closely with groups of Iraqi women who were continuing their education. She did a great job of attracting media to her area to cover the rise of women and democracy-building efforts there.

In the midst of the media firestorm fueled by the growing insurgency and the rise of Al-Qaeda in Iraq, the office also established a practice, with the consent of the White House, of booking coalition personnel as guests on local radio stations back home. In early 2004, we developed a list of people willing to do interviews. Beginning with their hometowns, radio stations began scheduling them as guests to provide updates on Iraq taken from their own experiences. We managed to hit dozens of stations in more than twenty-five states. It was a great way for folks to get some recognition for their work and to help people better understand what we were accomplishing. This was especially meaningful for the soldiers who didn't have access to phones the way civilians did. A soldier on a hometown radio talk show had the opportunity to feel really appreciated and let family and friends hear a strong, passionate voice from Iraq. They were celebrities for those few minutes. They loved it. One day, a reporter was standing in the Green Room while one of the soldiers was on a show. She actually asked me where his talking points were. Of course, she assumed that this was part of some new Bush administration propaganda effort. We didn't coach these folks. They were free to say what they wanted, of course not that anyone would believe that. We were confident that they would speak from the heart about the mission. Besides, anything negative that they might say would pale in comparison with the unbalanced reporting of the American press corps. By 2007, a Pew Research Center analysis found that confidence on the part of the American public in the accuracy of media reports had plummeted to just 38 percent by March of that year.

The hometown radio experiment that we conducted in 2003 proved an important point though. With the effective and aggressive use of broadcast outlets, a tremendous effect could be felt back home with an increase in the number of people on the ground who were able to tell their stories. During one interview with a San Francisco radio station, a strategist and commentator, Rich Galen, who had joined us to assist in strategic communications, mentioned that the soldiers liked Double Stuf Oreo cookies and asked people listening to send them on over. I mentioned it on another station the following week. Within two weeks of Rich's first interview, we began receiving boxes of Oreo cookies on a daily basis. People were sending cases of the cookies to us in the Green Room. On one afternoon alone, we received ten boxes. This went on for over a month. They were eventually distributed to the marines guarding the palace, some of the wounded soldiers at the 28th Combat Support Hospital, and military personnel whenever and whenever we could. Rich even brought some with him on trips around the country to present as gifts to soldiers.

As time wore on and the mission began to suffer from the increase in violence, the overall strategy changed. When we arrived in Baghdad, we were pushing out as much of what I would call "progress" news as possible on all fronts. As the security situation deteriorated, however, we had to be more selective. For instance, in July, if we hit a milestone in electricity generation, we would simply sound the trumpets. By the fall and the following spring, we had to decide whether we wanted to release the information at all. The announcement of milestones, particularly with respect to power and oil production, resulted in furnishing the insurgency with motive to bomb those facilities. As the mission matured, every time someone went out behind the podium or planned an event, they risked having a mortar hit near the building, or the power failing, or news of another bomb attack overtaking the story. To gain some traction at home, we needed to broaden our strategy. That broad strategy needed to reach into every aspect of the CPA's public face. It needed to analyze the impacts on public perception at every level.

From a structural standpoint, one of the first aspects of the strategy to sell the war continually at home that was overlooked was who was conveying the message during the first few months after the war. In those early months, we had good momentum back in the States coming out of major combat operations. We needed to continue to convey a balanced, credible message effectively. After Bush's "Mission Accomplished" speech, we were already trailing the critics. At least it was the early innings, I thought. The fall of Saddam really meant that we were starting over. This was a new phase of the policy, a new mission, and we needed to build credibility all over again with the public back home. One of the consequences of Washington's erratic communications planning was a failure to recognize that building credibility meant, in part, an American face for the mission beyond Bremer.

As I mentioned earlier, Charles was the principal spokesperson for the CPA in those early days. He was also a major driver of the Baghdad communications strategy. He was smart, capable, and articulate. His biggest problem was that he was British. I have nothing against our friends from the United Kingdom. They are steadfast allies and good friends. The experience of the British in the region, dating back nearly a century, also meant they had keen insight. Of course, they too shared the risks of the Iraq mission. It does present an operational problem, however, when the spokesperson doesn't connect with the people he is trying to address. Charles was very able to connect with European and Middle Eastern media; but, as I told Dan over dinner in the chow hall in August 2003, Americans want to hear from an American. Strategically, the British took a very one-dimensional approach to dealing with their press. They had all but given up on trying to push the story in Britain. The BBC represented the bulk of Britain's broadcast capability and the network's personnel were mostly loathed by the staff in our office. In fact, the BBC is the only news organization that Bremer ejected from the palace personally. After a *Frontline* interview in which a BBC correspondent outright accused him of being a liar, Bremer refused to deal with them and, consequently, the rest of the American staff followed suit.

If you were trying to drive the story in Britain, there were precious few choices. It was either BBC or SkyNews; the Fox News sister network decided to pull most of its folks out of Iraq in the fall of 2003. I don't fault Charles, Naheed, or the other capable British members of the strategic communications staff for the way they approached broadcast media. Media in many countries is far less complicated an animal than it is in the United States. For instance, the affiliate system and the large number of media markets that exist in the United States simply provide more options for tactical planning to ensure message penetration. It's just not present in other places in the world.

Ultimately, it was important for there to be credibility behind the podium in the briefing room from a civilian and military perspective. Both those voices had to be American to make a connection with folks in the United States and provide a steady, visible reminder that Americans were in control. Of course, it was a coalition, but for an American audience, whose sons and daughters were in Iraq in larger numbers than those of any other country (and whose tax dollars were being spent by the billions for the effort), they needed an American presence on their televisions.

Enter stage right Dan Senor, instant radio and television personality. Over time, Dan became a familiar face on cable news in the United States (in fact, he ended up marrying CNN's Campbell Brown), but originally he was somewhat apprehensive about being out front. I remember booking a number of radio shows for him at the beginning of his taking on this new role. He looked at the list with a degree of anguish, but in that one sitting he reached more people back in the United States than any coalition official other than Bremer had done in months. Teaming him up with Brigadier General Mark Kimmitt in November of 2003 completed the lineup and gave the mission two confident voices to articulate the CPA message.

We had lost valuable time. In an age of viral communications that requires real-time and constant responses, those two months were an eternity during which the coalition's ability to drive a positive message and build credibility suffered. When taken together with the barriers to information flow that were the natural consequence of an increasingly complex organization comprised of intricate relationships, the coalition's ability to stay on the offensive waned as summer turned to fall in 2003. The failure of the administration in Washington to manage expectations effectively or to broaden the strategy made our ability to counter the editorial filter all the more difficult. It made a tough sell even tougher.

NEW VOICES

There was a strange dichotomy. Back in the office, we would complain about the Western journalists driving their own perceptions and often doing the bare minimum, while we were watching the rebirth of their profession among the Iraqis.

To live and work in Iraq after the fall of Saddam was to see history unfolding in front of your eyes every day—the good, the bad, and the ugly. Back then, we were witnesses to and in many ways catalysts for an emerging democracy. The Iraqis we worked with were risking their lives to bring their people out of the shadows of tyranny and they were paying an increasingly high price for it. One of the most striking examples of Iraqis embracing their new freedom during the time of the CPA could be seen in the emergence of the free press. As I stated earlier, totalitarian regimes have many similar characteristics. The governments conform to a formula that is nearly universally followed by the despots that lead them. It is designed to maintain their grip on power and a grip on their people. One of the most prevalent of these throughout history has been and continues to be information management. Saddam's regime provided its people with a state-sponsored view of their country and the world around them. The television and radio stations as well as the newspapers of Iraq were operated by the government. It essentially reduced them to nothing but a propaganda machine for Saddam and the Ba'ath Party. This is of course well known. Remember Baghdad Bob telling the world that there were no American tanks in Baghdad?

What is important for those in the West to understand is how this information management is connected to the terrorist threat. The repression of free speech and a free press is a symptom of many Middle Eastern nations (both friend and foe) and can be linked to pervasive and fundamental mistrust of the West. The stifling of other news and information sources has cut off many people in the Middle East from ideas that empower individuals and promote free thinking. Repression creates ignorance, and ignorance breeds hatred and terrorism. To a certain degree, it is that simple. I used to get phone calls from Western media who would ask for comment from the CPA about various Iraqi protests that occurred in Baghdad, Basra, and elsewhere. You could almost see the smile on their faces through the other end of the phone. A big protest, after all meant that the reporter had found his or her story for the day—one that happened to support their notion that the country was in chaos. I would often give them a simple answer, "It's a free country." They didn't much like that answer, but it was the truth.

The Iraqis aren't a stupid people. Those Iraqis who were protesting were very cognizant of the fact that if they had exercised that simple right just a few months earlier, they would have been shot in the streets by their own government. The Western press saw protests and public assemblies as proof positive that the CPA, America, and the Bush administration had botched the peace. What they repeatedly missed was the incredible opportunities that the people of Iraq were now embracing as free people. They had a right to be frustrated about conditions and they had a right to say so.

It is in this area of freedom of speech and press that the Iraqi people progressed most strikingly during the period of the coalition's administration of the country. It is one of the great success stories of the Iraq mission. Those of us in the Strategic Communications Office of the CPA saw the evolution of the new free press perhaps more closely than the rest of our colleagues did. The staff of the new Iraqi Media Network, later named Al-Iraqia, worked out of the Green Room in the palace. Yes, they were supported and funded by the coalition, but at that point as satellite dishes popped up on seemingly every rooftop, we couldn't have the only thing Iraqis saw on television be the anti-American propaganda from Al Jazeera. We also had an Arabic Media Unit that worked very closely with the new Iraqi papers springing up across the country.

My area of responsibility was not Arabic or Iraqi media. One of the tenets of good communication is being able actually to articulate a message and, after all, I didn't speak a lick of Arabic. In late August, Charles and Dan let me take over the Baghdad Central press operation in the office and I saw an opportunity that couldn't be passed up. Baghdad Central was the CPA office that had jurisdiction over the City of Baghdad and the surrounding Province of Baghdad. The senior advisor of the office at the time, Hank Bassford, held executive authority in the city, meaning that (for all intents and purposes) he was the mayor of Baghdad. Bassford's somewhat chaotic operation was a combination of army civil affairs, Army Corps of Engineers, and civilian governance professionals who were involved in a myriad of projects throughout the city. In the mix with Baghdad Central's folks was the U.S. Army's First Armored Division, which also was aiding in the reconstruction in addition to their role securing the city and dealing with terrorists. Communication among these entities was a serious challenge and often simply didn't happen. The brigade and battalion commanders were spending Commander's Emergency Repair Program money on small reconstruction projects but often didn't report them to the division. The army civil affairs team was having difficulty getting information from its people in the field. No one was coordinating the activities of the all the NGOs that were also doing good work in the city. To top it all off, the office was understaffed, which naturally compounded the problem.

Despite the problems in the Baghdad Central Office and in the face of rising activity by former regime loyalists and terrorists, good things were actually happening throughout the city. From a strategic communications standpoint, it was difficult to do any proactive planning because usually no one knew something was happening until it already happened. It was hard enough to get the Western media interested in a "good news" story when it was fresh news. It was virtually impossible to get coverage when the event had already happened or the project was finished weeks ago. The coalition was spending large percentages of its money in Baghdad, yet from a press coverage standpoint, they weren't getting much return on that investment. The frustration with the situation was only compounded by fact that most of the media were located in Baghdad.

I decided to attempt to do something about this. With the permission and help of Gary Thatcher, we brought on air force reserve captain Paula Kurtz to assist me in getting a handle on Baghdad Central. I had envisioned her to act as a T-funnel of information, pulling together the reports for the various entities that contributed to the Baghdad effort and ascertaining what items could be developed into stories for the press. Hank Bassford had other ideas. He immediately demanded that Kurtz work for him, serving as his personal public affairs officer. This was in contravention of the CPA's press policy, which directed all interaction with the media through the main press office. With an operation the size and scope of the CPA, it would have been impossible to develop and execute any communications strategy if there were people in the building freelancing with the media without at least the knowledge or consent of Dan, Charles, or Gary. We went back and forth with Bassford and eventually reached a compromise whereby we both gave Kurtz assignments and all press contacts had to be cleared through me and the Strategic Communications Office. Captain Kurtz had a great deal of patience. Bassford wasn't known in the building for being the easiest person in the world to deal with, and I was getting increasingly frustrated with the lack of organization over in his office. I put her in an awkward position and felt bad about it, but Baghdad was too important to just be left alone.

The effort wasn't just about getting good press for the CPA. I came to realize that if the Western media didn't know what the hell was going on in Baghdad beyond the daily car bomb, then the citizens of Baghdad were also in the dark to an even greater extent. Charles, who spoke Arabic fluently, had been conducting press conferences almost daily with the Western and Arabic press to discuss the coalition operations, but the new local Iraqi papers did not seem to be engaged.

The rise of the free press was real. It was a result of the collapse of the regime often ignored in those early days by the media. On one occasion my colleague Shane Wolfe brought some Western press to witness the dedication of a new printing press. He tried valiantly to drive a message about how enterprising Iraqi journalists, authors, and activists were not going to be deterred by the violence. He did a good job and it was a good event, until the Iraqis decided to ritually slaughter a sheep. This further ingrained in the horrified Western reporters the false notion that Iraqis were backwards and barbaric, even though the Iraqis have been publishing since the days of the Ottoman Empire.

The CPA often touted the fact that somewhere between seventy and one hundred newspapers had sprung up across the country since the liberation. But the question remained, "Were these papers getting the information that they needed?" In Baghdad, most of these newspapers were small neighborhood publications produced out of someone's home and focused on mainly local issues. The national issues were far away from their needs for basic services. Neighborhoods in Iraq—or in any country where information is limited—are often the birthplace of rumors and misinformation that can easily spread and become accepted as truth. Such occurrences can have wide-ranging negative effects. My thought was to bring these fledgling news organizations together on their own territory, giving them the opportunity to interact with Iraqi officials and coalition representatives. Democracy is about transparency and accountability in government and, at that point, we hadn't been giving these new journalists a venue to ask their questions and get answers.

After discussing this with Charles, I asked the Baghdad governance staff to attend one of their frequent meetings, which included Baghdad city officials. As a side note, the coalition worked exceptionally hard to help the Iraqis build institutions of democracy and good governance. Assertions by critics that the coalition was not aggressive in building a culture of participatory government or focused on building political leadership are simply misguided. Building and then protecting the integrity of the political process was Bremer's top priority. After all, as Bremer often said, our job was to put ourselves out of a job.

The meeting was in one of the conference rooms of the convention center. It started late, as most meetings in Iraq did, and was a typical rundown from both coalition and Iraqi representatives of the state of the city. It was a wealth of information about street paving, traffic signals, electricity, and the selection of new district advisory councils. One person stuck out among the Iraqi group. Faris Abdul Razzak Al Assam was the deputy mayor of Baghdad for technical services. He spoke English fluently and was organized and action-oriented during the meeting. Faris was one of three deputy mayors appointed by the coalition to run the day-to-day operations of the city. The other two handled community relations, while Faris was in charge of infrastructure. He was a senior official in the Baghdad Water District before the liberation. After the fall of the city, the coalition identified Faris as someone whom they could trust to help get the city up and running again. Although the three deputies technically were equals, it was very evident that Faris enjoyed a special relationship with the coalition that made him senior to the others. In June, Faris had been part of a delegation sent to the UN as part of a team representing the Iraqi leadership. He had spoken confidently and passionately about the pace of reconstruction. Faris was relaxed and down to earth, often seen driving his pickup truck around town wearing a jogging outfit. He was the city's natural leader and was someone I knew would make the perfect Iraqi voice to articulate a story of real progress within the city—and he could do it for both Western and Iraqi press.

The first time we spoke about a new public relations strategy was a week later just prior to another meeting between the CPA and the Baghdad city officials. Faris sat just outside the meeting room at a small table as I asked him questions about getting the message of progress out to the people of the city. It was then I met Nidhal, his assistant, who spoke pretty good English and behaved as any good executive assistant would, taking down notes and phone numbers, recalling the schedule, and keeping Faris in the right place at the right time.

I told Faris that I believed that we could reach the Iraqi press with a positive message while reinforcing to them that the city government was functioning and accountable. I proposed calling a regularly scheduled press conference, mainly for Baghdad's bourgeoning population of new journalists. This would be a place for people to do something extraordinary—ask questions and get answers. After all, people weren't used to having access. I proposed to Faris that we give it to them—this time, however, on their territory, not in the coalition headquarters, not in the Green Zone in a coalition building, but at their city hall. At city hall, the coalition representative would be the invited guest of the city. It would be Faris's press conference. I would be there to answer questions about CPA efforts to improve the infrastructure and quality of life, while Faris would be able to answer questions as he saw fit, using his extensive expertise in city operations.

The concept was exciting to him. He liked the spotlight. Faris was already planning his presentation for the Madrid Donor's Conference, being organized by the CPA to encourage the contribution of funds from coalition nations to the Iraq reconstruction. It was clear from our first meeting that this was a man with a great vision for the city he loved.

We agreed that he could pick a day, and during the week Captain Kurtz and the folks at Baghdad Central would scour their reports to find news about each section of town. The information she compiled for the press conferences would serve a dual purpose. It would also help us with planning for Western media. Faris's meager staff would do the same. The information would then be developed into news briefs in both English and Arabic that would be distributed to the media in attendance. *It was important for the Iraqis to be able to walk away with something tangible from the press conference*, I thought. I would also bring with me the Arabic translations of all CPA press releases for that particular week. At the end of our conversation, he stood up, grabbed my hand, smiled, and said, "Tom, we will do this." We agreed to meet one more time before the first press conference. Faris wanted to introduce me to his media staff and he invited me to city hall to join him for some tea. That first visit to city hall would be an eye-opening experience.

People I spoke with back at home during this period had no idea that Baghdad had a city hall, let alone a government and nearly ninety citizens' advisory councils selected by local residents to address the concerns of their neighborhoods. How would they know? They were watching the evening news and reading the *New York Times*. In Baghdad, the CPA governance staff had developed a system of eighty-eight Neighborhood Advisory Councils (NACs) that reported to nine District Advisory Councils (DACs). These DACs then selected representatives to the City Advisory Council (CAC), which was in essence as close to a city council as Baghdad had at the time. It was an incredible achievement accomplished in a short period of time. The people on these various boards, especially at the neighborhood level, were diverse in their occupation, gender, and Islamic sect. Many of them had never served or participated in government before. It was the birth of community stewardship and participation in government for the new Iraq. True, these councils were not directly elected in the sense that we would recognize, but the process allowed for measured progress toward citizen rule that would have been impossible had the CPA waited to establish the infrastructure necessary for actual elections. Some councils were more representative than others. Some had greater participation than others. Overall, though, they began bringing people together and helped to develop leaders for the community. The councils were working closely with the Army Civil Affairs officers in their area and the local brigade commanders and the CPA to achieve real results.

For instance, one bridge project initiated by these councils reunited two Baghdad neighborhoods after thirty years of broken promises by Saddam's regime. Twenty-five years before the liberation, the Iraqi government built a canal separating neighboring Sunni and Shiite communities. For decades, the residents had petitioned the government to build a bridge traversing the canal to no avail. In June 2003, the NACs from the Gazeliyah and Al-Shula neighborhoods asked the city and the coalition for assistance in completing the long-overdue project. The project was headed by Basil Tawfik, a local Iraqi engineer, who employed more than forty people to construct the bridge with funding from the U.S. Army. Iraqi and coalition engineers worked side by side, and construction took only a month. The local battalion commander put it best when he told me, "The bridge is a small example of the community coming together. In the past this type of cooperation would never happen. Iraqis are now making decisions to ensure a better life for themselves." In this instance we had two communities—one Shiite, one Sunni—separated by a regime that sought to create great divides among its people, now reunited through their own initiative. *Is it too sappy and cute for Western media? Perhaps*, I thought, *but it couldn't be ignored.*

The councils raised issues to the CPA and the city government and it ultimately fell to the growing number of Iraqi journalists and activists to ensure that action followed to address those concerns. In any free society, the press plays an important role in holding government accountable to its people. However, in Iraq, during the summer of 2003, the culture of investigative journalism that seems to reach into the depths of every aspect of life in the United States barely existed, if at all. The councils were a voice of the people, and the proprietors and writers of these little newspapers were helping deliver the people's message. That was why I felt strongly about the press conferences at city hall or any attempt to get people information that would then allow them to express themselves. It was the infancy of an essential component of democracy.

Back in the office, amid covering interviews for the Ministry of Justice and running around pulling together information for the daily press briefing at the Convention Center, I was getting excited about the city hall project. Two of the biggest challenges constantly facing the members of the CPA were transportation and security. The Strategic Communications Office did not have its own security team and relied on the brave men and women of the American armed forces to share the risk of venturing downtown with us. Without their willingness to fill this role, we civilians simply wouldn't have been able to do our jobs.

In our office, security detail usually fell to Lieutenant Colonel Chad Buehring, our office manager and aide to the director of strategic communications. He enjoyed going out in town. Chad, as he preferred to be called, was U.S. Army Special Operations and, according to one of his colleagues, had "all the scary patches" on his uniform. He took care of all of us with a professionalism and confidence that made each of us feel safe, even in the most dangerous neighborhood. Along with Chad, the members of the psychological operations detachment who owned the most organized corner of our frenzied office also assisted us from time to time, especially when the trip provided them with material for psy-op products that they could use for their own assignments. To be clear, these soldiers and airmen didn't have to provide these escorts, but they did because they understood the important role that our office played in ensuring the success of the overall mission. I always felt uneasy asking the psy-oppers to run security for me. Most of them were young, lower enlisted soldiers like Sergeant Gibson who had become not just colleagues but also friends of mine. We played poker on Friday nights and hung out in our rare off hours. Several of them had new spouses and young children. I always worried that something would happen when we were out in town. I didn't think I could live with myself if I had been responsible for placing them in harm's way. I also didn't like the appearance of it all. Having them spread out in formation around me with their M-16s made it look like I was some big shot. I wasn't. They weren't just security. They were friends, colleagues, and equals, not to mention some of the bravest people I've ever known.

For my first trip over to city hall, Major J. R. Reiling, Sergeant John Lutz, and Specialist Corey Bostick offered to take me out into the Red Zone for my visit with Faris. In full "battle rattle," they loaded up in our dusty Suburbans and made the two-mile trip across the river without incident. John drove me—with an AK-47 shoved between the driver's seat and the armrest—though streets jammed with old, rusted cars darting about without regard for even the most basic traffic law. We drove past the blown-out Ministry of Communications Building, rotting along the river since it was ripped open by American cruise missiles.

Upon arrival, we parked on the ramp to the fountain plaza out front of the building and hurried inside. The city government or Amanat Baghdad was located on a campus that consisted of several build-ings, including the Water District Building and Tax Assessor's Office. *Who knew*, I thought, *that Baghdad had a government complex, which in many ways was much like one you'd see in any major American city?* The fact that there was a complex was really the beginning and end of the similarities. We entered the lobby of the building, which was dark, as they were conserving power by keeping off all but a few lights. The floor was covered by black tiles with white boxes outlined in a repeat-ing pattern and was in bad need of a wash and wax. One immediately got the sense that the building was once a very modern facility but like most Iraqi government buildings had deteriorated over time from lack of maintenance. Workers in the building took notice of the four Amer-ican men entering the building, three of whom had weapons bigger than a baseball bat. They stood and greeted us and showed us the ele-vators. I had called Nidhal from the car and she asked that we come up to Faris's office on the sixth floor. We piled into the small elevator, which already had two suddenly quiet and nervous workers coming up from the basement. The door closed slowly as if the elevator itself was unsure it could make the trip. The lift creaked and lurched up ini-tially but then appeared to only inch along. Suddenly, it stopped. The building had lost power and we were caught between floors. I looked at Reiling and asked sarcastically whether the army trained him for situations like this. We stood there in the dark with our nervous new Iraqi friends who were still trying to get upstairs from the basement. Sergeant Lutz made some wisecrack about the power. After a few of minutes of uncomfortable silence the power came on and we started moving again, stopping at every floor, regardless of whether anyone in the elevator was going there or anyone on the floor had called the car.

Just as we got off the elevator, finally arriving on the sixth floor, the lights flickered again. I asked a gentleman standing in the elevator lobby where Faris's office was located and he showed the way. Alright, I didn't exactly ask him where the office was. Given that I don't speak Arabic, I really just looked at the man and said, "Faris?" in an inquisitive tone. The hallways were dark. The yellow carpeting was musty and stained. The metal framed partition walls created a series of offices, plainly furnished and void of most equipment and supplies, including telephones. When we arrived at Faris's office, Nidhal came in to greet us. His outer office was simple, with some old leather chairs, a desk for the receptionist, and a few plaques on the wall. There was also a large replica of the sculpture at the Martyr's Monument located on the outskirts of town. After finishing a meeting, Faris came out and with a big smile, characteristic of his personality and general outlook, he called out, "Hello my friend." I introduced him to the guys with me, who insisted on staying outside the office during the meeting. We sat down facing each other in front of his desk, and we talked. His corner office was bright and airy, and it looked out over the city—in particular at several of the towering government buildings the Americans had bombed during the "shock and awe" period of the war. A few minutes into the conversation, he sent for some tea. I usually wouldn't eat or drink anything given to me that hadn't been blessed by KBR. I had to that point managed to avoid getting "Saddam's revenge" and I wanted to keep my streak going, but I couldn't refuse. The tea was delivered hot and sweet with a mound of sugar melting at the bottom of the small traditional glass.

The conversation flowed freely as we went over the plans for the first press conference. Faris was clearly excited. I stressed the importance of this being advertised only to local Iraqi media. It was vital that the Iraqis understood that this was going to be a venue for them, a gesture on behalf of the city government to engage with the people. I also didn't want Western or Middle Eastern satellite press hogging time at the expense of the local journalists. Faris asked about expanding the scope of the press conference to include Western media. He had already been bitten by the publicity bug when he was in New York at the UN with Akila Hashimi. Faris loved the spotlight. As much as I wanted to get news about the city out to the press more directly and efficiently, I gently pushed back, telling him that we should wait until after we had made progress with the locals before broadening the invite list. He agreed.

At that point, it was time to visit with the staff that would be contacting the local media and ensuring they knew about the resource we were about to make available. We went downstairs to the fifth floor, wisely forgoing the elevator. Faris stopped along the way to tell a maintenance worker to do something about the sewage smell that was for some reason filling the hallway. "They call me the nose," he said as we descended the stairs, emerging in what was their public affairs office. I guess I was still living somewhere else, because I was shocked to see that there was nothing. No equipment or even furniture in most offices. The Baghdad city "media staff" consisted of three people who read the newspaper and let Faris know what the press was reporting. That was it. In many respects, though, that was all they needed. When I inquired as to how he planned to communicate the date and time of the press conference to each of the papers, he told me that the staff would locate each paper's office and visit them each week. They would also create a banner that would be hung on the building with the day and time. I couldn't believe it, but when you live in a place with no land line phones, virtually no cell phones, no fax machines, and no computers, the old fashioned way is the only way. I wondered whether it would work. Faris asked me to trust him. "They will do it," he said reassuringly.

The group of us then took a look at the city council chambers. It was the largest room in the building, located on the opposite end of the sixth floor from Faris's office. The oblong chamber was lit by a large, star-shaped fixture which was flush with the high ceiling. Windows overlooking the city formed the far wall and a large ceramic tile map of Baghdad was affixed opposite the windows. The rest of the room was covered in plain wood paneling. The council members' desks were also made of dark walnut with black tops and at each seat was a microphone. With its stark, modern design, it was similar to any other large public meeting space constructed in the 1970s. All in all, it would work for the time being as the location for our little experiment.

From there, Faris took us into the mayor's ceremonial office where we talked about the city and Baghdad's future. In many ways everything was so close to normal. The city government was functioning to a degree. Workers came to work. Services were rendered. Even much of the usual municipal infrastructure was in place. Whether it worked well or worked at all was the issue that needed to be resolved. There was a legislative body and executive departments. I sat in the mayor's cavernous office, his bare desk collecting dust. I had to remind myself that this was a government that hadn't seen a democratic transition of authority in thirty-five years. The mayors—whose names were listed on the wall engraved in brass plaques—were appointed by Saddam, as were the chairmen of the city council and the heads of all the departments and offices. I was sitting in one of the great seats of Ba'ath Party power.

The soldiers took some pictures of Faris and me on the plaza outside of the building, and we left to return to the palace. As we drove out the gate, several Iraqis took notice of our vehicles and began yelling at the cars, pumping their fists in the air. They were a small group of perhaps ten. They made me nervous, but they didn't approach our vehicles. Lutz, who was driving me, had taken some Arabic before he was deployed. Once we were through the gate, he asked me whether I wanted to know what they were saying. "Devil. They called us the devil," he said. It was one of very few times in my time there that I was on the receiving end of animosity from a group Iraqis I encountered. It was a reality check. There would be more of those to come.

Over the next week, Paula Kurtz and I pulled together the first iteration of the news briefs and formatted them for distribution at the press conference. The coalition portion of the briefing would be an opening statement detailing that week's news on a variety of quality-of-life issues ranging from health care to governance. A typical litany would look something like this:

The Coalition Provisional Authority this week provided $100,000 worth of critical medical equipment to the al Hussein Hospital in Arashidia, Iraq just north of Baghdad. . . . The equipment will significantly enhance the intensive care monitoring of patients at the al Hussein hospital.

The equipment includes three electrocardiography (ECG) recorders, one defibrillator, three ECG blood pressure monitors, and three pulse oximeters. A generator is scheduled to be installed at the hospital in the near future. . . . The ECG recorders will provide enhanced monitoring of cardiac patients, and the defibrillator will help restore a regular heartbeat to patients with an unstable cardiac rhythm.

$1.4 million has been allocated for Personal Protective Equipment for the Baghdad Fire Brigade. The Iraqi Ministry of the Interior will review the price quotes and confirm the contracts for the Personal Protective Equipment within the next two weeks with the money that has been approved. . . .

The contracts for 300 new fire trucks have also been forwarded to the UN for the final approval. There are 120 fire trucks already in Egypt and are awaiting the response from the UN office. . . . There was a Ribbon Cutting ceremony on Tuesday opening the newly refurbished Rusafa Fire Station.

Baghdad Police will receive 5,000 of the 47,000 Glock pistols ordered for all Iraqi Police officers during the first shipment due to arrive on 16 September 2003. . . .

CPA will train liaisons to work with Baghdad DACs and NACs on governance fundamentals. This training will enable the DACs and NACs to establish effective Parliamentary rules and procedures, manage agendas, and develop minutes. These skills will assist the councils to better organize and address residents' concerns.

Still other news briefs contained announcements about major coalition initiatives:

Last week electrical power officials working with the Coalition surpassed their goal of 4400MW national output 5 of 7 days. Having successfully reached this milestone, fall power maintenance outages have begun and will remain on-going through December. . . . During this time, selected generators in Baghdad and throughout Iraq will be shut down to make preventive repairs. Locally, these repairs will be conducted on a case-by-case basis at Baghdad South and Doura through December to improve operating efficiency and reliability. . . . The maintenance program will increase the system's reliability and reduce unplanned outages due to equipment failures. In addition, considerable improvements in some areas have improved power capabilities from 2 on 4 off, to 4 on 2 off.

Much of this information wasn't readily available. The news briefs would be handed out to the media present along with the week's press releases from the CPA. There was an advantage to handing out the press releases about these items or other Baghdad news. Most of the new local papers had very small writing staffs, if any. The editor was the publisher and the beat reporter, much as with some small community papers in the United States. Giving them a press release is potentially the same as providing them with copy to fill the pages of the publication. Even papers in the United States often lift an entire press release with a few small changes for their editions. It was my hope that the Iraqi media would do the same, not because I felt that the CPA should be writing these publications but because it was an easy way to get a progress message out to the neighborhoods.

Faris agreed to prepare a similar document, albeit shorter and not as comprehensive. It was important for these new journalists to walk away with something official, something prepared especially for them. In a free society journalists deserve to receive information from their government, and the government has a responsibility to communicate effectively—and truthfully—about how the people's resources are being spent for their benefit. The responsibility is to the people, not to the media. The media are the conduit.

The day finally arrived for the first press conference at city hall, and with a sense of pride and clear trepidation, I asked the strategic communications staff at our morning meeting to keep their fingers crossed. I think Dan and Charles thought I was a little nuts trying to do this, but I felt that the potential was too great to ignore. Lieutenant

Colonel Chad Buehring offered to give me a ride across the river, and once again we piled into a Suburban and headed out. As I mentioned earlier, Chad was special ops and was the best person to have with you downtown. He carried a black knapsack loaded with guns, ammo, and an AK-47 he had acquired somewhere along the way. He was the driver, of course, and after getting into the vehicle he reached into his bag of goodies and placed a loaded 9 mm pistol on the armrest of the front seat. He also filled the cup holders with a smoke bomb and something that looked to me like a grenade. The AK was also within reach as it was easier to fire from the driver's seat than his M-16, naturally also along for the ride. He asked me whether I knew how to shoot the 9 mm. I hesitated and then told him yes. He then reached down and grabbed one of the canisters from the cup holders, explaining that should anything happen in transit, it was my job to pull the pin and then throw this thing out the window. I watched him demonstrate with what must have been a glazed look on my face. Chad was a good judge of people and their abilities. It is what made him a natural leader for his soldiers. After about fifteen seconds of silence, realizing who he was dealing with, he leaned over and said, "Now Tom—remember to roll down the window first."

We arrived without incident and pulled into the parking lot to see a large banner announcing the press conference hung on the façade of city hall, just as Faris had promised. No sooner did I mention to Chad about the less-than-reliable elevators than the lift abruptly halted its painfully slow ascent in between floors three and four. I was already a little late but could do nothing but laugh to myself that this would be just our luck. I hurried into the council chamber to find a handful of people standing around. This was another one of those times when I had to remember where I was. In Iraq, nothing started on time. Putting a time such as 10:00 on meeting notice meant that you were lucky if the meeting actually got underway by 10:30. It was more of a suggestion. I had a couple of minutes to breathe and distribute my handouts to the attendees.

A few minutes later, Faris came in, greeted me, and glad-handed everyone in the room. He too had his hand-outs. Without a copy machine in the building, his statement and news briefs were copied with an ancient mimeograph machine, leaving the purple hue of the carbon on the grey paper. We took our seats on the raised platform where the council chairman usually sat with the windows at our back. To my astonishment, the microphones actually worked and Faris asked the journalists who had come to take their seats. Six writers showed up that first morning, a pretty good start, I thought, but the cavernous room accentuated the fact that it would take time for the word to spread. I sat up there asking even myself, *Were they legitimate journalists or just citizens?* It didn't matter, everyone was a potential journalist. Everyone was legitimate to a certain degree. If one of these guys printed a leaflet in his basement that he distributed to his neighborhood, he was a journalist. Even if one little nugget of information he took away from the press conference helped dispel some misinformation swirling through his part of town, it was worth it to have him in the room and participating.

Faris began by welcoming everyone and explaining the goals of the weekly press conferences. Following his opening statement, during which he touched on some work being done in different parts of the city, it was my turn. I gave a brief statement being sure to thank the city government for the invitation to come and participate. I wanted everyone in the room to know that I was the guest and clearly in a subordinate position to Faris and the other Iraqi officials. Through the translator, I then began discussing the various news items of the week. In the middle of my remarks, ironically just after discussing electricity, the lights went out. Losing electricity meant that the room was now brightened only by the light of day coming through the windows. It also meant that the microphones didn't work either. I now found myself speaking very loudly to folks some twenty-five feet away, on the other side of the room. Within a few minutes, the power came back on. It would only cut out two more times during the remainder of the briefing.

Upon conclusion of my remarks, we began the question and answer portion. The first Iraqi recognized by Faris stood up and began what sounded like a tirade that lasted for several minutes. Speaking passionately and gesturing wildly, the bearded man wearing an open-collared plaid shirt went on and on about everything from electricity to sewage treatment. My translator could barely keep up. I grabbed

Faris on the forearm leaned in and asked him if there was a question buried in his rant.

"No." Faris replied, "He is just making a speech." In fact, everyone we called on that day—and we called on everyone—did the same thing. The briefing went more than two hours.

They simply didn't know how to ask questions. It was understandable. Yes, they were frustrated about the lack of services, but more important, nobody in recent memory had given Iraqis the opportunity to express themselves. These new journalists had to learn how to interact with government officials. In the United States, if a journalist grandstands and tries to verbally beat an official over the head, they usually get brushed off. The Iraqis had to learn, that if you wanted specific answers, you had to ask specific questions. If you want to hold people accountable or spur some kind of action, you had to ask questions. It was almost entirely foreign to the Iraqi press. They had been living in a country that hadn't seen a public budgeting process since the late seventies. They had been living in a country where questioning the authorities often left you dead and your family in danger. It just didn't happen.

Iraqi reporters also felt as though they actually did need to grandstand to get a response. For instance, on one occasion at a later press conference, one Iraqi journalist began complaining that his neighborhood did not have services, like water, electricity, and garbage pickup, and so on. "We have nothing!" he exclaimed fiercely, "No services!" Fortunately, I had electrical, water, sewage, and other statistics in a binder that Captain Kurtz updated for me with information about each of the nine Baghdad districts. I looked at him and to his shock explained that in fact services in each of the areas he mentioned had increased since the liberation and some were even above the prewar standards. A little deflated he smiled at me and shrugged his shoulders and said, "Okay, so we have services—but we want more!" It was a humorous exchange. He was intentionally exaggerating to elicit a response and we all saw through it. It wasn't hard, but he didn't really expect me to have a detailed response. Over time, the reporters became much better at this and began honing their questions to focus on the realities in their neighborhoods.

Faris helped me wade through the reporters' comments to find what issue they wanted me to address. Just when it couldn't get stranger, several folks entered the room about halfway through the briefing to serve tea. Hot, sweet Iraqi tea—at a press conference. It was a little bizarre, but then again, everything about this was a little bizarre. I was thoroughly enjoying myself. At the end of the briefing, I went over to the reporters and shook hands with them. Three formed a small circle around me and asked questions through Nidhal who had been there throughout. One of the men asked about roads and drainage in his neighborhood. Saddam refused to pave streets or provide essential services in several areas of Baghdad with large Shiite populations. During the rainy season, the streets turned to mud and flooded. I didn't know what to tell him, but I assured him that if he came back I would find the answer for next week's press conference. Nidhal relayed the message to him and the look on his face was clearly one of disappointment. His countenance gave the impression that he believed I didn't care about his question and I would not provide an answer. The following week he came back. I pointed him out to the group during my remarks, thanked him for his prior question, and then gave an update on the road paving projects in Baghdad, including his neighborhood. The reporter was shocked. He wrote furiously as I spoke and after the briefing he thanked me. Any observer could tell that, at that moment, he felt empowered. Iraq was about small victories. That was one, I felt.

Over the next few months, the press conferences continued and the numbers of journalists grew to about twenty per week. Some changes were made to the format of the news briefs. We also began inviting other Iraqi officials with a subject matter expertise to the briefings to answer questions about specific services. For instance, we often received questions about sewage and water. Under Saddam, the city's sewage flowed untreated into the Tigris River and backed up into the streets and buildings because the infrastructure could not handle the capacity. Cracked or broken pipes also leeched raw sewage into the ground, contaminating the water table. As the rainy season approached, Faris and I were getting a lot of questions about the sewage system and decided to have the head of the sewer district attend the meeting to help answer questions. The poor guy was practically assaulted, but it was another good gesture from the city to allow him to be questioned.

Faris began cutting off speeches and tirades, insisting on more succinct questions, which the journalists actually began to ask. We also planned and built a briefing room, separate and apart from the council chambers. The new room, which was ready to use in December 2003, was on the first floor of city hall and was laid out classroom-style with a podium at the front, much like most other press briefing rooms. The room had new chairs and bulletin boards where press releases could be posted. Faris and I worked on the design and installation of a backdrop for the podium as well as new lights, staging, and sound equipment.

Unfortunately, as the insurgency gained strength, we needed to alter the time, frequency, and day of the press conferences for security reasons. The decision was precipitated by city hall receiving threats and coming under fire from several rocket attacks. It cut into the attendance numbers at times, but through many challenges the press conferences continued into the spring of 2004.

There was a strange dichotomy. Back in the office, we would complain about the Western journalists driving their own perceptions and often doing the bare minimum, while we were watching the birth of their profession among the Iraqis. In any place where a culture of investigative journalism is allowed to flourish, the exchange I had with that Iraqi journalist would be a common occurrence. In Iraq, however, the new free press was just learning about the power they had to help represent the needs of the Iraqi people. They were discovering their important role in improving the stability of their nation. It was a very small but very important step forward. It was a privilege to witness. Those reporters were pioneers of their craft, a craft that just a few months earlier did not exist.

The groundwork laid by the CPA in 2003 and 2004 led to the drafting and ratification of a new constitution in 2005 that gave the Iraqi people a wide range of civil rights including freedom of the press, assembly, peaceful demonstration, communications, and conscience. Naturally the political and sectarian challenges that remained had led at times to uneven enforcement or outright contravention of those rights by the courts and government officials. Today, the press in Iraq remains highly politicized and, as was the case in the United States in the nine-teenth century, outlets are often mouthpieces for sectarian interests. In the United States, media outlets were often directly aligned with labor unions or political powerbrokers in a city. In Iraq, much the same culture has developed, unfortunately, along with the risks journalists take by expressing their opinion or accurate news-writing. Dozens of reporters have suffered from some form of retribution for their report-ing and analysis. Despite the legal, social, and political instability, Iraqis benefit from huge expansions of freedom of expression.

WHAT BLEEDS LEADS

Articulating the story was always a struggle because many reporters simply didn't believe a word we said. Some would even report the unsubstantiated rumors that ran rampant on the streets of Baghdad over the coalition's line.

H ere we go again," I'd groan, watching some American cable news channel in the office. The networks had a particularly misleading practice of looping footage of bombings, casualties, and burnt-out cars without labeling the footage as "old." For instance, a car bomb would go off at 9:00 a.m. The camera crew would race to the scene and take B-roll footage of the relative chaos that immediately followed. The crew would get footage of the bloody casualties, fires, coalition forces on the ground, emergency service personnel, and so on and rush back to their bureau. The network back in the States would then proceed to show that block of footage numerous times throughout the course of the day, leaving the viewer with the impression that the situation was always out of control. If nothing else of significance happened that afternoon, a viewer would be likely to see the same chaotic and graphic footage shot from different angles, every time they looked up at the television, often with no way of knowing whether it was a new incident or the same one just shown over and over. On several occasions, I had to call one of the Baghdad or New York bureaus to get them to indicate on screen that the footage was shot hours ago and in no way reflected current conditions.

We were in a real fight every day to get a foothold on the news being seen by millions of concerned people back at home. We didn't get battle fatigue in our office the way military personnel in combat sometimes do. We just got tired of reading, hearing, and seeing watered-down, oversimplified, incomplete, or just plain wrong information published or broadcast about the mission. We were exasperated by the sensationalism and shameless effort by many in the press who were so eager to tell people, "It's all going to hell." To paraphrase the Pulitzer Prize-winning columnist Tom Friedman, "When reporters stop reporting, they make mistakes." They also become advocates. When reporters become advocates, policymakers have a real fight on their hands. In Iraq in 2003 and 2004, we were increasingly on the defensive.

On one occasion, Ted Koppel showed up in Baghdad to do a series of interviews about coalition operations. He chose to interview Sandy Hodgkinson, affectionately known in the palace as the "mass graves lady." Sandy was a young State Department official and air force reservist who was doing outstanding work identifying and raising awareness about the mass graves that dotted the Iraqi landscape. She worked with torture survivors and relatives of victims to chronicle the abuses of the former regime. Sandy and her husband, Dave, also a CPA advisor, were additionally working on establishing the special tribunal that would try Saddam Hussein and other regime officials for crimes against humanity. Koppel sat down with Sandy in her office and proceeded to ask not a single question about what she had accomplished working for the coalition. He didn't ask about mass graves or crimes against humanity. He spent a half hour trying to get her to admit on camera that Iraqis were living in fear because of the American invasion. Sandy stood her ground and, as a good interview subject should, bridged back to the good work she and her staff were doing to give some closure to the millions of people whose loved ones were killed by the regime. After twenty minutes, Koppel got up from his chair, blurted out, "This is bullshit!" and stormed out of the room, ending the interview. His agenda was well thought out and established long before he entered the room. He had his ideas about what the Iraq mission was and he was going to use his show as a platform for those views.

Articulating the story was always a struggle because many reporters simply didn't believe a word we said. Some would even report the unsubstantiated rumors that ran rampant on the streets of Baghdad over the coalition's line. Like many left-leaning journalists, those covering the Iraq mission believed that the Bush administration—and by extension, the CPA—simply had no credibility from the start. Consequently, there was no such thing as a good news story. The piece always had to have a negative component or qualifier.

For example, in September 2003, while prying information out of Baghdad Central about quality-of-life improvements, I came upon what I thought was a great little story. No big headlines here. It was more of a news item than a full-fledged story, but little stories sometimes have bigger legs than you anticipate. This had the added advantage of being a subject matter that nobody back at home had heard anything about. Under Saddam's regime, only the most prominent Baghdad residents received garbage collection services. No consistent, universal garbage pickup existed except in the wealthier areas of town. Even then, garbage was collected only if residents tipped the city workers who came into their neighborhoods. This left more than a million residents without trash removal. Through the efforts of the CPA, all Baghdad residents— regardless of social or economic status—would have access to garbage collection for the first time in years, if not in the city's history. The CPA in conjunction with the City of Baghdad had established a pilot program for the first citywide garbage collection system.

Why was this important? Without a sanitation system, the vast majority of Baghdad residents left trash along the streets, incinerated it in their yards, or brought it to a neighborhood location where it was continuously burned. This led to significant environmental and human health impacts. Trash-burning and the piling up of waste have dramatic human health effects. The old system contributed to an environment where disease could spread easily, and the constant burning also released toxins into the air, creating dangerous breathing conditions. With the help of the CPA, more than one thousand trucks were beginning to run a series of new routes, reaching every part of the city. Under the plan the trucks would run two to three times per day to collect the more than twenty-two thousand tons of waste generated every week. The coalition and the city were in the process of developing a public awareness campaign about the garbage removal system to educate residents about the routes, pick-up times, and days. Plans were also underway for the creation of Iraq's first landfill designed to protect the environment and human health, and to construct the first recycling facilities.

This was a real need. In addition to the sewage backing up unto the streets, there was garbage everywhere. People just dumped it wherever they could—in streets, along major highways, or in neighborhood landfills. The trash would bake in the sun and the stench permeated everything in some areas of the city. This story had a clear human health component and showed that the city government was taking steps to break down barriers to essential services that had arisen according to religious differences or social status. After all, everyone deserves to live on a clean street. I wrote a press release and sent it out, making some follow-up phone calls to the bureaus to generate interest. Carol Williams from the *LA Times* responded favorably to the idea of doing a story, and I invited her to interview Susan Tianen, the Baghdad Central advisor who created the project and a host of other initiatives aimed at safeguarding human health. Susan was a dynamic and energetic woman. She talked fast, worked fast, and drove projects as fast as possible. In the four months that she was in Iraq, she was shot at on three occasions and often ventured into some of the most dangerous parts of town. She was the "trash lady," and her office was the ammunition and garbage dumps that dotted the city and the surrounding area. Williams, Susan, and I sat down in the mirrored room off the palace rotunda for the interview, and we spent an hour explaining the aspects of the problems posed by the mounds of trash, incineration, and the location of Baghdad's garbage dumps.

Saddam had placed the city's dumps on top of the water table that served the more than a million Shiites in the northern part of town. Toxins were leaching into the water and were being consumed by residents. Disease and high infant mortality rates could easily be tied to the conditions.

When the story hit newsstands in the United States the lede read, "Though Baghdad's streets are neater, a cleanup effort offers opportunities for corruption and the use of child labor." The article spent little ink on the health impacts of the current situation or the benefits of the joint coalition-Iraqi effort. Instead, Williams used the program as a way to highlight perceived rampant abuses of child labor in postwar Iraq. Williams was right, the program wasn't perfect. Some of the Iraqi workers were under the age of fifteen and were on summer break from school. Some of the workers were still trying to extort bribes from residents in an effort to make more cash. Operational difficulties presented themselves, requiring adjustments over the course of several weeks and months. The example of the Williams piece was all too typical when pitching a story. After a while, you could do nothing but plan for the worst and hope for something that wasn't terrible.

We were always mere inches away from a bad story. The line between good coverage and horrible coverage when dealing with the press corps was incredibly narrow. The media that would actually be willing to venture out to an event were usually looking to use the event or people at the location to prove a point they already had in mind. Of course, the coalition had an agenda and a message that we were trying to push. At the same time, many of the journalists and their editors had their own views that they were trying to prop up. It was something that we had to expect most of the time. The vast majority of the stories about the mission had a strong negative component to them. It increased the pressure, but that didn't mean we couldn't continue to push our message aggressively.

We had to be very careful about when and where we brought media. We weren't trying to gloss over the mission's growing challenges. We couldn't if we tried. We all knew that there were too few troops and that the security situation would get worse until that defect in the strategy was rectified. We had to adapt to the more hostile environment. This was especially true when a coalition official was involved. The task at hand was fraught with peril. You had to make sure that you did everything possible to ensure that the negative portion of the story didn't get bigger than usual. We also had to ensure that the message of the coalition was advanced and that the characteristics of the event sent that strategic message simultaneously to Western, Iraqi, and broader Middle Eastern media.

Two instances come to mind in which attention to detail saved a story from being overshadowed by potential outrage over subtle aspects of an event that highlighted progress. These are minor examples, but they are emblematic of the larger challenge. The first was the situation mentioned earlier where the Kurds had to be convinced to rearrange the flags at the memorial to the Halabja gas attacks. If the American flag had been first—or flown at all—the press would have universally seen that as an inappropriate symbol of American imperial power over the Iraqis. If the Kurdish flag had been first in line, the Western press in particular would have viewed it as further evidence that Iraq could never be one, unified state. After some prodding, the Kurds who were finishing the memorial agreed to fly the Iraqi and Kurdish flags at the site and in what observers would consider the appropriate order, with the national flag to the left of the provincial banner.

Another situation occurred at the Baghdad Police Academy. Obviously, a central strategic message for the coalition was to show progress in the training of Iraqi security forces. The media, to their credit, was interested in attending graduation ceremonies of the new classes of the various security personnel—at the beginning. After about a month, when the first battalion of the new Iraqi Army had graduated and the police had put through training the first groups of new cops, women cops, and Iraqi Civil Defense Corps battalions, the press's interest began to wane. In fact, when I was pitching some of the stories about new police officers, one producer from Fox News said to me, essentially, "Listen, I'm going to get my ass chewed if my folks back in New York see one more graduation ceremony. . . . Just give me something else." I respected that. They had in fact covered the initial graduations.

At the beginning of December 2003, I thought I had a good hook for them. The Baghdad Public Safety Academy was going to graduate 250 officers who had completed a three-week course that had been focused on international standards for human rights, modern policing and investigative procedures, due process, and applicable new Iraqi criminal laws. In addition, Major General John Gallinetti, the deputy commanding general of coalition forces, would be presiding over the ceremony. This might not sound like a big deal, but one must understand that not only did new police officers and security forces have to go through the most basic training, but human rights and due process were foreign concepts to the Iraqi Police and also had to be taught.

Gallinetti was a towering marine corps general. He was everything one would expect from someone who had risen through the ranks of the corps. He was a big guy, with a strong voice and imposing personality. The mention of his name brought instant respect and not a little bit of awe to the marines who worked in the palace. He also happened to be one of the most down to earth, genuine, and nicest senior officers I ever met during my time in Iraq. The day we met, he asked me to call him John. I respectfully refused. I had a great deal of respect for someone who could be tough as nails but then turn it off. I knew plenty of majors and colonels who had inflated opinions of themselves. Not Gallinetti.

I sent out a media advisory and did a "call around" to the bureaus. To my surprise there was actually some interest. I arrived at the police academy with a few staff members of the CPA Interior Ministry Office and began to mingle with the reporters as they came through the gate and over to the courtyard of the main classroom building. The building was a blue and white, two-story structure shaped like a U with a courtyard that was open on one end. The cadets used the area to drill in formation, but it essentially was like an academic quad on a college campus. There was a balcony that ringed the second floor overlooking the courtyard below. The building was under renovation following the war and was functional but with few modern facilities. The cadets often had class in darkened rooms because of the shortage of electricity in Baghdad.

On graduation day, the cadets were assembling in the courtyard along with their coalition instructors and dignitaries from the ministry and the CPA. They presented the impression of a ragtag group. Many of them were missing parts of their uniform. Many dressed with leather jackets and completely informally for such an occasion. It was the type of thing that would make a marine corps general shudder.

While the cadets organized themselves, the media set up their tripods in the only location I could find where they wouldn't be in the way. I strolled over to an open-sided tent that had been erected as a reviewing stand for dignitaries on the far side of the courtyard. As I approached the rows of mismatched plastic chairs under the canopy, I caught the eye of Ahmed Ibrahim, the deputy minister of the interior and the Iraqi in charge of the academy. Ibrahim was a boisterous and amiable figure. He sported a thick, black mustache and was always well dressed. He was probably the best-dressed Iraqi whom I dealt with on a regular basis. That afternoon, he was wearing what appeared to be a new black suit and, in a country where officials often wear an open-collared shirt, Ibrahim wore a red silk tie. He was a midlevel member of the police force during the time of Saddam and was imprisoned for speaking out against the regime. After Saddam's ouster, Ibrahim caught the attention of Bernie Kerik, the former New York City police commissioner under Mayor Rudolph Giuliani during 9/11, who was serving as senior advisor for the Interior Ministry in the early days of the CPA. Kerik took a liking to Ibrahim. He loved Ahmed's personal story, his passion, and frankly his willingness to work openly with the coalition. Ibrahim was gracious to a fault. He had pictures of American officials in his office, including an autographed photo of Mayor Giuliani as well as pictures with Wolfowitz, Bremer, Sanchez, and of course his good friend Kerik. He loved President Bush and Tony Blair and, despite death threats, he wanted to work with the CPA to build the police force. Not long after the war, Ibrahim was elevated to the rank of general. Soon after, he was shot during a raid on Fedayeen forces. On the surface, he was right out of central casting for the Iraqi who was needed to get the police force moving. He even was part of the Iraqi delegation to the UN in New York to discuss the postwar reconstruction earlier that summer. At Kerik's behest, he was appointed interim deputy minister of the interior and traded his light blue Iraqi police uniform for his trademark suit and the role of civilian government official. Kerik loved kicking down doors during nighttime raids with his new Iraqi friend.

From my perspective and that of Dan and Charles, he fit the bill as the Iraqi face on the new security forces. He spoke English—well, sort of—and like Faris, he loved to talk to the press. Show Ibrahim a camera and he would speed a path to its lens. At one point the coalition asked him to brief the media on Iraqi police operations after a major attack. He spoke passionately about protecting Iraqis from the remnants of the former regime and about the need for human beings to have respect for each other's right to life. With tears in his eyes, and his voice cracking, he thanked the American troops for liberating his people, saying that he wished he could give his life for each American who sacrificed to free Iraq. Elisa was standing next to me and burst into tears, which wasn't terribly unusual for her, but I couldn't blame her. It made the hair on the back of your neck stand up. In my position, I hoped that someone from the jaded press corps might be moved by his gratitude.

Like Kerik, Ibrahim would ultimately fall from grace for failing to manage the ever-growing rolls of the police force. Suspicion of widespread padding of the payroll and corruption under his tenure tarnished his reputation, forcing him out of contention for the minister's post and eventually out of the ministry altogether. He was also found to be stockpiling the weapons he confiscated, which were seized by the ministry in due course. Before we knew about any irregularities, it was apparent that he meant well and was publicly supportive of coalition efforts. Despite his serious shortcomings, which were dealt with by the Iraqi government, he was indeed risking his life to help the cause of protecting Iraqis and genuinely loved Americans and the overall effort.

Ibrahim came bounding over to me. He and I got along well. I had been part of the coalition team that media-trained him in October and briefed him for his press conferences. "Mr. Thomas!" he exclaimed as he took my hand in both of his, grabbed me and kissed me on both cheeks. "So good to see you," he said after which he asked me to sit in the second row of the reviewing stand. I respectfully declined, but he insisted and his assistant came over to show me to my seat. He and the general would be sitting in the first row in arm chairs that looked like they came out of someone's living room, just in front of me. I really didn't want Gallinetti to think I was overstepping my place. Eventually, I relented and took my seat to watch the final preparations before the ceremony began. The staff from the academy was checking the microphones and the band was rehearsing over in the far corner of the courtyard. Yes, that's right, a band. On the day that the regime fell, there wasn't a single police officer on duty in Baghdad. Now, six months later, they had a police marching band. I don't look at this as an accomplishment. It was more than a little ridiculous and a waste of resources. But Ibrahim, against the protests of his superiors in the ministry, wanted a marching band and spent the money to get one. You can see why he didn't last.

This wasn't like a police band in the United States, where the members are beat cops or have other policing duties. From my understanding, the band as it existed at the time was just that—a band, nothing more, nothing less.

Anyway, I was sitting on my wobbly white plastic chair listening to the cacophony coming from the instruments fifty feet away when I had a bad feeling. I didn't know why, but I was suddenly very uncomfortable. Have you ever been listening to music that sounds familiar but you just can't place the song? A few notes from a melody that is recognizable, but just barely? It often happens to me when I'm in an elevator or store and the re-recording of a popular song has been perverted into something other than its original form. That's what I was feeling as I listened to the band tune and rehearse. It was just a couple of bars, not much else and out of tune at that. Then I realized what it was. Ibrahim was going to have the band play "The Star-Spangled Banner" at the graduation ceremony. Crap. I grabbed his aide and told him that it was not appropriate for the Iraqi band to play the American national anthem at an Iraqi government–sponsored event. He didn't get it. I went over and asked Ibrahim. "You weren't planning on having the band play our national anthem were you?" I said sounding nervous and disbelieving. Ibrahim, grinning broadly, confirmed what I had suspected. They were going to start this Iraqi Police graduation the way we start a baseball game. He, still grinning broadly, said that it was in honor of the sacrifice of America for Iraq's freedom and in thanks to the coalition. Like I said, he meant well. I told him that it wouldn't be appropriate and would certainly garner criticism from other Iraqis to say nothing of the fact that the coalition was clearly larger than just the United States. He wouldn't budge. I also cautioned him that the general would be put in an uncomfortable position if the anthem was played. "This is your achievement, an Iraqi achievement," I told him. "We appreciate the gesture, but would rather that this ceremony be focused on Iraq, not the coalition," I urged further. He finally acquiesced just moments before the band was to begin playing.

We dodged a bullet. Had the anthem been played, that could have been the entire story. The Western press, who were using the event to prop up their contention that security forces were not ramping up fast enough to combat the escalating violence, could have used the playing of the anthem as another arrow to sling at the CPA and the administration. The Arab media would have thrown a fit altogether, using the incident as further evidence of American imperialism at a time when the coalition was trying everything it could to spread the message that Iraqis were in control of the government's day-to-day operations. Fortunately, it turned out to be a good event. Both Gallinetti and Ibrahim gave motivational speeches, telling the police that they were the first line of defense against those who wished to stop the progress and that their new training truly made them guardians of the freedoms and rights of all Iraqis. The stories picked up the high points but had more than their fair share of "it's all going to hell" language. It was almost a disaster. Little things mean a lot.

When fighting the communications war, it was critically important to build relationships and educate the media on an ongoing basis about a wide variety of issues. This is especially true in a mission as unique and complex as Iraq. The coalition did its level best to be accessible and provide information to the media. In my view, we were not as aggressive as we should have been, nor did we use the full range of possible tactics to drive our message, but we were charged with being as responsive as possible. The media on the other hand were guilty of routinely ignoring basic facts that were clearly articulated to them time and time again. The result was an oversimplification of the issues that were central to the Iraq mission. The coverage led Americans to believe that precious little was being accomplished, while the CPA was doing an enormous amount of work—and seeing real results, despite a deteriorating security situation.

The best example of this in my mind was the ever-raging debate over CPA General Order 2, which set out policies regarding the Iraqi Army under Saddam Hussein. Today, it is widely regarded as one of the most damaging decisions ever made by Bremer during that first year. For the media, opinion leaders, elected officials, and supposed subject matter experts, it was apparently too complicated actually to give readers or viewers the legitimate rationale behind the order. The press boiled it down to "Bremer disbanded the Iraqi Army." Not true. It became a myth that we in strategic communications would unsuccessfully try to beat back daily. I still find myself explaining the policy. The press convinced well-educated, intelligent people around the world of a complete falsehood by oversimplifying the complicated issues involved and beating them over the head repeatedly with misinformation.

This misperception made the decision one of the most hotly debated issues of the whole occupation. The policy didn't amount to a disbanding. It was a decision to not reconstitute the Iraqi Army. Not reconstituting the army made sense on a number of levels. The reasoning behind the decision was almost entirely ignored. It was grounded on common sense and an understanding of the realities of postwar Iraq.

It is true that the Iraqi Army employed thousands of people who, after the war, were out of work and were arguably susceptible to being recruited by insurgents or terrorists for operations against the coalition. However, that assumption is premised on the misguided notion that the majority of the army was somehow disgruntled by the collapse of the armed forces or for that matter wanted to remain in the Iraqi Army in the first place. It was also based on the flawed assertion that maintaining the Iraqi Army was even possible in the immediate aftermath of the war. In May 2003, when Ambassador Bremer signed the executive order stating that the Iraqi Army would not be reconstituted, he did so in the face of several indisputable facts. First, the Iraqi Army was not disbanded by the coalition but had already disintegrated by the time the order was signed. As major combat operations wore on, the command structure of Saddam's army collapsed from the top down. Saddam's army was made up mostly of conscripted soldiers who were poorly paid, poorly trained, poorly equipped, and poorly treated. Former undersecretary of defense under President Clinton and CPA senior advisor for security affairs Walt Slocumbe put it best when he said, and I'm paraphrasing here, "What happens when a conscript army's command disintegrates? The conscripts go home." And they did. To prove this, one need only take a look at the numbers of POWs the coalition took during the conflict. By the time Baghdad fell, the coalition had taken no more than seven thousand prisoners. After the first Gulf War in 1991, it had more than ten times that number in detention. The conscripts, who made up the bulk of the Iraqi Army, had taken off their uniforms, and most of them went back to their families.

There are some who have suggested that we could have called up certain units, but that was simply not practical. The coalition would have ended up with either not enough infantrymen or too many officers, to say nothing about having to scrutinize each person before letting them back into service to ensure they would be loyal to the new government. Consider that the U.S. Army and the old Iraqi Army were nearly the same size. The U.S. Army has approximately three hundred general officers. Saddam's army had nearly eleven thousand. You can't run an army with just generals and colonels. You need the lower enlisted personnel and the noncommissioned officers in order to operate.

Then add to these factors the realities of trying to operate an army with no equipment, no posts, no billeting facilities, no training centers, no ammunition, no vehicles, and no supplies. There was simply nothing left after the liberation from which to rebuild a viable force. Nothing. Nada. Zip. Zero. That didn't stop the press from criticizing Bremer and Bush in the days following the decision and beyond, as if the coalition would be able to simply cobble an effective army together with no resources, expertise, or personnel. They also ignored the fact that in 2004 during a battle against insurgents for Fallujah, the American military actually found the officers and members of a former Iraqi Army battalion. The coalition pulled them together, rearmed them, and engaged them in the fight for the city. The group was decimated and those who weren't killed either deserted or changed sides to fight against the United States.

The training of new Iraqi security forces began within weeks of the creation of the CPA, which enabled anyone up to the grade of colonel to reapply to a new professional army. Ultimately, 80 percent of the officers and the NCOs from the old Iraqi Army were retrained, re-equipped, and paid as a professional force rather than a conscript army.

The coalition made the right choice to move Iraq away from decades of conscription toward a more professional armed force. A volunteer force built with international expertise from the ground up would ultimately provide Iraq with better-trained and better-equipped forces. The concept was sound, but it required the luxury of time. The new forces needed to understand rules of engagement, international law, and specific skill sets for protecting their borders and working with neighboring armies—instead of killing them. It takes time. Ask anyone who has been in the military. They'll tell you directly that you can't mold a good officer overnight. It takes years of training, discipline, and constant support. The press knew all of these facts. They chose to ignore them, beating everyone over the head with this bullshit that had there been an Iraqi Army in the days after the war we would have prevented the looting and the rise of the insurgency. The criticisms that prevail to this day flatly ignore the very obvious operational realities.

Years of work were erased when American military support was reduced to a token force in 2011. Contravening the advice of our generals on the ground, who asked the White House for as many as thirty thousand troops to continue training and operating with Iraqi military, the Obama administration authorized retaining less than one-third of that number, which contributed to eviscerating the ability of Iraq to deter the advance of ISIS and the growing influence of Iran within its borders.

One of the other expressions from the media that I heard in person and, unfortunately, read nearly every day was the typical, "Why is [insert complex task here] taking so long?" Every press conference, every interview, every phone conversation was littered with this utterly ridiculous inquiry about any one of a hundred monumental tasks that the press believed should have been achieved with the snap of a finger. They passed this frustration on to their readers and viewers and, consequently, the perception grew that we weren't moving fast enough on reconstruction, developing security forces—you name it. Why was this ridiculous? We've already touched on the Iraqi Army. Let's look at another simple example.

Saddam neglected everything. One of the most shocking aspects of actually living in and traveling the country was the advanced state of decay that plagued the nation's entire infrastructure. I often used to say to my colleagues that we should not use the term "reconstruction" to describe our efforts to improve essential services. The term suggests that it (whatever "it" was) was working before we arrived and now we were rebuilding what we were responsible for destroying. I fought that battle in Baghdad and Washington and lost. The fact was, it wasn't reconstruction. We were literally building from the ground up.

The Baghdad sewage system for instance was a rotting network of overworked and under-maintained facilities. Some of the treatment tanks that I saw had shoulder-high weeds growing in them. It was next to useless. The sewage backed up into the streets and buildings. Rusty pipelines were so corroded that they leaked constantly into the water table, contributing to drinking water contamination. Decades before, the system had been built to serve one million people. Baghdad now had three million, many of whom in the Shiite areas had never had sewage service.

In the United States, constructing a new sewage treatment facility would take conservatively three to five years or more to build. It would need to be located, an environmental impact study would have to be completed, and several rounds of public comment would need to be done. Designs for the lines and physical plant would then need to be approved. Money would have to be appropriated. The new lines would be laid and the plant built. Of course that wouldn't happen until after the government contracting process ran its course to select all the vendors. If you pay taxes, I don't need to tell you that nothing happens on time and on budget when the government is involved.

Under the best circumstances, in a stable environment and with optimum equipment, the goal would take years to accomplish, but somehow it was reasonable for journalists in Iraq to question the coalition repeatedly about the pace of repair or construction of a sewage system the CPA had been working to rebuild for only a few months.

Nobody in the Bush administration ever gave anybody the impression that they could build a new power grid, sewage system, water system, or oil infrastructure in a few short months. Nobody. It didn't matter. The Western press felt duped by the Bush White House because they believed that no one ever suggested that this level of infrastructure development would be necessary in the first place. They were correct about that.

Still, the Western press perpetuated this foolish notion that the "reconstruction" was moving too slowly. I recall a *Washington Post* piece that I was involved with that ran in September 2003 about the Iraqi justice system. For days, I worked with the reporter to go over the sheer magnitude and complexity of judicial reform in Iraq, including the establishment of such basic entitlements as the right to counsel. When the story hit newsstands, it had those all-too-often-seen words and phrases littered throughout the reporting. The story told of judicial reforms as part of an "incomplete effort [and] . . . still under renovation" muddled by "American interference." No policymaker or policy communicator should discount the effect the word "still" appearing in a headline or story can have over the psyche of the reader.

Reporters were right to suggest that the coalition underestimated the state of decay of the country's infrastructure. It was also true that, as the insurgency escalated, the pace of projects slowed and costs rose dramatically. Inquiries about the effects of the insurgency on construction projects and prewar planning were legitimate. But suggesting to the citizens of the coalition nations as early as August 2003 that too little work was being done or that we were moving too slowly was an unreasonable criticism.

Perhaps the most striking divide between the media in the United States and the people they sought to inform was the undertone of fundamental distrust of government. The First Amendment to the American Constitution ensures that the press has the ability to behave as a check on government by questioning officials and holding them accountable to the people. This critical eye has always existed but has become far more pronounced since the days of Vietnam and Watergate. Although, on one hand, the decidedly liberal media would take the position that government is responsible, capable, and, therefore, required to solve domestic problems (thereby justifying higher taxes and more government programs), when it comes to national security, on the other hand, the view is often exactly the opposite. A fundamental contradiction exists on matters of foreign policy, particularly when a Republican is in the White House. The government can do no right if the strategy calls for any aggressive use of or threat of military force. This hyper-scrutiny, when not conducted responsibly or fairly, is counterproductive to our efforts as a nation to combat looming threats. It leads the American people into being bombarded with bad news that, consequently, aims to create a counter policy that competes with government decision-making. In the case of Iraq and the War on Terrorism, it affected our ability to win the war at home and is still affecting our ability to fight this very real conflict on a global scale. After all, the unpopularity of the Iraq War and its aftermath led to the election of Barack Obama and a dramatic shift in American foreign policy that has retreated from the aggressive, clear strategy of the Bush administration. By 2014, the Islamic State—which the Obama administration discounted as fantasy—was in control of Iraq's second largest city, Mosul, and the city of Ramadi and is still an active threat to both Baghdad and the Kurdistan region.

In addition, the coverage made the United States and other nations look weak in the face of the terror threat. Journalists ceased to simply report but instead posed as diplomats, military tacticians, and intelligence officials, fueling worldwide perceptions that the Iraq mission was a failure less than a year after the fall of Saddam.

Freedom of the press is a basic tenet of democratic society. There comes a time, however, when the combination of bias and the business of journalism lead to unconscionable reporting. That reporting often had the support and encouragement of editors and executives and was the result of journalists abandoning their ethics in an effort to further their careers.

Relations with the press and our ability to push out a broader message to the home front were also hampered by decisions made by the major networks when they established their Baghdad bureaus after the war. After major combat ended, and with it the successful media embedding process that allowed journalists to travel with coalition forces, the networks and newspapers established staffing and operations plans for their permanent Baghdad bureaus. Their decisions affected their ability to tell the Iraq story the way it deserved to be told. Most of the bureaus adopted similar staffing strategies, and they had far-reaching consequences. The level of coverage would come to suffer dramatically, once many of the reporters who were following major combat operations rotated out of the country back home.

Understaffing by the bureaus led to a decrease in the quality and quantity of coverage from the outset. The bureaus did not have the resources to send people out to different provinces or other parts of the country. This wasn't merely about reporters. On the broadcast side, there was a lack of equipment and technicians as well. The second, related circumstance that evolved within the news organizations was a near constant rotation of personnel into and out of the country. Many members of the media were there because they were sent there. This of course was in contrast to the CPA personnel, most of whom were in Iraq because they wanted to be there. A good chunk of the journalists in the country were "doing their time," as it were, counting the days until they could leave, hoping that having checked the Iraq box on their resume they would get a better assignment next time. It was like court-ordered community service for some of them.

The result of both of these conditions was that the CPA and its strategic communications operation were in a constant state of educating the press corps. Given the small number of journalists in each bureau, and the number of new people covering Iraq, you had to deal either with reporters cutting corners on stories because they were overwhelmed with other issues to cover or with reporters who had a complete lack of understanding of the complexities and history behind those issues because they had just arrived in country. The learning curve was steep for the reporters coming into the country, and few had the time necessary to get appropriate background or context for the issues that they were following. For instance, I often found myself explaining the intricacies of the Iraqi justice system to a reporter and then having to do it all over again when his replacement arrived just a few weeks later. It was particularly frustrating for Charles, Dan, and the military briefer. These reporters would ask questions that clearly telegraphed that they had not done the necessary research to get up to speed. Not having information meant making mistakes. It meant that wrong or incomplete information would surely make it into the story.

It also affected their ability and the desire to get out of Baghdad to explore the country. The press corps liked to present the impression that they were in the middle of the action. To be fair at the outset, a number of reporters placed themselves in harm's way during the war and subsequent occupation. Some were seriously injured. Some paid with their lives. Others will bear physical and emotional wounds that might never heal. Those few who stayed longer and traveled the country, choosing to balance their reporting of the car bombs in Baghdad with achievements in governance and the opening of schools and hospitals in the countryside, have my respect and admiration. Unfortunately, they were more often the exception than they were the rule. The fact of the matter was that it was a struggle to get the press to venture much beyond their hotels or to leave Baghdad altogether and travel to the relatively calm sections of the country. They didn't want to leave Baghdad because if you only had two camera crews and they were off in another province, the bureau might not have the bandwidth to cover the obligatory car bomb story in the capital. I had reporters and technicians from multiple news agencies admit to me on several occasions that, despite the limited resources, it was policy to keep a camera crew dedicated to filming the more sensational Baghdad attacks.

In addition to the constant rotation and understaffing, the reporters who were either assigned to the bureaus or willing to come to Iraq for an extended period of time were virtual unknowns. We had a saying in the office: "What was the one thing all the Baghdad reporters had in common?" Answer: "Nobody ever heard of them before." By and large that was true. Many of these journalists cut their teeth in this most undesirable place on earth for reporting the news. After all, it wasn't like this was a big story or anything. (Note the sarcasm.) This led to an overzealousness and a drive for sensationalism that contributed to the difficulty in pushing out more positive stories. They knew what their bosses wanted and they were going to deliver. If they made a front-page headline, it could make their careers. Sometimes that attitude is compatible with a journalist's responsibility to inform. Sometimes not.

The overzealousness and biases often led to outright unethical behavior and a disregard for journalistic integrity. One reporter from the *New York Times* decided to file a story about a bombing across from the former UN headquarters, listing the wrong number of fatalities. The real number was much lower. When asked why the wrong information ended up in print, the reporter told one of my colleagues that he had been given the casualty information from someone near the scene. He actually heard several numbers but instead of waiting for the coalition to respond to requests that would have provided him with accurate information, he just picked the highest one and inserted it in the piece. He told my colleague that he was up against his deadline and had to file something. She could do nothing but reply, "At least it's good to know how you make your editorial decisions." Some weeks later, the *Times* ran a piece by the same reporter detailing the gruesome scene after several Oil Ministry officials were killed near Kirkuk. The *Times* claimed that they were killed by U.S. Marines. The only problem was that the deaths were caused by an IED and were not the fault of the marines. The reporter actually admitted to our office that he filed the story without speaking to military officials or credible witnesses. Even a cursory examination of the bloody scene, which he explicitly described in the story, would have poked holes in the notion that marines using M-16s could have been responsible.

In the final analysis, there were in fact a few journalists who did their level best to be fair, take a broader view, and seek to contribute to a real public discourse about realities on the ground in Iraq. Those journalists who succeeded were the ones who stayed, some of them for a year or more, to immerse themselves in this complex mission. Those who succeeded were the ones who hoped to explain the realities of the hard work being done and the real challenges that remained rather than simply fill their stories with thin perceptions, misleading labels, and sensational sound bites.

We didn't expect great news, or even outright good news, but we felt that we were entitled to fair news. When a bombing occurred, we didn't expect it to be ignored. We did expect that more positive stories would not be relegated to one column inch at the tail end of a print piece or to a passing reference with no footage in a broadcast package.

It is an unmistakable truth in our world that, when it comes to mass communications, what bleeds leads. Death is more interesting to the public than life, and what went wrong is going to be more interesting than what goes right. It is a fascinating and, some would say, sad commentary on our society. Regardless, it is the truth. Journalism is a business. It's about selling papers and advertising. That was and is the foundation of war coverage. Operational decisions that prevented news organizations from telling the story effectively clearly hampered our home-front efforts, but the editorial direction made for more compelling coverage. The biases of editors, producers, and reporters interfered with their obligation to be factual. The reputation of our leaders and that of the mission suffered. America's standing on the world stage was dealt a massive blow.

Those of us who followed the Iraq story from on the ground have good reason to criticize the media's handling of the coverage. To be sure, though, they were not solely to blame for the difficulties in winning the war at home, but the power of the press permeates every aspect of daily life. People are bombarded with more noise and messages through more mediums than ever before. The story of the Iraq mission also had to compete for attention with the rest of the stimuli that we encounter every day. Nothing can cut through all that noise and leave a lasting impression like the steady drumbeat of often exclusively bad news. It had a psychological effect on the public. There simply comes a moment when even strong convictions can be overtaken by the emotional response caused from a consistent rhythm of negative news, graphic images, and depressing sound bites. They create perceptions that become reality. It is the Walter Cronkite effect. The former CBS News anchor dubbed "the most trusted man in America" had a practice of beginning each broadcast during the Iranian hostage crisis with a running count of the days that Americans were held in Tehran. It had an effect on the viewers and, consequently, Jimmy Carter's bid for reelection. A decade before, he had let it be known that he believed that Vietnam should end, and public support for the war plummeted.

This war, like all wars, had its painful costs and personal sacrifices, but an uninformed American public grew quickly impatient over Iraq and turned it into something as bad if not worse than our more than ten-year involvement in Vietnam, which took the lives of more than fifty-seven thousand brave Americans. Perception becomes reality. In the absence of an aggressive counterpunch to the media bias and misinformation, the car bombs and insurgent attacks not only became the story, but they also came to define the entire mission.

Tragically, the media's treatment of the Iraq story has also fueled a culture of distrust that encompassed both government and the press. It is a distrust that contributes to historically low ratings for both government and the Fourth Estate. The bully pulpit that was once dominated by government has now clearly been overtaken by media in all its various forms. Policymakers, on the wrong side of the editorial filter, must now play hard to create a balanced discourse. Governments who play defense with the media risk ceding to the press their ability to control public policy. That can have far reaching and negative effects on global security.

DISCONNECT

Upping our resolve to articulate better the facts and policy is essential if America is to continue to be the world's leader and a moral authority, regardless of who is president of the United States. It is the nature of policymaking in the twenty-first century. Never surrender the microphone.

We truly fail as a government and as a people when we refuse to acknowledge our mistakes. Furthering some policy or program in and of itself is not a failure, so long as its intentions are in keeping with the best traditions of democratic society. Some policies work. Some programs don't. For others, assessment of success is more complicated. I believe the broad, long-term vision to fight the War on Terrorism by expanding freedom and reinstituting a policy of active deterrence can be effective despite the shortcomings of the Iraq mission. As we continue to prosecute the War on Terrorism and fight Islamic extremism it is important to assess the successes and failures of the Iraq policy. This assessment is not about beating the Bush administration over the head or partisan political maneuvering. Our public discourse shouldn't be based on the desire to embarrass but rather to assist future policymakers in their ability to establish and articulate a set of values and goals. Ultimately, it's about the future rather than the past. For those of us fighting the media war, it is also about acknowledging that some of the crippling wounds we suffered were self-inflicted. It's about acknowledging that, early on in this conflict, we surrendered the microphone to its critics. In so doing, we have affected the ability of the United States to develop, articulate, sustain, and defend policies that will make the world safer.

The question I was asking in 2004 was one that for many persists today: Why? Why were we so clearly losing the war at home, and why were we on the defensive while our people were making some historic strides in an increasingly dangerous and volatile situation? After all, we were sailing in uncharted territory right from the very beginning. The answer to the question can be found by analyzing a series of acts and omissions that led to the breakdown of our ability to articulate our message to a broad audience and combat the editorial filter.

The problems of the media's antiwar bias, staffing, and methods combined with internal communications difficulties within the CPA get us only so far. Also, opportunities were clearly missed and flawed strategies were employed by the administration in Washington that contributed to a perceived failure of policy with respect to Iraq. After all, it was the administration's responsibility to articulate its policy effectively. We heard a great deal in those early days about how winning hearts and minds was a central component of a successful mission. What policymakers repeatedly miss is that winning hearts and minds in the age of digital media is not merely about indigenous people on the ground in the midst of conflict. It's about winning and maintaining support at home. We need to reach back to those lessons from Vietnam and other conflicts about the political war or the war on the home front. Call it public relations. Call it a media war. It doesn't matter. It is the same thing in essence today as it was decades ago, and the United States has historically done a poor job in managing public opinion while executing foreign policy. At least in the case of the Iraq conflict, Bush had the fortitude to stay the course and not permit the polls to undermine his longer-term vision. His surge strategy, while coming late, was one of the boldest presidential decisions in decades. His strength of conviction might be recognized fondly by the judge of history, but it can do little to protect a policy during its implementation from a tsunami of misinformation and bad press.

At the outset here, let me be clear that winning the war at home is obviously more complicated now than it has ever been. The penetration of the Internet, social media, the blogosphere, twenty-four-hour cable news, and the ever-expanding variety of platforms that people have today to express their views make it difficult to push out a message. I'm not saying that had we done a better job at communicating a coherent message about Iraq public opinion would show that a majority of

Americans would be in favor of a long-term military presence. I'm not suggesting that the problems were the result of widespread incompetence or deliberate deceit. I'm not saying that we would have won the media war at home outright had we not made these tactical errors. I am suggesting that had the government been more aggressive, more strategic, and more focused in its communications planning, the Iraq War would not be as susceptible today to the label of a fool's errand. Public support for the war simply would not have waned so dramatically in such a short time.

Again, this isn't about fault-finding or pointing fingers. This is about learning from mistakes and acknowledging that, even after the hard lessons of communicating Vietnam, the U.S. government went ahead and made the same mistakes all over again. Add that to the other factors mentioned earlier and you're left with a mission and a message that was destined to suffer.

The discussion must start in the run-up to the war and the expectations game. Whether you're pitching American foreign policy or a new brand of soda, if your product doesn't measure up to the advertising, you're not going to sell it. The administration's prewar rhetoric was dominated by the accusations about Saddam's WMD. Though almost universally ignored by the mainstream media, messages about addressing the freedom deficit, human rights, and other compelling reasons for regime change were indeed articulated by administration officials. These messages took a back seat to the sexier and more compelling reason for invading Iraq: to prevent Saddam from transferring WMD to terror networks. I don't fault the Bush administration for using the intelligence that they had to bolster their opinion that Saddam's ouster was in the best interest of Iraq, the Middle East, and the free world. You couldn't blame them. Congress and the international community were screaming for some UN authorization for the invasion. Given the fact that the UN, as an institution, cares little about democracy-building or addressing the freedom deficit in the Middle East, something more potent was needed.

We can criticize the media for oversimplifying the complexities of the mission; but to be fair, we must also levy that same charge at the government. George W. Bush had a wonderful way of breaking down complicated concepts into their most basic form. He did this throughout his career in public service. It was arguably a large part of his ability to connect with people. Bush saw certain things in black and white. Liberals have criticized him for statements about the War on Terrorism such as, "You're either with us or with the terrorists." It is important to realize that Bush lives his life with a very real sense of right and wrong. There is no moral relativism in his view. Some might say that it's a strength. Some might say that it is evidence of a simple mind. Whatever the psychology behind it, this thought process, which had previously helped him successfully articulate and promote his values to millions of voters, now hung around his neck like an albatross. Throughout the prewar maneuvering, major combat operations and the aftermath, administration officials failed to realize that they were behind the eight ball from the beginning.

Regime change in Iraq had long been the policy of the U.S. government. But the Principals Committee of the National Security Council (NSC), composed of the president, vice president, secretary of state, secretary of defense, national security advisor, CIA director, chairman of the Joint Chiefs of Staff, and White House chief of staff, had never reached agreement as to the time or manner of such an action. That was true during the preceding Bush and Clinton presidencies. Bolstered by the Afghanistan operation and buttressed with evidence supported by the international community of an active WMD program, the concept of Iraq as the next destination in the War on Terrorism gained support. The capable sales job of Iraqi expatriate Ahmed Chalabi convinced the Pentagon that a new, secular, democratic Iraq was possible and added to the fervor. In the minds of the National Security Council (NSC) Principals Committee, after more than a decade, the government finally had all the reasons act.

Ultimately, as the administration did its high-wire act on the global stage at the UN, it began to emphasize the most compelling reason why the war needed to be waged. The administration found an issue that, when wrapped in the context of the War on Terrorism, made military action necessary at that time when it had in the past seemed imprudent. That issue was WMDs. Sources inside the administration, close to the Homeland Security Committee at the NSC and the White House, agreed in discussions with me that, by the end of 2002, the Principals Committee of the NSC was unanimous that the need to effectuate regime change was clear. It is believed that they felt it would be clear to everyone. As they would find out in their first attempt at a UN Security Council resolution, they were going to need more. Sources close to the White House and Pentagon have confirmed to me that there was utter shock at the blowback from the international community.

Their use of the WMD threat as a vehicle to gain UN, congressional, and public approval for the use of force tied success in Iraq to the finding of the dreaded weapons. The short-term gain in focusing on the WMD threat that Saddam posed to America overshadowed the more nuanced policy objectives of fighting terrorism through democratic reform and active deterrence. In those early days, from a communications standpoint, the administration should have done more to promote greater discussion about democracy-building.

At its foundations, little about the Iraq communications operation seemed coordinated. Links with Al-Qaeda, the need for democracy-building, advancing human rights, WMDs, and other messages created a cacophony of themes for the public to absorb and debate. From a communications standpoint, it was—as one former administration official put it—"like throwing spaghetti against the wall." Officials in Washington were slowly backing themselves into a corner as the media coverage and the rhetoric was overtaken by the WMD discussion. What the administration desperately needed was aggressively to counterbalance the WMD message with an articulation of Bush's broader terrorism strategy, including efforts that the administration was undertaking around the world with the cooperation of dozens of governments.

From the earliest discussions about Iraq, careful attention needed to be paid to the expectations game. The strategy was to use words like "win" and "success" when talking to the public about Iraq, the War on Terrorism, or any military action for that matter. It's a decades-old practice. The public, however, didn't quite know what those things meant in the Iraq context, and arguably they never did. Was success ousting Saddam? Was winning about finding WMDs? The Iraq conflict would pose many questions to a public who still looks to World

War II for their archetype for a military victory and Vietnam as their definition of a military defeat. Iraq would be markedly different from both situations.

Iraq wasn't something to win or lose. It was a set of unique potentials. There are simply too many shades of gray involved in such significant social, political, and economic change to use black and white language. Public policymakers in the era of digital communications must be extremely careful. A speech isn't a speech. It becomes boiled down into a sound bite that is replayed possibly hundreds of times.

The wrong sound bite can create the wrong emphasis. The right sound bite today can create perceptions that won't hold up tomorrow. It's up to the policymakers to know when their message is getting away from them, when they are losing control, and when they are backing themselves into a corner. Effective crisis communications planning could have possibly made a marked difference in the home-front war— even before the first shot was fired.

Military planning should never be based on optimism. Neither should policy communications. A military operation, especially one as broad and complex as Iraq, can't be seen through rose-colored glasses. I'm not saying that officials at the Pentagon didn't understand this. Certainly, questions will always be asked about whether Rumsfeld's view of the new military as a lighter, sleeker, high-tech force supported by air power was compatible with postwar Iraq. Many would say no. A variety of contingencies were indeed planned for within the walls of the Defense Department. Whether or not the resources would have been available to address them adequately is another issue. One can assume that some outcomes matrix was being constructed at the NSC or the Pentagon to look at the possibility of this mission going off the rails. What is vital to point out is that there is no evidence that those in charge of communications and public affairs took steps to integrate their own planning into any potential matrix. There is also no evidence that they developed a plan that paralleled any outcomes assessment then being done. There is no evidence that, from the beginning of 2003, any effort was being made to develop communications strategies and responses to a variety of outcomes once the full-fledged military operation transitioned into the CPA. A crisis-planning matrix in communications, as with anything else, is not something that an organization properly develops in response to a crisis. The organization must effectively anticipate crises to permit pre-planning. That planning prevents us from being blindsided. It also enables us to see trends in coverage, minimize response time, and get ahead of potentially negative stories.

From the outset it was an uphill battle. By the time of the president's speech on board the USS *Abraham Lincoln*, the expectations game was already in full swing. Pollster Frank Luntz, in his book about effective communication, says it clearly: "It's not what you say. It's what people hear." It didn't matter what Bush said that night. Read the speech. He was cautious. He said the right things about the hard work yet to be done, a longer engagement, and the need for strength and patience, but the "Mission Accomplished" banner was viewed as a clear and unbelievable expression of hubris and became emblematic of the disconnect that existed between Washington and the public. In the age of digital and increasingly visual communications, attention to detail is essential. Increased scrutiny should be expected. Engagement on every level is critical.

As time passed and the Iraq mission grew more perilous, there was an absence of focus on aggressive communications and effective planning by those who had the power to establish those strategies. One sign of this was obvious to those of us in the Green Room. Consider that in the seven months that I was in Iraq, during some very critical times for the coalition, virtually no senior administration officials—whose jobs it was to articulate the Iraq message—spent time in the country. Some never set foot in Iraq. Astonishingly, these officials included the White House communications director, the White House press secretary, the White House director of media affairs, the director of communications for the National Security Council, and the acting assistant secretary of public affairs at the Defense Department. Even the director of the White House Office of Global Communications never bothered to spend a few days working with the strategic communications operation or just seeing for themselves what was going on. It was astounding to me and many others working long hours and taking great risks in the Green Room. The folks in Washington preferred to do video teleconferences and conference calls rather than make the trip. When articulating a message, credibility is key. There is no substitute for living in the environment, breathing the air, and sharing the risk. There is no substitute for being able to say, "I was there and I saw it with my own eyes."

There were realities that existed within the walls of the CPA that affected our ability to articulate our message effectively. These realities—including the difficulty in gathering information from the coalition, military, civilian, and NGO sources—could only be understood from spending time in the theater of operation. The Baghdad press corps was driving the message, and those officials had no shot of understanding the dynamics of the Baghdad-based media without actually being there. Most important, each of those officials, especially those who regularly acted as administration surrogates, never benefitted from the enhanced credibility that comes with on-the-ground experience. Credibility is essential to one's ability to convey a controversial message. Credibility is earned and must constantly be proven to the audience.

The situation was unnerving and conjured up thoughts of the quite possible collapse of the administration. Over the preceding several years, throughout the campaign and during the first term, I had come to admire the Bush team's ability to develop a simple, coherent, yet malleable communications strategy and then aggressively push out their message, whatever it happened to be. They were also incredibly disciplined in their pre-planning. They collected and disseminated the information necessary to ensure that everyone was on the same page. The Bush White House had built a well-deserved reputation as having an outstanding communications and media operation, but when it came to the war in Iraq, there was a lack of focus and a lack of confidence. By the beginning of 2004, some in Baghdad were openly speculating that our Washington counterparts were just hoping Iraq would go away, permitting them to focus on smaller, simpler, more manageable domestic issues. I didn't buy that premise, but at times that was the way it seemed. Public perception was not in line with reality. The White House saw that they were losing their ability to get their line to stick when it came to the war. I believe that they felt the communications disconnect with the public. Integrated communications planning was lacking, so officials spent their time looking for answers rather than adding new tactics to their operation and executing a plan.

Earlier in the chapter, I referred to the acting assistant secretary for public affairs at the Defense Department. Buried within that long bureaucratic title was yet another operational misstep that affected the ability to fight the home-front war and added to a disconnect between Baghdad and Washington. Most people probably don't remember that after Tori Clark's departure from behind the podium at the Pentagon in June of 2003, the Department of Defense did not have an assistant secretary for public affairs until April of 2006. That's right, with America in the middle of a war overseas and a communications battle at home, the public affairs operation's leadership was in a perpetual state of flux. The Senate confirmation of the individual nominated by Bush to replace Clarke was held up for over two years. During that time, no deal was ever struck to get him through the Senate, and the individual wasn't asked by senior administration officials to withdraw his name until late 2005. The result was that the Pentagon didn't have a face other than the secretary.

During the Afghanistan operation, Tori Clark was the face of the Pentagon. She was a fixture on television and was readily identifiable with a solid media operation in the building. She also formed a critical buffer between the press corps that works in the Pentagon every day and Secretary Rumsfeld. Now, while I believe that Secretary Rumsfeld is a very capable spokesperson, I also believe that a buffer should have existed to protect the secretary and better solidify and manage the department's relationships with the media. There was a lack of direction within the public affairs operation and an unwillingness to be aggressive in pushing out positive news. It was not that the department's leadership didn't want to get some good news out about Iraq, but they clearly didn't dedicate the resources to accomplish that goal.

Our CPA communications team and the ambassador's staff was ultimately augmented by former *ABC News* executive Dorrance Smith. The creator of *Wide World of Sports* and longtime executive producer for *Nightline*, Smith served on the White House staff of President George H. W. Bush. He brought a breadth and depth of experience in dealing with broadcast networks in particular. Smith would go on to fill the assistant secretary's post in the Pentagon Public Affairs Office in January 2006, nearly three years after Clark's departure. His expertise was an asset to us, but the communications challenges weren't with the CPA's depth of experience. They were increasingly grown out of a stilted and incoherent strategy coming out of Washington.

The White House too was suffering from not having a strong, credible presence behind the podium in the briefing room. After the departure of White House press secretary Ari Fleischer, the president named Scott McClellan to take the reins of the Brady Pressroom. McClellan was an unmitigated disaster. He stammered and spoke in a tone that telegraphed uncertainty and lack of conviction. I spoke with several members of the White House press corps during that time and none of them respected him. We would sit in the Green Room in the palace watching his press briefings and being completely baffled by the fact that not only did he get the appointment but he also hadn't been replaced. By the time Tony Snow and later Dana Perino stood behind the microphone at the White House, the damage had been done.

In October of 2003, a "Rumsfeld snowflake" landed on my desk. "Snowflakes" as they were called, were memos from the secretary that demanded action on some issue that he felt needed to be addressed. This particular snowflake inquired about why members of the Baghdad press corps were not traveling around the country to get a broader view of what was going on. In the response that I was asked to craft, we developed a plan to move media throughout the county by putting together tours of various provinces. Each tour would have a military component, including coalition and Iraqi security forces, a reconstruction element, and a governance component. I figured we would do it once every other week. Yet again, approval was slow in coming, and the Pentagon would not dedicate the transportation resources to make it happen. In this instance, it didn't matter. By then, many of the Baghdad bureaus were limiting their travel by air. Filling even one helicopter would have been a serious challenge.

An effective strategy needed to be driven by Baghdad with the support of Washington. If Washington dithered then resources and necessary support from military assets would not be available. Several examples come to mind to demonstrate this point. In February of 2004,

I began working on a project that I hoped would help cut through at least some of the negative news coming out of Iraq. Rob Tappan, the new director of strategic communications, teamed me up with Rich Galen, who had joined the office in November as a senior media advisor. Galen was a well-known Republican strategist whose long list of credits included working for Newt Gingrich during the development of the Contract with America that helped the Republican Party take control of the House of Representatives back in 1994. Galen was instrumental in establishing GOPAC, a key grassroots political action committee and, in addition to being a fixture on the speaking circuit, was a frequent analyst on cable television news in the States. Rich was the last person you would have expected to see fitting into our merry band, but the White House wanted his strategic experience sitting in the Green Room. I didn't mind that, though I can see why some folks in the press would be outraged at the thought of his involvement.

Rich had pitched and won approval for an idea that I thought might solve some of our problems. The concept was simple. Use the talents of the armed forces video production teams already in Iraq to create high-quality news packages to chronicle the contributions of soldiers and civilians in Iraq. These news packages would be produced in Iraq and then pitched by the Pentagon to network affiliates in smaller markets throughout the United States.

Here was the rationale: We were having a tough time getting the major networks to bite on good news stories, while thousands of talented and brave civilian and military personnel were doing great things to help rebuild the country. They were building hospital systems and power plants, sewage treatment facilities, and hand-holding new citizen councils. They were training Iraqi security forces and constructing new schools. The list went on and on. The problem was that, in the face of the increase in violence, the press in large part weren't biting. Affiliate stations and their news programs from smaller media markets did not have personnel in the country. Their network counterparts were understaffed and not about to spend any resources to do a feature on a hometown boy or girl done good. At the direction of Rich and me, the army cameramen and editors would develop the packages in either fully edited form or with B-roll and interview footage included as separate components. The hard work would be done for the stateside news organization so we could get some positive coverage on a major network–affiliated news broadcast without going through the network's headquarters in New York or Washington. The footage would be sent electronically to Washington, where it would be copied to tape and shipped directly to the local stations. Keep in mind, this was before the use of high-capacity memory cards and other forms of digital storage and transmission that exist today. The local station then had the option to air it or not, to re-edit or rewrite the piece, or add interviews with family or friends.

It was information people should know. It was about people whom America and the world should be proud of.

Rich asked me to spearhead the coordination of the crews, stories, interviews, and production schedule. I was happy to do it. This was the kind of outside-the-box thinking that we needed. Sending out press release after press release wasn't working, and the homegrown surrogate operation wasn't developing as fast as we needed. These people deserved recognition and the American public deserved to know that progress was indeed being made despite the ever-growing interference of the insurgents. I think that Rich was as surprised as I was at the quality of these productions. The Broadcast Operations Detachment (BOD) team moved into the CPIC and we began shooting the stories. The teams, made up of army public affairs specialists from the National Guard, were professional, creative, and genuinely excited about the opportunity to get the word out about the progress and coalition's best and brightest. Over the next month and a half, they shot nearly thirty of these news pieces. They featured everything from civilians working on the electrical system to enlisted soldiers making their five-thousandth mission into downtown Baghdad. Their interview subjects ran the gamut from CPA senior advisors working to create institutions of democracy to the lowest-ranking enlisted soldier just doing his job with unswerving dedication.

In between the now nightly mortar attacks, we did our part. The question was, would the Pentagon do its part? Here is where we again hit a snag. We requested and were assured that the Pentagon public affairs operation would dedicate time and resources to transferring these stories, pitching them to the news programs, and sending them out. They were also supposed to help us assess the effectiveness of the program by keeping track of which tapes made it on the air. It seemed like there was a lack of will or focus by officials to make this work. In the end, the program was discontinued without being given the full attention it deserved over Washington's concerns that the media would criticize the strategy as using military assets to push out Bush administration propaganda.

The CPA and the administration were getting raked over the coals in the press every day, but the Pentagon shelved the program because they were concerned about criticism. Of course, someone would write that story. We developed a program intended to honor those making a positive contribution to the mission. It was a risk worth taking and, even if there was blowback, some midsize market in Kansas would likely still air a piece about a local hero. It was frustrating, but disappointment was not an uncommon feeling, as we tried day in and day out to take back some degree of control over the message.

Across the river at the White House, it appeared (at least from afar) that the Bush spin team had allowed their reputation for discipline get in the way of a robust strategy. As early as November 2003, the White House began developing a program that would have also helped to inject at least some balance into the coverage of both national network news and smaller markets. The program was called Ground Truth and was essentially a massive surrogate operation. Developed in part by former CPA advisor Ali Tulbah, the program would have culled large numbers of civilians and former military personnel who were beginning to rotate out of Iraq and back home and would help them tell their firsthand accounts of their work in Iraq. Many of the civilian advisors were private citizens who were pressed into service by the administration to help in areas in which they had expertise. For instance, Michael Fleischer, former White House press secretary Ari Fleischer's brother, was a successful New York–area businessman who volunteered to spend months in Iraq working on economic development. There were people from the health care and telecommunications industries, former military officials like Brigadier General Hugh Tant, then in the banking industry in South Carolina, who oversaw the Iraqi Currency Exchange program mentioned earlier. The list was long and impressive. All of these folks made tremendous sacrifices and took great personal risks to help further the mission. The thought was that these people were from all over the country so they should be encouraged to talk about their experience on radio and television and through personal appearances and speeches to interested organizations.

Without question, there was a need for this kind of proactive planning and organization. When I came back to the States in March 2004, I spoke to several groups who were astonished to learn about all the work that was going on—even as the violence worsened. Americans, and for that matter the rest of the world, had little information about the steps being taken to aid reconstruction and to improve the quality of life for the Iraqi population. There were successes and failures to report. It seemed to matter little to the folks with whom I spoke. They were just surprised to hear what was actually going on.

The folks involved in the Ground Truth program would be divided into categories according to an assessment of their abilities and expertise. In other words, if someone on the list was an excellent policy analyst but might not do well in a short television segment, it would be recommended that they be used for audiences who would benefit from their unique style and experience. People with experience with radio and television would be put in another category. The White House and Defense Department catalogue vast amounts of information about conferences, events, and constituent groups. On the media side, they have the ability to reach every producer and correspondent in the country. Ground Truth would help target and arrange for surrogates to appear at times, places, and outlets where they could help deliver an appropriate message. Just so you don't think that the federal government was going put these people on payroll, everyone on the list would give of their time and participate at their own expense. They would have access to current information, but their remarks would not be edited or reviewed prior to their appearances. Just as with the hometown radio initiative discussed earlier, it was believed that anything negative these folks might say would certainly be more factual and more balanced than the media reporting.

The process of development began in November 2003, as Ramadan in Iraq saw attacks rise by an order of magnitude and coalition casualties increase. Unfortunately, Ground Truth went nowhere—to the frustration of many in Baghdad and in Washington, not to mention these potential surrogates who ended up either promoting themselves or just staying quiet. Many did little else than speak to their local rotary club or chamber of commerce. Upon my return, I asked both the White House Office of Media Affairs and the Office of Global Communications why it was taking six months to get the initiative off the ground. The response was as shocking as it was shortsighted. I was actually told that the only people who would be talking about Iraq would be the president, Cheney, Rumsfeld, Powell, and Rice. That's it. There would be no larger coordinated effort. I'll never forget standing in the White House Office of Media Affairs with my mouth gaping open in disbelief as I was told that the White House wanted people to focus on the economy and job creation in the run-up to the 2004 presidential election, not the war. As if the administration was in control of the message. As if domestic policy issues could cut through the noise of growing insurgent attacks and an increasing body count. They were facing a well-organized opposition from the media, Democrats, and liberal opinion leaders. By not designing some larger coordinated surrogate operation, the White House effectively surrendered the microphone on Iraq to their opposition.

When it came to Ground Truth, the sad fact was that officials were again not committed to marshaling the resources to make it happen. They might have recognized that there was a problem, but communications and policy officials were not willing to put structures in place to execute a robust strategy. There was indecision about who should have that responsibility in the first place. They spent months trying to figure out who would run and fund the program. The army, the Office of Global Communications, State Department public affairs, the White House Communications Office, the White House Office of Public Liaison, the CPA, the Pentagon, and the NSC could never agree on ownership. There was simply nobody authorized and empowered to champion it or any other broad communications strategy.

The home-front strategy was breaking down. It came back to the issue of credibility. As violence escalated and hopes of finding any WMDs faded, administration officials began losing credibility on the Iraq issues. Many of the advisors and potential surrogates who would have participated in the program were not political or at least a few layers removed from the inner circle. By the end of 2003—and certainly after the spike in violence in the spring of 2004—anyone who made their living from the Bush administration was going to lack a degree of believability with the public. The president was being accused of lying to the public about the WMDs, failing to plan for the postwar period, deploying too few troops, prematurely calling an end to major combat, and supporting a systematic regime of torture against detainees. The administration needed people on television and radio who were not directly affiliated with the administration and had firsthand experience in the Iraq theater. Limiting the number of folks who, on a coordinated basis, were talking about Iraq to solely high-level government officials ignored the potential benefits of having more independent voices expressing a positive view.

Back at the Pentagon, 2004 was shaping up to be yet another rudderless year from a communications standpoint. The Iraq reconstruction operation was in full swing, administering the use of the supplemental funding dollars that had been passed by the U.S. Congress for Iraq's infrastructure development. The Abu Ghraib crisis hit the staff over the head with an anvil of bad press that was getting worse. The presidential campaign, much to the chagrin of the White House, was becoming more about Iraq than anything else. Abu Ghraib was particularly disheartening. Within days of the news breaking about the alleged abuse, Secretary Rumsfeld established a Detainee Task Force within his office to address the onslaught of criticism and unanswered questions. The group, headed by Major General Mike Maples, met every morning at 6:30 a.m. for a daily "who shot John session" about new revelations and reports of alleged systematic prisoner abuse in Iraq, Afghanistan, and the Guantanamo Bay Prison.

I compiled the daily media analysis for the group and was part of those crack-of-dawn meetings. I was up at 4:30 a.m., in the office by 5:15 a.m., and in the secretary's suite by meeting time. Every day it was like groping through the dark, trying to appease furious members of Congress and a ravenous press corps naturally out for blood. At the same time, we all were sitting back and listening to the likes of John Kerry and his surrogates, using this horrible situation as yet more evidence that Bush had created a new Vietnam.

It was another offensive by the press. Yet again, the administration was on defense from a communications perspective. This was especially true in beating back the impression that these incidents were systematically engineered by the government. The media blitz was so effective that, to this day, I'd wager that most Western audiences don't know even the basic facts about the Abu Ghraib abuse. What kind of information you might ask? For instance, that the abuse in the photos could not have been part of standard interrogation techniques because the detainees pictured had little to no intelligence value. Oh, and by the way, they were never interrogated. Another little tidbit of information would be that the supposed inhumane technique of restricting someone to a diet of bread and water is actually on the books as a punishment for our own navy sailors under certain circumstances.

The media were even getting away with rehashing old news and previously reported information just to make another morning's headlines. The piling on of the International Red Cross and other human rights organizations added to the barrage of criticism; they went so far as to suggest that forcing a Gitmo detainee to stand for four hours constituted torture or inhumane treatment. Through it all, the Pentagon spent more time culling records to placate Congress than it did organizing a robust media operation in its defense.

Back in the previous fall in Iraq, it was decided that a proper filing center for the media should be built to help consolidate the press in the convention center. For those who are unfamiliar with filing centers, they are typically large rooms of workspaces dedicated for journalists' use. The White House traveling press corps or groups of Western media in remote locations are used to having such a resource to facilitate the preparation and transmittal of their stories to their bureaus. In Baghdad, it made sense to provide the press corps with a base of operations inside the Green Zone where they could get information quickly. The filing center would be outfitted with satellite capability,

Internet hookups, and phones for each of the Baghdad bureaus. Often times, there would be multiple press conferences or events occurring in the Green Zone or at the convention center each day. Due to the lack of press facilities, reporters would have to leave and go downtown to file their stories. It made communication between the CPA and the media more difficult. Difficult communications made it harder to respond to a crisis before misinformation was released by the media. Additionally, to make CPA and coalition military personnel as accessible as possible to television shows back in the United States, it was decided that a studio would be constructed that would permit news organizations to dial in to satellite feeds and pick up video of Bremer, Sanchez, or whomever without having to send a crew to the palace. It was another sound idea. All of us in the Strategic Communications Office had high hopes that with the appropriate support for the projects from officials both in Iraq and in Washington it would improve press access to the CPA and quicken our response time to the news cycle. It also gave us the ability to reach those smaller markets who lacked resources in Iraq.

However, although the CPA briefing room was given a much-needed and speedy overhaul by White House production guru, Scott Sforza, the money, support, and equipment for the other two arguably more important projects were slow in coming. Both the studio and the press filing center took more than six months to complete. It was maddening. Even when it came to facilities envisioned for use by the ambassador, just acquiring space in the palace for a small studio took months to nail down.

At one point in 2004, with the torrent of bad news consuming the mission, Deputy Defense Secretary Paul Wolfowitz realized that we had to do something to get a handle, not just on Iraq but also on our messaging about the War on Terrorism, which had fallen off the radar screen amidst the growing emphasis on the Iraq mission. *Finally*, I thought, *maybe we could get organized*. Under the direction of a former press secretary at the Interior Department (if you don't know, they handle national parks and Native American issues), who had inexplicably been hired at the Pentagon to support the public affairs operation, I and a Wolfowitz staffer were asked to come up with a strategy.

The strategy was to create a new Global War on Terrorism Task Force to implement a broad-based communications plan and wrestle back some control of our message. The plan had several components, including an improved and more strategic scheduling operation for senior Pentagon leadership, a surrogate operation, a congressional relations group, and overall a more specific and tactical approach to communications planning for the global terror war. When the plan was presented, everyone seemed to agree that it was what was needed to get us back on offense. It died a quick death. Months went by with no staff being hired, save one poor soul who couldn't even get office space or computers in the building.

It seemed that some administration officials believed that the existence of a task force so aggressively pushing out the War on Terrorism message would generate criticism during the '04 elections that Bush was using the Pentagon to help the campaign effort. So apparently the answer was to do next to nothing. God forbid the administration be accused of promoting a more complete picture of an operation that was perhaps the most complicated foreign policy initiative the nation had undertaken in decades. Heaven forbid that the administration should be aggressive in fighting back against the obvious media bias that was perverting a bold vision into an utterly misguided and failed policy in the eyes of the world.

The War on Terrorism message was clearly an additional casualty of the administration's Iraq communications planning. Since the 9/11 attacks, the Bush administration had participated in operations in more than one hundred countries, capturing or killing more than two thousand suspected terrorists. Increased cooperation on intelligence-gathering and information-sharing that allowed governments to respond to threats in ways not contemplated prior to the attacks on New York and Washington. Efforts to engage governments in Yemen, Somalia, Pakistan, and other nations allowed the United States to continue an aggressive posture pursuing terror cells. Financial resources had been seized, and communications between terror suspects were being watched more closely. Active deterrence and engagement was working and yielding results. Unfortunately, any success of the broader strategy was obscured by the constant bludgeoning of bad news from

Iraq and the frequent charge that the administration had abandoned its other efforts in the larger war for the sake of the Iraq mission.

It wasn't until the White House advanced the surge strategy in 2007 that the administration finally found its footing when it came to the messaging about the war. With the new increase in troops, the administration pivoted back to the anti-terror message it had used in Afghanistan after 9/11 but only irregularly in the aftermath of major combat operations. The surge messaging was simple and direct: prevent Iraq from becoming a caliphate used by Al-Qaeda and its affiliates to gain influence and launch terror attacks on a broader scale. Bush was still criticized for again oversimplifying the complexity of the realities of the situation on the ground; but, as we would see during the Obama presidency, the notion that Islamic terror groups could grab territory to create an Islamic State is a stark reality of our current fight. The shift in message worked and the public supported the surge as a vehicle to protect our gains, advance freedom, and prevent Iraq from becoming overrun by the same kind of fanatics that perpetrated the 9/11 attacks.

Articulating the surge messaging was done with much better planning and coordination. The administration, organizations like the Foundation for the Defense of Democracies, and individual surrogates coordinated to ensure message discipline and real-time responses to critics of the increase in troops to salvage the situation. There were both earned media and paid media components to the mini-campaign that actively engaged the media, thought-leaders, and the public to garner and maintain support for the new policy. As with the war itself, that communications program needed to be sustained and sustainable over a long period of time. It wasn't.

So what do we learn? That is the point of the discussion after all. What we learn is that you don't win games by playing defense. Regardless of the message, breaking through the noise of opposing viewpoints and everyday life must result from a relentless and aggressive strategy. The media war required serious planning, staffing, and strategy, much like the military operation. Every imaginable contingency must be addressed with robust pre-planning. Corporations do this. Even large nonprofits do this. I encourage my clients to do it in the private sector. Those on the front lines of any public debate need to have a stronger voice in shaping that strategy, and those in the rear need to continually show support.

If the tactics of your opposition change or intensify, yours must do the same. Consistency, in terms of communications tactics, can at times be essential to success, but there comes a time when changes in strategy and message are required to counter opposing viewpoints and misinformation. Rolling out the president to give an address to the nation every few weeks was not an aggressive strategy to combat a barrage of bad news and misinformation. This is not 1941. The world doesn't work that way anymore.

War changes; it evolves like everything else. It becomes more efficient and more effective. The human race has been inventing better ways to kill for millennia. Just as the nature of war changes, so too do ways of communicating. It requires harnessing new avenues for communicating, new technologies, and adjustments to standard operations. Upping our resolve to better articulate the facts and policy is essential if America is to continue to be the world's leader and a moral authority, regardless of who is president of the United States. It is the nature of policymaking in the twenty-first century. Never surrender the microphone.

REALITY CHECK

We would have to change to cope. Our strategy with the press, our lifestyles, and our attitudes all would have to adapt while we kept our eyes on the mission. There could be no mistaking it: this war wasn't over and we were in the middle of it.

When I arrived in Baghdad, the security situation had already started to deteriorate. Earlier in the mission, CPA personnel could travel almost without concern through the streets. I did it a few times, heading out for Italian of all things one evening with some of my colleagues from the Green Room. Even Bremer ate out at restaurants downtown with only minimal security. Coalition staff shopped in the markets, ate at the restaurants, and explored the city much like tourists. That began to change in June as former regime loyalists and a growing number of foreign terrorists linked to Al-Qaeda began a renewed offensive against coalition forces. We needed more troops, but help wouldn't come to the extent required until long after the CPA had dissolved.

Life for those living in the Green Zone was changing and, unfortunately, it wasn't for the better. Despite the violence, progress continued at a rate that outpaced any similar effort in history. If you were sitting in the Strategic Communications Office, an increase in violence made it more difficult to push out positive news by an order of magnitude. News that didn't bleed became at times nearly impossible to sell to reporters. Shortly after the August 29, 2003, bombing in Najaf that killed the Grand Ayatollah Mohammed Baqr al-Hakim, my colleague, Elisa Pruett, called Reuters to offer them an exclusive on a story about several million dollars in reconstruction aid and projects that were awarded in the Najaf area. The CPA was obviously attempting to show that progress continued despite the tragedy that had recently occurred. The money was for schools, health clinics, and local government support. Reuters flatly told her it wasn't news. That scenario would be repeated dozens of times over the course of the year, and it became far more prevalent as the violence escalated.

The situation started to hit home on August 20, 2003, following a low rumble that shook the windows in the palace. It was early afternoon, and the sound of the distant explosion gained little attention in the office. That was until word came ripping through the building that there had been a bombing at the UN headquarters. It was a larger and more brazen attack than we had ever seen before. The media were in a frenzy, calling for information, and there was little information to be had. Intense worry and uncertainty could be seen in furrowed brows in the front office and on the face of others throughout the palace as we waited for word on casualties. There are almost as many opinions about the UN as there are people in this world, and many to most at this point are not favorable. Indeed, there are many questions about the UN's efficacy, ethics, and purpose. In many respects, the UN has proven to be a corrupt, often anti-American organization and a platform for dictatorships to find legitimacy on the world stage. Those perceptions aside, the staff that they sent to Baghdad, which was led by Sergio Vieira de Mello, was well respected by the CPA personnel. De Mello was an experienced diplomat and Bremer trusted him to do what was right for the goals we shared. Despite the constant and unfounded assertions by the news media that President Bush was adverse to a UN role in Iraq, Bremer and the CPA were working closely with the UN team.

The casualty numbers started coming in. When Bremer heard that De Mello was buried in the rubble, he decided to go down to the scene. In the Green Room, the crisis communications strategy was twofold. First, show the Iraqi people that the former regime loyalists and terrorists were killing those who were trying to help build a new, free Iraq. Second, get Bremer and Iraqi officials out on as many television outlets as possible to demonstrate that the attack would not stop the progress. As the security team hurriedly put together a motorcade, I scrambled to get a television crew from the Iraqi Media Network hooked up with the convoy heading out to the UN headquarters. I later went over to the convention center with some other colleagues to set up the television live shots that Bremer and Iraqi Governing Council member Akila Hashimi would do that evening for the international press.

The death of de Mello and his staff hit everyone hard, even those who didn't know them or work with them. His last words were reportedly, "Don't let them pull the UN out of Iraq." It was perhaps the first time that people realized that we could be next. The more we succeeded, and the more it became evident that our troops were spread thin, the more of a target civilians would become. The shock and sadness surrounding the UN bombing was an expression of that reality. Moving forward, we would have a major terrorist attack on a civilian, military, or Iraqi target nearly every week for the next few months.

The day after the bombing, Ambassador Kennedy came in to the office to ask me for a favor. The senior staff from the UN were reeling from the tragedy. Many from among their ranks were dead and still being identified. They were in the throes of the grieving process while having to make arrangements to notify the families of the dead. Hanging in the balance was the future of their mission in Iraq. At the same time, Sergio de Mello needed to go home. His body needed to be returned to his family in his native Brazil in a manner befitting a man of his experience and station. Bremer offered the CPA's assistance in ensuring that de Mello was memorialized appropriately in Baghdad by those who benefited from his work and friendship. Kennedy wanted me to serve as a liaison to the UN team for the purpose of planning the repatriation ceremony for de Mello's body. That day, we met with a battered group from the UN in a small conference room off of the JOC at the palace. It was difficult. It was emotional. As we sat down and began discussing the arrangements, I could see these men straining to keep back their tears. They all must have felt in some way responsible for the death of their boss and so many colleagues. Even if security wasn't in their job description, their helplessness fueled an anguish that surely weighed heavy on their hearts. We discussed the program, the music, and how to display the plain metal transfer case used to carry the body. We would do everything we could to make it a proper memorial.

Aaron Gibson and I went out to BIAP for the service. We used a section of plywood platforming covered in black drape built by KBR as a catafalque upon which sat de Mello's casket. His body, draped in the pale blue of the UN flag was brought through an honor guard of UN troops and workers out on the ramp next to a Brazilian Air Force plane sent to Iraq for his remains. Bremer, the members of the Iraqi Governing Council, senior coalition officials, and surviving UN staff stood to one side of the casket as tributes and prayers were read. Bremer was obviously emotional, along with many others in the crowd. I had arranged for two bagpipers, one American and one British, to play "Amazing Grace" as the casket was carried to the plane by de Mello's surviving close aides.

It was nearly 130 degrees on the tarmac. The heat was simultaneously coming down from the sun and up from the concrete. A distant column of thick black smoke from some unknown fire cut across the otherwise clear sky as the soldiers and airmen saluted a fallen friend. As I watched the body pass by, I thought about Bremer and my colleagues. *What would it be like to lose a principal or a friend in all this?* I thought. I wondered how we would be able to carry on with the mission so soon after losing someone so close or so critical to the operation. Would I let resentment, fear, and hate form a barrier between me and the mission? Would I become too hard a person to deal with the legitimate emotions I would face in the event of such an eventuality? I would find out.

I began October 26, 2003, in the early morning hours with a return to the Al Rashid Hotel, following a barbeque with the folks from ABC News at the Sheraton Hotel in downtown Baghdad. My roommate, David, from back home, was a staffer in the White House Communications Office who had recently arrived in town to help his boss assemble those badly needed press facilities, and we had taken him along with us for his first trip outside the Green Zone. He was a "Red Zone virgin" as it were, having been working in the confines of the palace for the past few days. As we left work that night for the Sheraton, he commented to everyone how living over here in Iraq "wasn't as bad as people made it out to be." Along with David and me that evening was Lieutenant Colonel Chad Buehring, who was playing his usual role as part social planner, part security guard, and driver extraordinaire. It was actually Chad's idea to go to the party. I wasn't feeling especially well and could have used a good night's sleep, but I wanted to be there when David had his first Red Zone experience. David's boss Scott Sforza, Major Ed Smith, and Mike Spiros were also with us as we headed out into town. I was sitting in the middle of the back seat of one of the Suburbans and, therefore, was unable to serve as the vehicle's second shooter. As I stated earlier, it was recommended that we travel downtown Baghdad with at least two guns in each car and in two-car convoys. Chad looked back and asked David, who was sitting next to the window, whether he knew how to shoot. David, being a Texan and (like most Texans I've encountered) fancying himself as a bit of a cowboy, gladly accepted Chad's 9 mm pistol and along with it the duties of second shooter.

The trip to the Sheraton was uneventful and normal as nighttime jaunts through Baghdad go. We drove at high speed, with a CD in the stereo, along largely empty streets as Baghdad prepared for Ramadan. The party was a good time. We in the press office had a pretty good relationship with the folks from ABC News. Tina Barabovich, her husband, and the rest of their bureau were a fun group as reporters go. Yes, you still had to put up with the usual social repartee about the pure futility of the Iraq mission, but they weren't nearly as morose as many of the others. Unfortunately, they weren't on-air talent. Around 11:00 p.m., I went over to Chad and told him that there were some folks who needed to get back. We piled in the cars and left. After dropping David, Scott, Mike, and the major back off at the palace, Chad and I set out alone back to the Al Rashid. We pulled into the parking lot just outside the gate and cleared our weapons. Chad packed them up in that black backpack he carried around with him. As we walked back to the hotel, I was commenting on my sore throat and general fatigue. The office had instituted a policy of one day off per week for staff. It was a policy that I and most others had chosen to largely ignore for some time. It was taking a toll on my health and productivity. Chad was concerned and he that knew I was hitting a wall. He was typically concerned about everyone. That was his personality and, as Gary's assistant, it was part of his job. Walking through the parking lot, he looked at me and said, "You should take better care of yourself." I halfheartedly agreed. A few moments later in a very assertive tone, he instructed me to take tomorrow off, to which I gave my usual response of, "I have too much to do." As we moved through the glass double doors of the hotel, he now a few steps ahead of me, pressed me further, "Take just the morning. I don't want to see you in the office tomorrow morning." I told him I'd think about it. I stopped at the reception desk to get my key, and he went on to the bar, wearing his Hawaiian shirt and carrying a backpack full of weapons. For me, it was time for bed. Watching him walk slowly away, I decided he was right. I'd sleep in tomorrow. I'd feel better.

There are experiences that never leave you. They never fade. It was 6:30 a.m. when I heard the first explosion, when I felt the building shake. Jolted awake, I opened my eyes wide, staring at the ceiling. I knew this sound. I had heard it before. It wasn't an IED or a mortar shell. It was a rocket. Rockets have a very distinctive sound when they impact a target and explode. At least I thought so. First there's a crack, like taking a stick and whacking the metal rim of a drum. That loud crack is followed a split second later by an explosion and a vibration you could hear and feel. If you're near the impact, sometimes, you can hear the hissing sound of the rocket engine before the impact as well. The hotel had been hit before. A projectile hit the building one morning in September. But this time it was different.

I heard another. The building vibrated again. There was another. At that point I looked over at Pearse and yelled, "Holy shit. Those all just hit the building." Another crack and boom. They were getting louder. The building made a whirring sound as it vibrated. It was taking a beating. Suddenly, I heard a massive explosion that sounded as if it were above us. The eleventh floor had been hit. I dove in between the bed and the wall and covered my head. I could hear rooms being ripped apart. For a split second I thought I was certainly dead. I remembered what the survivors of the World Trade Center said it sounded like when the building started to collapse. When eleven was hit, I thought I heard the breaking apart of concrete. For an instant, I was sure the ceiling was coming down on top of us. They say that when you think you're going to die that your life flashes before your eyes. That didn't happen. Perhaps it was because my faith penetrated most of my fear; perhaps it was because it all happened so fast. I did for an instant think about my father, waiting for me on the other side of this life. I wondered for an instant whether this was my time.

Just then the windows in my room blew open and the door blew off its hinges. Another explosion this time rocked my floor of the shaking hotel. Smoke and dust started to fill the room, and for the first time I heard yelling and screaming in the hallway. Pearse jumped from his bed in nothing but his white briefs, and in a peculiar moment of sitcom humor in the midst of a grave situation, grabbed his most prized possession exclaiming, "Nobody's going to blow up my guitar!" and ran with the case into the bathroom. Everyone has their priorities, I suppose.

Within a few seconds, the explosions stopped and, while I wasn't sure the danger had passed, I knew that the rocket launchers used by the enemy were typically standalone devices that were not used in tandem with others. We had never seen a coordinated attack using multiple devices to my knowledge, but I just couldn't be confident that we were in the clear.

Then, it was time to get out. I threw on the clothes I was wearing the day before, which were slung over the desk chair in front of me, grabbed my glasses, identification, and camera, and went to the door of the room. The heavy solid wood door, which had been blown off its hinges, nearly fell on top of me when I tried to move it. I picked up the door and moved it to the side, throwing it against the closet as more dust and smoke billowed into the room. Smoke and dust filled the room and hallways. The hotel had lost power and the hallways looked like caves. I remembered seeing *Towering Inferno* as a kid and having nightmares for a week. *Is that what we were going face on the way out?* I thought. Sunlight from the adjacent rooms pierced the blackness and bounced off the clouds of smoke. People were struggling to get out of their rooms. Some were calling to friends just down the hall where the rocket had hit. I yelled down the hall to see whether anyone needed help, and started moving down the passageway, tripping over debris. Broken furniture, molding, and plaster covered the floor that was now soaking wet from broken pipes and sprinklers triggered by the smoke. I began to choke. My throat began to burn. I got about twenty feet and realized that Pearse wasn't behind me. I started walking back to the room yelling back encouraging him and others down that end of the hall to get out quickly. People were moving to the only stairwell in the hotel, located in the center of the building near the elevator bank. The stairs were across from where one of the rockets had decimated a guest room. The Gurkha guards were standing with flashlights helping residents move through the darkness.

I made it to the stairs. Residents from floors eleven and twelve were moving down the steps as I started for the lobby. Looking to my feet I immediately noticed blood smeared down each marble step. People were slipping on it. It was a trail that I followed down ten flights. Glass was broken everywhere and barefoot residents, blown out of their beds, wearing little else but their underwear, were cutting themselves walking through the debris on their floors. There was blood on the walls at several points, perhaps where injured residents had grabbed onto the wall for support. With each floor, as people saw the blood or recognized an injured friend, crying could be heard. We tried to keep each other calm. I stayed focused on getting down fast.

I remained calm until about the third floor. At that point an overwhelming feeling came over me that the building was coming down. I felt like I was suffocating. I knew I was near the lobby, and I just wanted to get the hell out before the building collapsed. I arrived at the bottom of the stairwell and headed for the lobby. As I rounded the corner of the elevator bank, I slowed down to see more blood smeared across the lobby floor. One man was sitting on a couch in nothing but shorts, his arms and legs covered in blood. People were carrying the wounded through the lobby. Soldiers and medics were tending to the injured. I proceeded past reception to the main lobby, where hundreds of residents were gathering, many of them in their nightclothes. I saw Elisa in her pajamas, barefoot and standing with her arms folded covering her chest, making her way around without her glasses or contacts. She was visibly shaken, as most everyone was. I began rushing about looking for people I knew, and I called Chad and several others, not being able to reach anyone. I called Gary, in an attempt to tell him what had happened and let him know that Elisa, I, and others were unhurt. After I called him several times with no success, I contacted one of the press officers who lived on the palace grounds. He had heard the explosions but was still in his trailer unaware of what had transpired. I asked him to find Gary and get everyone he could together in the office. It was going to be a busy morning. I tried Chad again.

As we stood in the lobby, every couple of minutes a medic, soldier, or someone from Force Protection would yell through the crowded area to clear a path for the stretchers that were bringing wounded down from the floors battered by the rockets. We'd be pushed to the sides as they came through. With each passing gurney, I looked to see whether I recognized the faces.

It was then that I saw a television camera. I was shocked at the time because, in the midst of everything, I had forgotten that Deputy Secretary of Defense Wolfowitz had stayed in the hotel the night before and his press pool was also in the building. The NBC cameraman was standing near the front door of the building taking footage of bloodied CPA personnel sitting on the front steps, being treated. Not only was taking footage in the Al Rashid forbidden, but taping the faces of those injured was potentially disastrous and, in my opinion, unethical. I approached the videographer and calmly asked him to turn off his camera, which he did. I left the lobby for a couple of minutes, running down the hall to the cafeteria and the small courtyard nearby to check in with my colleagues. When I returned to the lobby, the NBC cameraman was taking more footage, this time of a stretcher being brought through the crowd out to a waiting ambulance. I approached him again and explained more forcefully who I was and the rules regarding cameras in the hotel. Just then, I looked across the room to find Elisa and Naheed, in tears arguing with NBC correspondent Jim Miklaszewski, who was the network pool reporter for the Wolfowitz visit. Adam Levine from the White House Office of Media Affairs was also present.

The argument was over the rules regarding taking footage in the hotel and showing the faces of the victims. Imagine learning that a loved one had been injured in an attack by seeing it on television. As the altercation became more heated, I tried to calm both sides down. Instead of supporting the CPA personnel, the White House official openly contradicted Naheed and Elisa regarding what was permissible. Naturally, Miklaszewski accepted the White House position as the real policy. I told both women to let it go, and I approached the NBC correspondent myself. What happened next would be yet another moment from that morning that I will never forget. When I (calmly I might add) asked him to instruct the cameraman to stop taking footage, he stood toe to toe with me, looked up, pointed his finger in my face, and said, "Listen buddy, when the first shot is fired, all the rules go out the window. I have a story to get." He turned around and hobbled off.

I needed to resolve this fast. The only way, at that point, to get rid of him was to get rid of the whole press pool. The Wolfowitz pool was what is called a "protective pool." It is a group of journalists who are at any given location for the sole purpose of covering the official to which they were attached. From my time traveling for President Bush and through my work with the Secret Service, I knew that once a dangerous environment presented itself, Wolfowitz's security detail would have removed him from the building. Nearly an hour had passed since the attack and I assumed that he had been taken to a secure location. That being the case, the pool had no reason to be in the hotel, as he was no longer there. Not even Levine could legitimately argue with that. Still, watching Miklaszewski walk back toward his videographer, I spun around and marched over to the press handler from the Pentagon Public Affairs Office who was in charge of the traveling media. I told him that the deputy secretary was gone and the pool should leave the hotel. He asked me if I was sure that Wolfowitz had left, and I told him yes. I admit it. I had no idea, but I wanted the media out of the building. He took me at my word and brought the pool across the street to the Coalition Press Information Center.

While this scenario was playing out with NBC, Ambassador Kennedy arrived at the hotel and took charge of the evacuation effort. Force Protection began moving everyone out of the building to the convention center in an effort to get an accurate count of survivors. Elisa and the others went across the street. I stood near Kennedy as he spoke by phone with Bremer, who was in Washington for meetings, along with Dan Senor and other senior staff. "They hit the hotel again," he told Bremer, "and this time it's bad." As folks were being asked to leave, I asked Kennedy whether I should stay with him in case he needed anything. He had no staff with him from the front office and I wanted to be a resource if I could. He agreed and I stayed behind, making calls and taking calls as he sought to grasp the extent of the damage and the number of casualties. We moved from the outer lobby to the reception area, and to my absolute amazement, Wolfowitz suddenly appeared, walking near the elevator bank with members of his staff. I saw his press secretary, Kevin Kellems, and informed him that the press pool was across the street. Wolfowitz leaned on the end of the reception desk. He had just come from some of the damaged floors and insisted on staying in the hotel to visit with some of the wounded and watch the medics tend to the injured. As two more wounded staff members were carried out past him, he began to write a statement. He leaned on the edge of the counter at the reception desk and scribbled his thoughts on paper. As he wrote, Kellems asked me to take down the pool report for the press waiting across the street. I grabbed a piece of hotel stationery from the bellman's desk across from the reception area and scoured the lobby for a pen. On the back of a message slip with the Al Rashid logo, I wrote as he talked:

The Deputy Defense Secretary was in his working office at the time of the attack. Immediately following the attack, he exited the room and asked to be brought to the casualties. He came downstairs, checked on some of the injured and then consulted with military officials at the hotel.

As soon as I was done writing, more medics and still another casualty appeared at the far end of the lobby near the bar and fountain. Wolfowitz looked up when he saw the group. Instead of moving quickly through the lobby, they had placed the victim on the floor. Kennedy, General Sanchez, and those few of us remaining in the hotel followed the deputy defense secretary to the far end of the lobby near the fountain to see the injured. As I approached with the others and watched the medics work, I caught a glimpse of the injured man's feet. They were pale and had a slight blue hue to them as they hung off the end of the stretcher. I thought, "This person isn't going to make it." The man looked lifeless and cold as he lay there in only a pair of shorts. I assumed the person was still in bed when the attack began.

I moved closer, trying to get a better view of the valiant efforts being taken to treat this obviously critically wounded person. The medics had covered his face with a breathing apparatus. Nobody from our group spoke that I can recall except one person who softly uttered, "Hang in there," under his breath in the hope that the man would pull through. We all just watched. The shutter of the official photographer pierced the relative quiet of the scene, capturing not the wounded man but Wolfowitz's reaction. After a couple of minutes, the activity around the body slowed. They picked him up. I saw the face. It was Lieutenant Colonel Chad Buehring. His lanky frame was limp and milky white. His head bobbed side to side as they lifted him.

He looked so different, not the towering presence that I trusted with my life, not the man who strode out of view the night before carrying a bag full of guns and ammo, not the man who insisted that I sleep in that morning. He seemed smaller, almost entirely different. But I knew that face. As they carried him away, I knew that another brave soldier had closed his eyes upon the world. I didn't know whether he was really gone at that moment, but I knew I would never see him again.

I was numb. I looked at Kennedy as we all walked back to toward the front of the lobby. He was drawn, but focused. I asked him whether he needed anything. He said he was fine. At that point, I took my leave of the Al Rashid and rushed across the street to deliver the pool report still clutched in my sweaty right hand. As I entered the convention center and saw some of my colleagues. I knew that I couldn't tell them what I had just seen. I knew that I couldn't answer their questions about our friend who ordinarily would have been helping us through this ordeal. They didn't know his fate. They would soon learn that his room had taken a direct hit. They would soon learn that, instead of leaving when the first rockets impacted the building, he sprang from his bed, grabbed his gun, and tried to locate the origin of the firing platform in an effort to take out those responsible for launching the weapons. Seconds later, one of the rockets impacted his room. Hearing the groans of a wounded man, residents of the eleventh floor, including Dave Hodgkinson, helped free Chad from his splintered room so the medics could try their best to save him.

Throughout the morning, I tried furiously to reach Dan back in the United States. I must have called him fifty times. I finally reached him while I was standing in the press center. I was trying to hold it together, pushing the emotion further down inside my body and fighting the numbness that I felt consuming me. I was the first person to reach Dan. Gary had confirmed to me that Chad had in fact died, and he instructed me not to tell anyone until the staff was back together at the palace. But I had to tell Dan. Dan asked me what happened and I gave him a quick recap of the morning's events. He was obviously concerned about everyone. He asked about everyone's condition. I was standing by the window. Looking through the cloudy glass, I told him Chad didn't make it. He was the only person killed in the attack. After a brief pause, Dan said, "Our Chad?" To which I responded "Yes." "Our Chad?" he asked again in disbelief. Before we hung up, I just blurted out a simple request, "Come home, Dan." I was trying to deal with what I had just seen—and what the future held for all of us. Yes, he was one of the bosses, but he was also steady and reassuring, and his absence that day was felt deeply, at least by me.

I saw Elisa, Naheed, and others as I wandered the second floor of the convention center. They asked whether I had seen Chad. I told them no. I had no choice. Later that morning, Gary called everyone in the office together to tell them the news. In telling the staff, he pulled out Chad's army extension form from his desk. It had just been approved. Chad's tour was ending, but he wanted to stay, even if just for a little while longer. He believed in the mission. He saw the positive results. Now, we would carry on without him.

As my colleagues tearfully faced this blow, I stood stoically, trying to be strong and focused. Gary asked me to keep an eye on folks for him, to help them if I could as they came to terms with their loss. I walked out of the Gary's office and passed one of my colleagues. He was sitting at his desk, his arms propping up his head and his hands covering his face. I didn't know what to say. Nothing would help at that moment. I placed my hand on his shoulder and held it there for a moment before walking on out of the Green Room. In the rotunda, Pearse grabbed me and hugged me tight, saying as he wept, "I was the last person to see him." He and Chad had stayed up at the bar until after 2:00 a.m., singing songs and playing the guitar. He grabbed me so hard that I could barely breathe.

I think that some people in the office might have resented the fact that I kept my emotions to myself, that I tried to stay focused on the job. If that is true, I could understand. It's my way. When the first funeral you ever attend was at age ten and was that of your own father, you tend to deal with death differently. You look at the world differently. Perhaps I had grown too hard as a person. I wanted to help them. I wanted them to know that I was there for them. I wanted to make sure that they would keep going. In the days that followed, I hope that in some way I did some good as we all grappled with our new reality. That's what Chad would have wanted—for everyone to go on.

On Wednesday of that week, we gathered in the Chapel along with more than five hundred others to pay tribute to our fallen soldier. It was a simple ceremony. Chad's boots, gun, helmet, and dog tags were placed on a platform in the front of the room. His unit was seated, facing the assembled to one side with the program participants and eulogists to the other. Kennedy, Greenstock, McManaway, and other senior staff sat in the front row. Pearse played "Dixie" on the guitar, the Iraqis who worked in our office read tributes, Gary gave an emotional eulogy, and I spoke for a few minutes as well. I had asked Gary whether I could speak. I wanted to share my thoughts on Chad with the rest of the team and pass on a lesson that I had learned during a difficult time in my own life. It might have seemed unusual. I wasn't his closest friend in the office. In fact, there were times when we butted heads a bit. It was my way of finally releasing how I felt to the group—and to him. Since I saw him in the lobby of the hotel that Sunday morning, I felt an attachment to the man. Indeed, his face will be with me for the rest of my life. At the service, I quoted my late father, who wrote,

> Memories are like antiques. Not only because they get older each day, but because only certain kinds of people like to keep them. Some people believe that the past should be forgotten, whether because of hardships or because they convince themselves that the past is of little or no consequence. Fortunately, I am not one of those people. Confucius reminds us that "one who can look back with pleasure, lives twice."

I went on to say that Chad would undoubtedly continue in his new life the mission that he held dear in this life. I believed that he would still be taking care of his people.

The morning after the attack, as we gathered for our usual 8:30 a.m. meeting, it was as if a pall had fallen over everyone. Toward the end of the meeting, Captain Kurtz came in and pulled me out of the room. She was shaken. Her eyes were filled with tears. Faris was dead. He had just returned from making a successful presentation to the international community at the Madrid Donor's Conference. He was by many accounts the star of the program. He had told one reporter that he wanted to turn Baghdad into a "paradise on earth." Two men had entered the café where he was eating the night he returned from Spain and shot him in the head three times. He died instantly. I turned from her and interrupted the meeting to inform everyone that the deputy mayor had been assassinated. I barely got the words out. I left straight away to see Bassford and get more details. It was at that moment that I started to feel the strain of all the grief and pain. I became almost disoriented for a time. My head was spinning. Another friend was dead. The work I did with Faris was some of the work that I was most proud of during my time in Baghdad. *Had everything suddenly come to an end?* I wondered.

What was worse was that I was pretty sure I knew who killed him. A couple of weeks before, just minutes before U.S. secretary of commerce Don Evans visited city hall, I was waiting to speak with Faris when two men wearing black robes and black turbans came into the outer office asking to see him. Faris brought me into his office and then went back outside to speak with the two men. As he left the room, he closed the door behind him leaving it open only a crack. I didn't know the two men. I had never seen them before. I did, however, have suspicions about whom they were associated with. The men were part of Muqtada al Sadr's organization. It was a serious security concern that two of Sadr's people would be in the building around the same time as a member of the president's cabinet.

I went to the door and watched the brief exchange. After motioning for the translator, I asked him to tell me what was being said, but he could barely make out a word. It was very disconcerting. When Faris returned, I pressed him about the conversation. He explained that they were waiting for an answer about a concern they had raised. I asked him about his response. With a smirk, he jokingly uttered an old Arabic saying, meaning, "You will hear good things." Of course, the "good things" might not be about the subject of the person's inquiry, but they would be "good things" about something nonetheless. It was apparently a polite Middle Eastern way of blowing someone off. He then told me that he would rather resign than have people dictate terms to him the way this group was apparently trying to do.

I only later learned that Faris was trying to move a city official in one of the districts to another part of town. Sadr apparently wanted to stop the transfer. The deputy mayor refused to back down from his decision. I believe that he paid the ultimate price for it.

Faris never accepted security from the coalition. I asked about him getting bodyguards on several occasions and each time he told me that his was fine. He liked to spend time in the neighborhoods and, while he enjoyed the notoriety that came with his new position, he made every attempt to remain just like everyone else. He also understood the need to maintain the appearance of independence from the coalition. I never told security officials about the exchange. As it turns out, Bassford knew about the issues with Sadr and the risks, as did other CPA personnel, but I will always ask myself whether I should have pushed the issue. If I had made a big deal about them coming to the office, perhaps the coalition would have forced Faris to accept a security detail. I'll never know.

Later that day, I went into Bremer's outer office to see Ambassador Kennedy. With Bremer still away, he was shouldering much of the burden and I wanted to see what I could do to help. He took one look at me and pulled me into Bremer's office. We sat down around the coffee table. I couldn't look at him. I knew why I was sitting there. Kennedy saw the stress building in my face. He knew that I was in pain and yet numb all at the same time. He counseled that it was alright to take the time to deal with my emotions. Kennedy said, "You've lost two people you knew in two days. It is especially hard for you now, I know." At that moment I nearly broke down. It was the closest I had come to letting it out in front of someone. In retrospect, I should have. He wouldn't have cared. I think he wanted me to let it out. I could barely say a word to him. I just stared straight ahead and then down at my feet. I assured him that I would be fine and that I'd take the time to recover. I went back into the Green Room and my roommate, David, from back in Washington got up from his desk. He came over to me and tried to give me a hug. I pushed him away and still feel guilty about doing it. He wanted to help. He knew I needed someone and that I needed to allow myself to grieve. I spent the afternoon in my new home, a trailer out behind the palace, to collect my thoughts.

Everything changed. Ramadan would see mortars falling on the Green Zone almost nightly. Military casualties increased sharply and threats to the CPA and civilians rose. After the bombing of the hotel, the mood changed. It led to the premature departure of a number of civilians. We would have to change to cope. Our strategy with the press, our lifestyles, our attitudes, all would have to adapt—while we continued to keep our eyes on the mission. There could be no mistaking it: this war wasn't over and we were in the middle of it. We needed to rise to the occasion. I believe in many ways we did.

BURNT ORANGE

As the violence escalated, many of these people, whom the media and war critics would quickly pan as inept neocon drones, would extend their tours of duty one after another. Every day, they'd keep taking the risks.

It was morning in the palace in mid-January, 2004. I had just grabbed a bowl of Sugar Smacks and milk from the dining hall and was walking at a good clip through the corridor back towards the rotunda. I didn't want to be late for our 8:00 a.m. staff meeting, as I had overslept the day before and didn't make it into the office until 9:00 a.m. As I neared the main entrance to the building, about fifty feet from the door, an explosion rang out. The concussion seemed to rip through the building as the marines from the FAST team tore down the corridor, almost instantly responding to the detonation. Yelling, as marines tend to do, at the traffic in the corridor they plowed through everyone to take their defensive positions. I ended up dumping half my cereal on the dull-white marble floor as I squashed myself up against the wall. This wasn't a mortar. This was a bomb, and it sounded like it was right next to the front gate of the palace. I ran into the Green Room, where everything had ground to a halt. Within a few minutes, it was confirmed that it was a car bomb, but to my surprise, the explosion occurred out at Assassins' Gate more than a mile from our location. Beyond the busiest of the Green Zone's heavily fortified gates now laid melted cars, incinerated bodies, and a crater several meters in diameter, the aftermath of a suicide car bomb. More than twenty Iraqis were killed, some of them fused with their vehicles from the heat of the explosion. Miraculously, no coalition soldiers were killed in the attack. The dead were mostly Iraqis who worked in the Green Zone. Some of them worked in the palace. There would be yet another

249

memorial service in the building that week, but the Iraqis who worked in the palace kept coming to work.

For the CPA's civilians, life was in a constant state of transition. This wasn't caused just by the challenges posed by the insurgency and terrorists but also by the nature of the CPA as well. For most Americans who believed what they've been fed by the press—that the coalition's effort in Iraq was an impotent effort—they also didn't realize that, over a five month period, the CPA had grown to more than three thousand personnel, mostly civilian. Contrary to the impression left by the media, those staffers were not all cloistered in the Green Zone. Many Green Zone residents traveled the country and throughout Baghdad regularly. Many of them left the Green Zone daily for meetings at the various Iraqi ministries, at project sites, or with community councils around town.

Unlike the British personnel attached to the CPA, who were provided with security and bulletproof vehicles, American civilians often traveled in military convoys or thin-skinned cars, with minimal protection. Force Protection was even warning us about insurgents who were tampering with vehicles by placing homemade detonators in gas tanks. One morning, I came out to the car and the tank was open. Not willing to bet that the gas had just been siphoned, I spent a half hour with a soldier examining the car before turning the key. Despite the threats, we pressed forward and people went on traveling regardless of the risk. If the job had to be done and it required you to travel, then you just did it.

As Al-Qaeda and other terrorists impacted the security situation, it forced changes in our daily lives. Every morning, I'd come into the office and read the daily SITREP (situation report) on the attacks of the previous day. The reports were getting longer as activity by both the terrorists and our troops intensified. The reports listed by grid number the areas of town that had seen activity. It also classified those areas as green, orange, or red. One of the very obvious differences between the SITREPs of August and those of November was the number of orange or red areas. They were getting closer to us. We were still dealing with Chad's death, and there were days when I couldn't get Faris's voice out of my head. Through it all, we continued to do our best to advance the coalition's message. The strategic communications staff continued to travel downtown and around the country. We tried to keep it business as usual.

Since the bombing of the hotel in October, it had been anything but usual. One night, I was sitting at my desk banging away at my laptop when I heard a low rumble. It sounded like thunder, but considering that I hadn't seen a cloud in the sky in weeks, I knew it couldn't have been a natural phenomenon. "Mortars! But where?" I asked myself while still sitting at my desk, as the other Green Room inhabitants nervously rose from their seats. Mortar attacks became an unnerving part of life along with other threats that were directed specifically at the Green Zone. On one occasion, Force Protection, the military operation charged with implementing the security strategy for the CPA, had picked up what they believed was credible intelligence about a terror threat to the zone. They recommended that CPA personnel spend the night in the palace rather than their trailers. The palace, like so many other government buildings, was built from reinforced concrete. It would provide more protection in a mortar, rocket, or other attack. A number of us dragged sleeping bags and pillows up to the office that coordinated international donors for Iraq. Someone grabbed a couple of bottles of wine and an LCD projector. About fifteen of us watched movies spread out in the dark on the floor, well into the night.

As the mortar attacks became more common, procedures were put in place to direct CPA personnel, most of whom would have preferred to stay at their desks working, into the basement of the palace. We even dubbed the time between 7:00 p.m. and 10:00 p.m. as "mortar time," being the part of the day when we were most likely to have an attack. Everyone would be ushered into the basement—or, as the basement came to be called, the bunker. Some wore their helmets and flak jackets. Others just carried them, having long ago resigned themselves to the possibility of getting shelled. We'd hang around in the basement, ignoring the phone calls of the media who were clamoring to hear about the devastation, carnage, and chaos that wasn't. We eventually would release one simple statement about the attack, which thankfully almost always resulted in only minor damage. On one occasion, a shell impacted the parking lot where many CPA vehicles were parked. Eight cars were demolished by the mortar, including one that I used with the other staff in the Strategic Communications Office. For those watching at home, any mortar attack on the Green Zone was automatically treated by the press as a breaking news story, regardless of whether they had confirmation of any damage or injuries. It undoubtedly took years off the lives of the staff's friends and relatives who were watching some reporter wearing a flak vest and giving people nothing more than speculation from his perch miles away at the Baghdad Sheraton.

Then there was the new Giant Voice. Yes, the Giant Voice. Sitting in the middle of an inbox full of new emails one morning, one in particular stood out. The subject line read simply and strangely, "The Giant Voice is Now Operational." "What the heck is the Giant Voice?" I asked out loud to the bullpen. Force Protection had come up with the idea of a siren and series of lights to let people know we were under attack. Alright, I accept that it was necessary to have some sort of mass communication system for the growing population on the palace grounds, but this seemed a little silly. The loud siren and Giant Voice, which said "Take Cover! Take Cover!" would only sound after a mortar or other attack had begun. That's right, after. Often times, it would sound a full minute or more after the impact of the mortars. This was supposed to be particularly effective in warning the hundreds of civilian and military personnel who were living in the trailers on the palace grounds in the event of an attack. We were instructed to put on our flak vests and get under our beds. More than a few mornings, we were awakened by the thuds of mortars or the cracks of rockets, followed by the siren and the Giant Voice. We began joking that the Green Zone was false advertising. After the word went out that we should not travel alone within the zone after dark due to kidnapping threats against civilians, it really was more like "burnt orange" than green.

Part of life in the "Burnt Orange Zone" was living in trailers. After the bombing of the Al Rashid, the building was too damaged and too dangerous for large numbers of people to live there. Ultimately, only a few security personnel were moved back into the hotel's lower floors. All of us were moved into trailer parks on the palace grounds. New trailers for the growing number of CPA personnel seemed to always be arriving. Date trees were cleared on the property, and eventually rows of trailers stretched from just beyond the road that ran along the back of the palace to within a few feet of the wall along the Tigris River. It was a new city of white trailers and dusty sidewalks. The trailers were white metal outside and typically accommodated four people. A trailer park resident usually shared a ten-by-twelve-foot room with a colleague, giving them each less space than your average prison inmate. A bathroom separated the two rooms in the trailer. The walls of the rooms were a thin wood paneling. The floors were a gray epoxy or plastic composite. On the plus side, the trailers were air-conditioned and the water and electricity nearly always worked. The downside to living in the trailers was one of security. The coalition had hired Iraqi workers to install the trailers and sidewalks and to perform maintenance in the area. They were vetted and supervised during the work day, but I felt that it was a security risk. In fact, at one point at the beginning of 2004, bomb-sniffing dogs detected residue on some workers working in another nearby camp during a routine search. Consequently, all of the trailers had to be searched for hidden explosives. None were found that I knew of, but the mere idea that a device could be planted by a terrorist near our bunks unnerved many people. That, along with the constant attacks, certainly affected my ability to sleep.

As the number of trailers grew and the terrorists were getting more brazen, the park became a target. At one point, there was a perceived credible threat that a number of terrorists were planning to come over the wall of the palace grounds at night to murder coalition officials. The marines killed several potential attackers in boats and, one night, we were all ushered into the basement of the palace because of a reported infiltration on the grounds. Marines patrolled the trailer parks, and it was a comfort to see them walking through the rows of white boxes as I made my way back to trailer 69 each night. Still, I didn't feel safe. The hotel might have been a target, but at least it was made from reinforced concrete. Even the windows were bulletproof. The palace was also a hardened structure. The trailers, on the other hand, were like tin cans. A bullet would pass through the walls like a knife through butter. If a mortar landed on your trailer, you were dead—and not just you; the shrapnel would shred the trailers around you as well. At night, I'd pray for the marines, the soldiers, and my cousin John, who was stationed at that point in Tal Afar. I would say the prayer to Saint Michael in the hopes that we all would be protected "from all the evil spirits who prowl throughout the world seeking the ruin of souls." I knew the odds were that nothing would happen, but I still felt better at night when I heard the helicopters overhead making their runs in the skies over Baghdad. Any kind of air power overhead served as a deterrent to those who set up the mortars and rocket launchers.

Although the attacks changed our routines, the people of the CPA pressed on. In December 2003, the Green Zone Café expanded and became a favorite haunt for CPA personnel for a number of months. The café, which opened in the remains of an old gas station along the road to Assassins' Gate near several of the old ministry building complexes, opened not long after the war. The owners were shrewd Baghdadis who were involved in the business community. They were a well-connected family with at least one member on the newly established City Advisory Council. Originally, the place was outdoors and had seating for about thirty patrons on various sets of plastic furniture. The restaurant's meager menu boasted a couple of local chicken and lamb dishes as well as pizza—well, something close to it. The expansion saw the addition of a large tent on the property and extended hours of operation. It became a hangout for CPA personnel who were tired of waiting on the long lines at the chow hall, or who were just plain tired of eating KBR every day. The place served beer and probably the worst wine I've ever had. I remember the bottle having a picture of the Virgin Mary on the label and assuming it was probably church wine. Nevertheless, the place was constantly packed.

Past the hospital and behind the second bombed-out building on the left, a takeout Chinese food restaurant popped up in early 2004. How a group of Chinese people made their way into the Green Zone and set up shop, I'll never know, but they did. They were probably a front for some Chinese intelligence operation. The food actually wasn't that bad. On one occasion, I headed over to the place, stepping around the rubble of the building next door and thinking out loud about how great Peking Duck would taste right about then. As I opened the gate to the building where the establishment was located, standing in front of me and looking up was none other than a plump white duck. He took one look at me and waddled off in between the tables of patrons enjoying their food. I had the sweet and sour chicken.

In addition to the Chinese food place, the Green Zone also developed a souk or market where Iraqi vendors would rent booths and sell their wares. The souk became a popular "tourist trap" for civilians and soldiers alike who were either living in the area or visiting the zone from the field. The vendors sold rugs and old Iraqi Army uniforms, headscarves that came in handy during sandstorms, and bootleg DVDs of American movies. They hocked artwork and old Saddam dinars, little trinkets, and hookahs. On the other end of the zone was a little mini-mall, so to speak, with several enclosed stores that sold pottery, jewelry, rugs, and clothes.

As I alluded to earlier, the CPA had also constructed a gym within the shell of an old warehouse. The frame of the old building was still standing, but the engineers had built new inner walls and installed florescent lighting, a drop ceiling, and all the usual refinements of your average health club. There were new step machines and treadmills, Nautilus-style machines, and free weights. Stepping inside was really just like being back at my Gold's Gym in Alexandria, except smaller and with the addition of the mortar rounds that seemed to hit somewhere nearby whenever I was in there.

The Thursday nights at the disco picked up again, although they were much less well attended than before, and people began adapting to the new security situation. There always had to be a social outlet. Some offices had movie night. Others liked to grab a few people and go to the gym. Still others liked to congregate out around the pool or the trailers, since the usual haunts at the hotel were no longer available. It was not unusual for a trailer to have a small repository of beer or hard liquor on standby for such an occasion. Around Christmas 2003, Harvin decided to have a party together with some other folks from nearby trailers. We piled into the car and headed out to BIAP along that infamous highway that the U.S. Army First Armored Division somehow could not secure. The destination was the duty-free shop on the now dormant commercial side of the Baghdad Airport. The duty-free shop sold, at great prices, many things, but especially brand name alcohol. As we sped down the road at about 90 mph, one of us kept watch on the overpasses for trouble while another watched the roadside for possible IEDs. This might sound crazy, but people did it constantly. If you wanted beer, you had to either get it from a distributor downtown, who was a perpetual target of Islamic militants, or you went out to the airport. Most chose the airport. If you needed American snacks, drinks, other food, and clothes, the only place you could get much of it was the post exchange at BIAP. The military had built something resembling a small Walmart out there to support the soldiers coming in and out of theater. They also brought an unmistakable piece of Americana to the desert heat. It was the famed BIAP Burger King franchise. It didn't matter whether it was early morning or late at night, the lines were long and worth the wait. In fact, the BIAP Burger King became for a time the second-busiest restaurant in the entire chain. You went out there, got your supplies, and before long were weaving back through the maze of concertina wire and concrete barriers onto the open road for home.

We ordered food from somewhere for our little extravaganza outside trailers 68, 69, and 70. We strung some Christmas lights along the walls of our sheet metal homes and broke out our score from the duty-free. It was a chance to have a couple of drinks under the Baghdad night sky and spend some time as friends. Even Gibson, Kimmitt's aide, Lieutenant Berdiner, and some other military colleagues hung out and had a good time. About 10:00 p.m., we all froze at hearing an all-too-familiar sound: the crack and boom of a rocket impact. Silence fell over the revelers as we looked up we heard the hiss of a rocket engine overhead. I for one thought it was coming at us. I had never heard the hissing of the engine before and was sure that it would hit the trailer park. I hit the deck. I felt kind of foolish standing next to Berdiner, an artillery officer, who did nothing except look at me as if to say, "What's the big deal?" To me it seemed like the right thing to do. Needless to say, the party broke up about then.

I always had to keep repeating to myself the two little pieces of advice that General Kimmitt had imparted to me one night when we had come under mortar fire while at the Convention Center: "When it's your time to go, a toothpick will kill you" and "If you can hear the explosion you were going to make it." It was very indicative of life in the Green Zone during the rise and height of the insurgency. Relaxation or something approaching normalcy happened in very small spurts. Rest assured, however, you would be reminded sooner or later that all of us who worked for the CPA were targets.

On a February afternoon, a group of us from the office took a ride downtown to scout out a location for a press event highlighting the Iraqi Olympic wrestling team. They were going to be leaving Iraq to train in the United States in advance of the Athens games. We stopped into the Olympic swimming facility and then headed over to a gymnasium and amphitheater to look at locations where Bremer could announce the formation of the Iraqi Olympic Committee. Bremer was especially interested in events that featured youth and sports. On one occasion, in his office, he said to me that he wanted one announcement a week about some youth or sports program in the country. The ambassador understood the importance of sports to the Iraqis. Any sports programs, soccer games, or athletic competitions would be a symbol of the restoration of national pride and normal life. Throughout the short lifespan of the CPA, several of us in the office worked the youth and sport beat.

Our venture out was an uneventful excursion until, on the way back to the Green Zone, our Suburban was walled in by traffic. Our driver, an army lieutenant colonel, wasn't much for aggressive driving and took a turn into a clogged Baghdad artery. Instead of hopping the barrier of the road to get us moving he insisted that we sit there in traffic. Traffic back in the United States or anywhere is an annoyance. It simply means that you're not going anywhere fast. In downtown Baghdad, sitting in a 2003 Chevy Suburban meant you were a sitting duck. It was obvious to anyone within blocks of you that a group of Americans was immobile and vulnerable. The name of the game was if you got stuck, get the hell out of the jam. We sat in traffic for five minutes, while our guts were telling us we could be in trouble. Snipers in buildings along the street could pick each of us off easily. In addition to our vehicles being soft-skinned, the windows weren't tinted. One person in the car had the courage to take the initiative. He was an Iraqi who had spent much of his life in the United States, living and raising his family in the Midwest. He volunteered to move back to Baghdad with his wife and daughter to assist the coalition, first in the development of security forces and later in the establishment of the Youth and Sport Ministry. Ahmed Hassen Auda was a great guy. He spoke the language and blended in with the population. Ahmed believed so much in the possibility of an Iraq where he could again be united with his relatives, in an Iraq better than the one he fled. His enthusiasm was palpable. He jumped out of the car wearing his body armor and began speaking to the Iraqis in the cars around us. He started directing traffic to free us from our risky predicament. After a few minutes of him running around in the roadway-turned-parking-lot, we were moving again. We popped the curb, hung a U-turn, and found an alternative route back to the zone.

A couple of weeks later, while leaving his home in Baghdad, Ahmed, who had obviously been identified by terrorists as someone working with the coalition, was gunned down in front of his house. He was not much more than thirty and left a young daughter. His murder hit several members of our communications team hard, including Dallas Lawrence, who had recently arrived in country and was working on the youth and sport beat. On a trip to Sulaymaniyah the week before the murder, Dallas had spent a night at the hotel bar getting to know Ahmed. Dallas and I sat together at the memorial service in the palace. It was yet another reminder that the terrorists would stop at nothing to disrupt the mission.

The press were always suggesting that the CPA was just a bunch of hermits in Baghdad's Green Zone. What should be obvious by now was just how wrong they were. Fully one-third of the CPA personnel were assigned to—and lived and worked in—the provinces. Life went on in the regional offices of the CPA during this time of transition for those of us in Baghdad. Some of the regional operations were, for a time, unaffected by the rise in violence around headquarters. Hilla was one of those places. Hilary White arrived in Baghdad in much the same whirlwind fashion as I had in July 2003. The difference between our two trips was that hers didn't end in Baghdad. Much to her displeasure, she and her luggage were thrown into a truck the day after her arrival at 9:00 a.m. for the two hour drive to Hilla. She wasn't really thrilled. Who the heck had ever heard of Hilla? She had signed up to live and work at the CPA's headquarters in Baghdad. Dan wanted her assigned to the Strategic Communications Office, but the CPA Personnel Office had other plans for Hilary. Never one to keep her mouth shut, she complained, but to no avail. Dan was on vacation back in the States and couldn't fight to keep her in Baghdad. So it was off to Hilla for Hilary. It was understandable that she would want to be near the hub of activity. It was also safer for her to be in the Green Zone. A Bush administration appointee and campaign veteran, she also wanted to be closer to the political leadership. She had never run a public affairs operation before, but she was going to get a trial by fire.

Hilary didn't exactly blend well. She is about 5'4", blonde, and blue-eyed. I used to tell her to wear a headscarf to cover her hair. She was from Texas and knew how to shoot a pistol, and to be sure she compensated for her diminutive appearance with focus, enthusiasm, and more than a little courage. Within a few days, she came to like the challenge of living in a provincial office. They really needed her help. Then the game became how she could stay. The plan was to stay in Hilla and avoid Baghdad long enough for Dan to see some positive results and just how important it was for her to be there. Hilary was the only public affairs person for the CPA in the region. She replaced an army colonel who had two Iraqis working for him. Now those two Iraqi men, who were certainly not used to working for a woman, were working for this little spitfire from Texas. After a few days of dealing with that little staffing issue, she began cobbling together a communications operation far away from Green Room's 8:00 a.m. meeting. She was virtually alone. After she figured out how to push out press releases to whatever constituted local media at the time, she began obsessively reaching out to Western media, begging them to come to Hilla.

The little CPA compound in Hilla had air conditioning and a KBR dining facility. Baghdad was another universe. There were few social outlets and she was the only political civilian assigned there. It was a lonely existence. As so many civilians did time and time again in Iraq, Hilary buried herself in her job and rose to the occasion. She even worked out one of those "drug deals" I talked about earlier to get Dr. Pepper in exchange for letting some soldiers use her computers at night. They'd go up to BIAP and get cases of it for her. Hilary also benefitted from having Mike Goefeller as regional coordinator for South Central.

To produce results and push out a positive message, the region needed somebody who was willing to do just about anything to get the mission done. Normally, many FSOs wouldn't work with the military or do some of the tougher, hands-on work to accomplish the CPA's goals. Mike did what needed to be done and let Hilary do her job.

As the security situation in Baghdad worsened, Hilary's little operation in Hilla paid dividends for the coalition and the media war. Reporters began trusting what the regional office was saying over what the Baghdad communications operation was putting out. By the media's logic, the Baghdad operation was too close to the administration. It was too much like a Washington press office, despite the fact that Hilary was about as big a "Bushie" as you could get. The region was perceived as having more credibility because the staff members were out there in the middle of the action rather than supposedly holed up in the Green Zone. It always fascinated me that they gave more credibility to regional staffs because they were away from Baghdad even though the journalists increasingly stayed in Baghdad and refused to travel.

For most of the time that the CPA had authority in Iraq, Hilla was an example of success. It wasn't perfect, but there was a budding participatory government taking shape. A local cleric had put together a Regional Democracy Center and a women's center that provided vocational training, and a small business assistance center was also developed. Hilary would pitch a story and the media naturally didn't believe it. They didn't want to believe it. They came down to prove her wrong. They couldn't. As the attacks in Baghdad increasingly defined the mission, Hilla was still thriving. So was Hilary. Sometimes she had better success talking about the mission with Western media than we did, and she managed to push out positive news. She even got good press out of the BBC. Hilary was racking up a great record.

She had also developed a good enough relationship with the local population to execute a communications strategy focused on countering the terrorism message from the Iraqi perspective. For instance, if a truck bomb would go off somewhere near Hilla, she would travel to the scene and take photos. All too often, as with most insurgent or terrorist attacks, the pictures would be of a child's doll or a woman's clothes ripped apart by the bomb. The photos would then be coupled with a statement, not from the coalition but from the local police chief commenting on the tragedy and who the Iraqi officials believed was responsible. It was a solid approach that kept public opinion on the side of the coalition for a time. Hilary would also have statements from President Bush about the Iraq mission translated into Arabic and distributed. Not that anyone in the Western press would tell you, but the local Iraqis in that little town couldn't get enough of George Bush. "They felt like he was speaking directly to them," Hilary told me. Even I was astonished by it. "They want him to come visit," she said.

From a Baghdad perspective, what was going on in some of the regions, especially South Central, was a breath of fresh air. Of course, some journalists attempted to blunt the momentum. In early 2004, the *New York Times* came to Hilla to do an event at the Regional Democracy Center. The local Shiite religious leader, who was the driving force behind the center, gave remarks at the event saying that his father and Muqtada al Sadr's father were friends, but that he was appalled by the behavior of the young man now threatening to disrupt the progress toward democracy. The *New York Times* ran a piece essentially calling the pro-coalition leader a Sadr supporter. The reporter had relied on a Sunni translator, who we rightly suspected either sabotaged the interview or just didn't translate the dialect properly. The reporter never bothered to speak to coalition officials about what would have been a 180-degree reversal of position on the part of the Iraqi leader. You have to remember that the coalition pitched the story of the Democracy Center to the *Times* as a pro-democracy and pro-coalition initiative. The story gained the attention of many in Washington. Their confidence shaken by the allegations, and fearing potential embarrassment, folks in the administration began to distance themselves from that local Iraqi leader.

For the *Times*, this was another coup in the battle to humiliate the backers of the war. When approached about the inaccuracy of the reporting, the reporter and editor refused to write a corrected piece or retraction. They instead committed only to running an opinion piece written by the local Iraqi official to correct any misperceptions. The piece was promptly delivered to the paper. They never printed it. The story of Hilla would be irreparably damaged.

The regional staffs knew what was going on in Baghdad. Our lives were changing. We were back on our heels, fighting both the insurgency and the media war. Hilla was insulated for a time from the life of being shaken awake by the concussion of a car bomb and the rush to the bunker during the nightly mortar attack. Perhaps because the staff lived on a smaller compound, they knew they could get hit any day. They lived with the threat differently. They couldn't be insular. They couldn't even think about it. They had to travel around the provinces. One night, Hilary called me to tell me that she was in the middle of an interview with a reporter but "men with guns are outside our compound and security is telling us to get into the bunker." She was very calm about the whole thing. Hilary was more concerned about the interview. I was more concerned about her. She wanted to know what she should do about the interview. I told her to end the interview and to get herself and the reporter into the bunker. Incidents like that happened from time to time, but the civilian staffs in the provinces kept marching on and moving forward.

For Hilla, that too would come to an end as spring 2004 approached. Months later than Baghdad, but much in same way, the situation changed for the CPA there overnight. March 9, 2004, Hilary had just left for Amman. While there, she received word that her roommate, Fern Holland, and colleague, Bob Zangas, were killed when their car was ambushed, allegedly by rogue elements of Sadr's militia. Fern had been one of the CPA staffers who had aided local leaders in building the Democracy Center. "The life I came back to was completely different," Hilary would recall later. "We hardly left the compound. Transition was looming, and it was now going to be up to the Iraqis. It was clear that they weren't ready." Within a year of the transition of authority, Hilla became a hotbed of activity for ethnic militias. The Regional Embassy Office set up by the U.S. government was staffed with FSOs and contractors, who rarely engaged with the local population in the way the CPA attempted to do. From reports I received, by late 2005, the staff also didn't travel as often or as widely as their CPA predecessors.

"Burnt Orange" time also meant that Bob Goodwin and his boss, Jim Haveman, would have to forge ahead, despite the increase in violence. Bob and Jim would head to the Health Ministry every day and meet regularly with the minister of health. They'd work late hours, sometimes venturing to the minister's residence in Baghdad for meetings and to host discussions with Iraqi doctors. On one occasion, Bob and Jim were hurried out of the house through the kitchen because a sniper had taken up in the building across the street to take them out. A convoy that Bob was traveling in was hit by an IED. He escaped unharmed, but the attack killed an Iraqi family and blew out the windows in one of the cars in the convoy. Despite the risks, Jim and Bob kept reaching out to the Iraqis across the country. They kept focused on creating a new and better health care system. They knew that the Iraqis were taking risks and paying a price for working toward a better life. It was vital to press on.

There were some bright spots during the "Burnt Orange" time, if sometimes only symbolic ones. One day in December, a crowd of staff gathered out in front of the palace to witness a little piece of history. As we sat along the empty fountain imbedded in the front lawn, hundreds of CPA personnel watched with great anticipation as a large crane slowly lifted the first of four busts of Saddam Hussein from the roof of the palace. As the huge statue broke free, a round of applause went up from below and a rainbow appeared in the sky above us. We would no longer be working in the shadow of the tyrant. Those imposing busts of Saddam came to rest on the driveway for a while, prompting the military to install signs that read "NO URINATING" on the ground near the statues, in response to some Iraqis who apparently desired to relieve themselves on their former leader.

Yes, there were certainly bright spots as the Green Zone turned orange. There were always bright spots. Little flashes of hope and progress that would pierce the shroud of the violence. They were important. Some were historic and critical achievements for a democratic Iraq. The signing of the Transitional Administrative Law at the beginning of March was a truly powerful moment. Although the media dismissed the possibility that it would be signed at all, and later faulted the CPA for delays, it was a tremendous achievement for the coalition and the new Iraq. Article Twelve read,

All Iraqis are equal in their rights without regard to gender, sect, opinion, belief, nationality, religion, or origin, and they are equal before the law. Discrimination against an Iraqi citizen on the basis of his gender, nationality, religion, or origin is prohibited. Everyone has the right to life, liberty, and the security of his person. No one may be deprived of his life or liberty, except in accordance with legal procedures. All are equal before the courts.

Was it perfect? Of course not. Were tensions running high? Naturally. Regardless, the CPA had set out a roadmap for the transition of control back to the Iraqis months earlier, and they were one step closer. Bremer would say, "There is nothing good about being an occupier and certainly nothing good about being occupied." Despite the charges of American imperialism, it was our every intention to provide a transition of authority and prepare the country for national elections and the establishment of a constitution in a measured, thoughtful way. The talking heads on television back in the States were clamoring for elections as soon as possible. What the media couldn't bring themselves to comprehend was that even the most basic infrastructure for elections didn't exist during the spring of 2004.

The whole concept of the CPA was to get in, rehabilitate the country, put in place certain institutions, and turn over responsibility to the Iraqis as soon as possible. One of the first strategic shifts that the CPA made was to slow that process down to ensure that we could create a political process in the context of the occupation. Pushing too fast would have left a bureaucracy and new political leadership ill prepared to operate the government and move the country toward stability. The administration actually went back to the UN after the fall of the regime essentially to get permission to allow the coalition to make executive decisions for a period of time. The UN, therefore, effectively established the occupation.

This was the only way to avoid a total collapse of the country in the immediate aftermath of the war. The infrastructure of the state had dissolved. The United States had assumed that, after the war, there would still be an army and a functioning set of ministries that could be responsive to new leadership. After the looting, that simply wasn't possible. Communications had been cut off by the looters. Government buildings were unusable. Equipment had been stolen. Even the copper wire that ran through the walls of government facilities and that was part of the electrical system was ripped out.

The once highly centralized structure of the country was decentralized virtually overnight, cutting off the provinces from the capital. The penetration or influence of the state was initially very limited beyond Baghdad. Bremer and his Governance Team ultimately turned a perceived negative into a positive. Being cut off from Baghdad meant that there was an opportunity from a governance standpoint for local control to be established. The governance staff led by Carpenter would establish elected provincial councils and local councils through a series of caucuses in nearly every corner of the country.

Bremer and the CPA slowed the train down to ensure that the initial Iraqi Governing Council could be constituted with more than merely a diverse group of expatriates and also include leaders who could interface with Iraqi citizens. That first governing council, which included women as well as all major religious sects—including Christians and Turkmen—was appointed in July of 2003. They were ultimately empowered to make decisions and to take actions to earn increased legitimacy during that first year. Bremer understood that transition and elections needed to be done on a responsible timeline—not on Washington's timeline or the media's timeline or the so-called experts' timeline. This again went back to the moral obligation that I discussed at the outset.

As the media war and home-front battle waged on in the press and the disconnect between the activity on the ground and the reporting back in the States widened, the domestic political timeline started to shrink. It would keep shrinking until, ultimately, our time horizon was set at June 2004. The press chided Bremer for (as Rajiv Chandrasekaran would later recount in his book) making Iraqis "jump through hoops" before holding elections. What critics and the press often refused to acknowledge was that the country lacked all of the vital conditions for legitimate elections—secure balloting, reliable tabulation, polling places, electoral boundaries, and election laws. Clearly, when starting from scratch, some body of law, some expression of rights, and some national government structure were needed first. For months the media and war opponents would downplay the significance of the Transitional Administrative Law, but the mere fact that Sunnis, Shiites, and Kurds were able to cobble together a progressive statement of rights and commitments to their people remains an extraordinary achievement. It took more than ten years to finally craft and ratify the governing documents for the European Union, but the Iraqis managed to write both the TAL and a permanent constitution in under two years. Although law enforcement in a fair and just manner continues to be clouded by serious sectarian, tribal, and political issues, those documents remain the most liberal government documents in the Middle East.

The most famous of these bright spots occurred in December. "Ladies and Gentlemen, please turn off all pagers and cell phones. The press conference will begin in two minutes. This is your two-minute warning." Having said my bit, I quickly walked back into the CPIC, where Bremer, Sanchez, and Iraqi Governing Council member Adnan Pachachi were waiting to formally announce the capture of the Ace of Spades in the deck of Iraq's most wanted. Bremer kidded me that my delivery could have been better. Two minutes later, we all walked in together, with me and Charles bringing up the rear. "Ladies and gentlemen, we got him!" Bremer said at the suggestion of Charles, who stood next to me on the side of the packed room brimming with excitement. The briefing room instantly erupted in cheers and for some, uncontrollable tears. The Western media thought it unseemly for the Iraqi press to express their delight in the news so openly. Nothing could stop them. "What? They weren't supposed to be biased?" I thought as some of the American reporters sat there looking pissed off. The video of Saddam's medical examination sent chills down my spine as the emotion poured out of Iraqis in the room.

After the press conference, Bremer, several members of the Iraqi Governing Council, and a few staff visited the new residence of the deposed leader out at a fortified BIAP detention cell. Later that evening, a group of about twenty of us had a little reception in the conference room to celebrate. Bremer, wearing an open-collared shirt and a green fleece vest, stood there and gave us the play-by-play of his experiences that afternoon actually being in the room with the Butcher of Baghdad. I never saw him more relaxed. Our soldiers and the Iraqis had reeled in the big one. Scott Carpenter, the senior advisor for governance, who had also been out at the airport for the meeting, was positively giddy. He couldn't stop talking about what he had just seen. I ran back to the Green Room and grabbed my handheld tape recorder. I gave it to him, telling him to sit down alone that night and record every feeling, every sight and smell, and every word uttered, before it all faded from memory. He did.

Bremer was happy. We all were happier than we had been in a long time. If you think that we stood there with an inflated sense of self-satisfaction, you're wrong. We knew little would change. Saddam was one man. Just like bin Laden was one man. This fight was about religious extremism. It always had been. It was part of the War on Terrorism. The killing of Osama bin Laden years later would do little to break the will of ignorant Islamic fanatics around the world who were bent on killing free people. We see it today in the form of the Islamic State's unimaginable brutality. So too the capture of Saddam would do little to end the violence that threatened Iraqi freedom.

As time wore on and the Green Zone became more of a target, optimism turned to frustration within the civilian ranks. Confidence faded at home as people buckled under the bad news. I continued to be impressed, however, with the people working around me. The civilians in the palace kept taking chances. They kept traveling around the country. They continued to bounce back. Since the CPA dissolved at the end of June 2004, critics have worked hard in every forum imaginable to portray CPA civilians, particularly those affiliated with the Bush administration, as nothing more than a cancer on the organization. To be sure, as in any organization, there were the unqualified, the opportunists, and the adventurers. Many of the staff were certainly very young and up against a huge learning curve. I won't dispute those observations, but many of these people simply don't get credit for their passion and willingness to get something done with their time in theater.

They were brave. They believed. They impressed me, and they impressed themselves as they threw themselves into their surroundings. As a civilian in Iraq, I think you made a critical decision early on in your stay. Probably within the first two weeks you figured out whether you would be there for a month or two or more like six, seven, or ten.

As the violence escalated, the media and war critics would quickly pan many of these people as inept neocon drones, but they would extend their tours of duty one after another. Every day they'd keep taking the risks. We believed in something greater than ourselves. That's not idealistic drivel. In an environment like Iraq, it was fuel for the soul.

UNFINISHED

Living and working for the Coalition Provisional Authority gave each of us a glimpse into the glory and imperfection of humanity. It made us more cynical, more measured, and more balanced in our view of the possible. Tragically, lost in the ubiquitous press coverage of the worst of the war was the best of people.

In the third week of February, we received word that the White House was sending over to Iraq a group of six governors to visit National Guard troops and to tour the country. The bipartisan group of officials included Idaho governor Dirk Kempthorn, Minnesota governor Tim Pawlenty, Louisiana governor Kathleen Blanco, Hawaii governor Linda Lingle, Oregon governor Ted Kulongoski, and New York governor George Pataki. I was brought in to plan the schedule and to handle the media for the visit. This was something new. I was excited about the prospect of something other than the run-of-the-mill congressional delegation (CODEL) blowing through town. CODELs typically followed a cookie-cutter format with the obligatory troop visit, meetings with Iraqi officials, and a press conference. With the governors' visit, we would have an opportunity perhaps to be more creative in showing these chief executives examples of progress.

Governors deal with quality-of-life issues, infrastructure, and economic development every day. It's what they do. They understand the difficulties in making progress with public programs and initiatives. In addition, they would be traveling with their own media, and we would supplement their press with Baghdad-based reporters. Anything new was good. The press were tired of us pitching what they viewed as more of the same old crap. This had a new hook. What added to the intrigue was that this was one of those occasions when I was asked to put together a group of traveling media but was not allowed to tell them who was coming. The trip was planned in secret, with the coop-eration of the military and security personnel. From a planning stand-point, it wasn't as difficult as one might imagine, having to schedule so many high-profile officials. There was one overarching reason that the planning and execution was a success: they were not permitted to bring any staff with them. No straphangers, as we called them in Washington. None. The White House sent Maggie Grant from the Office of Intergovernmental Relations to accompany the group, but otherwise they were ours.

We came up with a wide variety of activities to highlight economic progress in the country. They needed to see that private enterprise was beginning to thrive again. That story, among others, was also not getting out back home. I enlisted the assistance of Michael Fleischer to help us craft the schedule. Michael was a senior advisor to the Finance Ministry and was one of the "go-to" folks on the coalition side when it came to economic development. Michael, along with Tom Foley, a corporate executive who was later appointed by President Bush to serve as ambassador to Ireland, was working to set the economy back in motion. Rather beefy with a somewhat contemplative and deliber-ate personality, Michael's enthusiasm for his great task was palpable. I called him and told him the mission. I needed ideas for good examples of private businesses thriving in postwar Iraq. His voice was confident and resolute. "Meet me in the parking lot in fifteen minutes," he said. I grabbed my helmet and my vest, ran out to the lot, and searched for a Suburban. After a few minutes of my wondering, wandering, and waiting, Michael pulled up in a rotting, white pickup. "What's this?" I asked him through the rolled-down window. "It's a pickup truck," he replied. "Get in." He said it was the only way to really see Baghdad without having a big target on your back. He was right. I got in the truck, its shocks creaking as I sat down, and I inquired as to the loca-tion of his flak vest and weapon. No weapons. No protection. We were on our way. Not sure why I trusted him, but over the next two hours I toured the city in that rusty truck and had actually never felt more relaxed downtown. "You see that?" Michael would ask pointing out the window. "That's new construction," he'd say with excitement. "Over there are new homes. That's a building that was unfinished before the war, now being completed." It was a remarkable education. You didn't notice it unless you really looked. We all used to marvel at the number of satellite dishes newly perched atop hundreds of Baghdad buildings, but Michael spent enough time watching the businesses and activity that he could notice the subtle changes. New stores, new signs, new merchandise, new construction—it was all happening, and was largely unnoticed or at least unreported by the media.

We drove down Karada Street into one of Baghdad's main business districts. I had been through there before and it was my favorite part of town. Karada was a real symbol of normalcy, a real symbol of Iraq's potential, a real symbol of life. Stores line the street on either side. Within a few months of the war, new stores were opening with an enormous inventory of new products unavailable during the reign of Saddam. Storeowners had so much new inventory that they piled it up on the sidewalk and paid security to guard it at night. Brown boxes filled with televisions, refrigerators, stoves, washing machines, microwaves, and even computers formed a wall along the curb. There were new electronics stores with colorful new billboards. It spoke volumes about the entrepreneurial spirit that had made Iraq a once-great civilization. After all, these people had been doing business long before even the Romans.

I had my showplace for the governors. In addition to the plastics factory and some other manufacturing facilities on the outskirts of town that were experiencing marked growth since the war, I pitched to security personnel the idea of having the governors actually get out of their armored motorcade on Karada Street and meet with shopkeepers, patrons, and anyone else who might happen by. It said everything that we wanted to say about the potential for a vibrant Iraq. After a lot of convincing, the military and security personnel agreed to dedicate the assets to protect the group, and approval was given for the stop. It ended up being the highlight of the trip. Even the Democrat governors were hard pressed to be too critical or pessimistic. Six American governors actually stood on a Baghdad street corner, spoke with shopkeepers, browsed the merchandise, and shook hands with residents. A couple of them even met some children playing nearby. Apache helicopters hovered overhead and armored vehicles blocked the street from traffic. While moving reporters around the washing machines and microwaves, I engaged them about the significance of the visit. Most were characteristically unimpressed. It was just a photo-op. No news here. That was until one of the shopkeepers began complaining about the lack of electricity. Then of course the spiral notepads came out and the pencils began scribbling furiously. The reporters' faces showed signs of life again. They had their negative story for the day.

After listening to the owner of one business discuss essential services, Governor Pataki of New York told the man how proud he was to hear him complain about the government in the same way a New Yorker would. The Associated Press used almost none of the information about the economy and described little of the scene in its reporting. They of course found plenty of space to highlight a complaint that the governors heard from one entrepreneur about American troop patrols on Baghdad streets.

Inordinate attention during the governor's visit was paid by the press to the security measures taken to protect the group. Whether it made it into a story or not, the Baghdad-based Western media always seemed utterly dismayed by the amount of security for Bremer, congressional delegations, governors, and other dignitaries who made the trip. The grumbling could be heard constantly. On one occasion, Bremer went downtown with some press to visit a new electronics store that had opened along Karada. After talking with the owner and browsing the merchandise, I stood out on the sidewalk before his arrival, watching coalition forces prepare to close the street. It was also obvious to me that security was placed on the rooftops and in the buildings in the immediate area. Later, even some air cover would arrive, hovering overhead to give security a bird's-eye view. The scene was actually not much different from what it might look like back in the United States when the president or vice president would do a similar event. If George W. Bush visited an electronics shop in New York, the Secret Service would design and implement a security plan over the course of a week prior to the visit, using many of the same tactics and techniques that the military and Blackwater used to keep high-ranking CPA officials safe in Baghdad.

Bremer was in effect the president of the country after all. We never liked to put it that way, but he had executive decision-making power.

He was also a marked man with a price on his head. On at least one occasion, the terrorists almost got him. But for some reason, the media didn't quite understand—or want to understand—that visible security measures were necessary. They used the tight security as yet another example of a nation in chaos, when despite it being more visible, it was little different than the security used for any head of state or head of government, even in the friendliest environment.

Some of the Baghdad-based Western media were actually pissed off when they found out that they had signed on to be part of the traveling press for the governors' visit. Due to security reasons, I couldn't tell the bureaus that I had contacted who was coming into town, only that there were some special visitors arriving the following day.

It was a similar drill to what occurred when President Bush made his surprise visit to Baghdad for Thanksgiving Day the previous year. In that instance, virtually nobody was told that the president was coming. All of the planning was done in secret. Dan asked me to build a press pool with Iraqi and Western journalists for Thanksgiving Day, only saying that I should tell the reporters that "it would be worth their while to come." Many of the reporters, including some of those with whom we had the best of relationships, declined to come out to BIAP that day. They asked me on the phone, "So, it's just going to be Bremer and Sanchez meeting with some troops?" They couldn't be bothered with that, of course. Many of them had plans for dinner with colleagues and other journalists and simply didn't want to go. I couldn't tell them exactly who was coming because, frankly, I didn't know for sure and it was very clear that absolute secrecy was essential. I couldn't even intimate that there was going to be a surprise visitor. Writers from the *New York Times* and the *Washington Post* turned me down. A major news service accepted the invitation and then backed out, forcing me to give the exclusive on this little excursion to the Bob Hope Dining Facility to one of their competitors.

Those who made the trip on that Thanksgiving Day—perhaps those who had nothing better to do—were certainly not disappointed. When Bush walked out from behind the green camouflage netting onto the stage, the reporters who came with me were stunned, along with everyone else in the dining hall. They were part of the collective gasp that, for an instant, seemed to suck the air out of the room. They knew that they had a front row seat to something truly historic. The room shook from the roar of every man and woman in the place. Television didn't do it justice. It was a scene of absolute euphoria. Soldiers were in tears, standing on their chairs, applauding, and shouting. While the media back home began to piss and moan about being left in the dark about the trip, the president hugged, thanked, and took photos with everyone. He spent nearly forty minutes serving meals to the soldiers. It was emotional for everyone, especially the Iraqi media who were there. They too had tears in their eyes. In the midst of the endless ovation, they came up to me shouting, "Mr. Tom! Mr. Tom! We must meet him! We must speak to him!" The CBS Radio Network correspondent Lisa Barron, who had been complaining in the hours leading up to the event about not being able to file her story, sat on a folding chair repeating a series of four-letter words out of complete shock. Her phone was locked in the bus, as was all the other electronic equipment. She had anticipated the event being such a dud that she didn't even bring a pad and pen and ended up writing her report on scraps of paper and maybe a napkin or two.

The governors' visit would be a different story. Once I had convinced several reporters to sign on to the two day trip, we again headed out to the airport for a briefing and the arrival of our clandestine visitors. Standing in the VIP lounge out at BIAP, I told them who was coming. One producer from Associated Press Television actually came up to me and complained that if had he known it was "only" going to be these governors, he would never had agreed to cover it. I guess it just wasn't as important as keeping that crew at the hotel ready to pounce on the potential car bomb downtown. It was shocking to me. After nearly seven months of this kind of reaction, I'm not sure why it shocked me, but it did. Here was a broadcast service, with subscribers in dozens of markets represented by these officials, that was actually complaining about being invited to cover the first visit of its kind to Iraq. It goes to show you that, in Iraq, it wasn't about news. It was about bombarding the public with a consistent diet of dreadful imagery.

When it was time for the governors to depart, I stood in front of the terminal at the airport as the sun dipped below the horizon, leaving a lavender barrier in the sky between the land and the black of night.

Streams of tracer fire shot skyward every few minutes as I waited for the C-130 carrying the governors' delegation to take off. The trip had been a success in many ways. I too was nearing the time when it would be necessary for me to head home, to leave this place, its people, and its challenges. It was an unsettling feeling. Our media war was looking more and more like a lost cause. Of course, I relished the idea of being home with friends and family. I didn't want people to worry about me any longer.

Yet, on a professional level, it was a gut-wrenching decision. It was hard to let go, to leave so much work unfinished, to leave the game while you were behind in the score. "I have to be going back," I said to Rob and Dan sitting in their mirrored office just off the Green Room. Like so many of those buildings under construction, left uncompleted for months and years, I too would leave unfinished work behind. It was one of the most difficult decisions I have ever made—and one I still regret. I wanted to stay, but I made a deal with my family that I would be getting back. After all, I had told them I'd be gone for a few weeks, and I was rapidly approaching the seven-month mark.

So much had changed in the office since my arrival. I had watched the CPA and the strategic communications operation grow, change, adapt, and overcome. I had watched as the CPA grew to fill the palace and then overflow it. I had seen colleagues grow from a few loosely organized folks doing four jobs apiece to an operation of more than fifty people. I had watched the Green Room develop from a something just short of a disaster area to a modern and functional office space.

Over Chinese food and soda crammed on a small table in the Green Room, colleagues from around the palace came by to wish me well. Dan, Rich, and Rob said a few words and presented me with a few gifts, including a little poster with my name that everyone had signed. It was a nice little sendoff. It didn't happen for everyone, and I appreciated it more than they knew. When it was time to say my piece, those present gathered around. I chose to quote the one person who more than anyone else had brought us together. It wasn't Bremer. It was President Bush. During his commencement address in 2002 at Notre Dame University the president spoke about the importance of public service. He encouraged the graduates to help a neighbor in need; because a life of service is a life of significance. Because materialism is ultimately boring and consumerism can build a prison of loss; because those who are not responsible for others are those who are truly alone. Because the same God that endows us with individual rights also calls us to higher obligations.

No other group of people I had ever worked with had embodied those words more than those attached to the CPA. The civilians and the soldiers of the CPA decided in coming to Iraq that they were committed to helping these battered people, that they would make a significant contribution to a cause much greater than the accumulation of wealth or position. It was an honor to be with them for a time. The time had come for them to continue the mission, while I would leave the circle. It was unfortunate for me but would be just another day for this interim government that, like any large bureaucracy, would go on virtually unfazed by the departure of one person.

I'm a nostalgic person by nature. I think about the past a lot and I strive to come to grips with changes in the present. Over the next day, I walked around the palace and the grounds quite a bit. Like a phantom, I spent a lot of time just watching everyone work, observing the bustle of activity while still in its midst but removed from it at the same time. I organized my files and passed them along to the folks taking over my responsibilities in the office. I saved my documents on CDs and pulled together my digital pictures. I went back to the Al Rashid one last time and stood at the place where I last saw Chad. I called Nidhal at city hall and said goodbye. After my last press conference a week earlier, all of the Iraqi reporters posed for photos with me. They asked, "You will come back? Yes?" I told them I hoped to someday.

A couple of guys from the office helped me lug my bags out to a Suburban for my last trip out to BIAP. Standing in the rotunda, Dan gave me a hug. Bremer thanked me again and wished me a safe trip. The day before, I had come by his office to thank him for everything he had done. We spent a few minutes. The day of my departure, I left a note for him on his desk with a quote from his patron saint, Jerome, and wished him God's protection in the days and weeks ahead. He would need them.

Rich was nice enough to walk me out to the parking lot. Before I jumped in the car, he thanked me for what I had done for the office and for him. We had gotten pretty close in the past few months, as people tend to do in these high-pressure circumstances. All I could say was, "Reed is a lucky guy," referring to his only son back in the States. "Stay safe," I said. It was a poignant moment for both of us.

Into the car, locked and loaded one last time. Off we went, through the razor wire, around the Jersey barriers past the Ba'ath Party head-quarters and out on the road to BIAP. The Green Room, the palace, and the Green Zone were behind me now. Little did I realize how wrong an assumption that was. I stared out the window soaking in my last view of Baghdad. With each second, the landscape passed before my grimy window. Beyond the roadway I could see the small, sunbaked homes packed together in their neighborhoods. They seemed so normal in many ways, but what was happening on the streets and in the country—both the good and the bad—was at the same time extraordinary and deadly. I thought back to those kids I saw playing in the garbage on my way into town for the first time. There was an innocence about them; there was an obliviousness to the dangers that surrounded them. I wondered whether they had been able to hold on to it as these mon-umental changes were being made in the very fabric of their society. I hoped their lives were better in some way.

We passed the checkpoint on the outskirts of the airport and around the concrete barriers. It was a series of final times: the final time that I would drive out there; the final time that I'd pass through the check-point; the final time that I'd feel the hot Baghdad sun on my face—or so I thought. I had scheduled passage back to the United States on a C-5 Galaxy cargo plane direct from Baghdad to Germany, then to Bangor, Maine, and finally to Andrews Air Force Base, outside Wash-ington. I liked the idea of traveling on the same aircraft and not flying commercial. During my time in Iraq, I had come to feel safer on mil-itary planes than on commercial aircraft. I booked a seat for myself and one for Scott Sforza, who was also heading back after the long-awaited opening of the new press center.

What I didn't realize about C-5 Galaxy planes is that they break. That is apparently a technical term used by the military that means they well, break—often. The mammoth plane, one of the largest in the world, had an impeccable safety record, in part I assume because they are always being repaired. We arrived at BIAP for our final flight and waited for our transportation until well after dark, long after it would be possible to return to the palace for the night. The plane never came. We were stranded. The airmen manning the terminal offered to put us up in their "VIP" quarters for our long last night in Iraq. Scott and I accepted with appreciation and promptly dragged our mountain of gear to our lodging. Our lodging was actually a shipping container parked just outside the rear of the terminal building and not two hundred feet from the ramp where the helicopters landed and refueled. It was a tin can with a fluorescent light fastened to the interior roof and an unnecessarily loud heater that gave out about halfway through the night. It was either noisy or freezing.

I couldn't help but laugh as I lay there freezing and shaking in my army-issued sleeping bag. It was my last night in Baghdad but my first time in a shipping container. No concierge to complain to. I had gotten used to that. We were lucky that we had a place to sleep at all. Literally a day didn't go by when I didn't have some new experience or learn something or surprise myself. It was a way of life here in Iraq right to the last moment. Nothing went as planned. You were always forced to challenge yourself to deal with varied and taxing situations—situations to which you never thought you would be exposed. Not that this was big deal. It was just typical. This was one of those little curve balls that just made you laugh.

We were up early the next morning, as the sun made its way over the horizon and warmed the chilled air of the desert. We booked ourselves on a C-130 bound for Kuwait and we would then take a commercial flight back to Washington by way of London. So, it looked like I would leave Iraq much in the same way I entered. After another few hours of waiting in the terminal and being strangely engrossed in an *Iron Chef* TV marathon with about a hundred members of the Big Red One (aka the U.S. Army First Infantry Division), it was time to get moving. I boarded the plane and took a seat on the left side of the aircraft. We were a diverse group of cargo that morning. A couple of photojournalists sat near me, along with several army colonels and other officers, in addition to the requisite band of soldiers heading out of theater. Over the months, my nerves had dulled somewhat to the point where I could not only handle a BIAP takeoff but also be happy about it.

We began our climb into the clear skies over Baghdad when suddenly the plane's nose rose sharply placing us on what seemed like a 45-degree incline. Something was wrong. I gripped the bar that connected the red webbing of the jump seats with both hands and stared at the floor. I began to sweat as other passengers, including the officers, began to look visibly nervous. After a few seconds of a steep climb the plane banked sharply to the right, placing it almost on its side. My drenched palms gripped the bar on either side of my legs even more tightly to prevent myself from falling forward. Then I heard the countermeasures deploy. We were being shot at. I started to pray as the plane went into a dive so steep it lifted me and everything in the cargo area up off the floor. This was it. The blood rushed to my head and my stomach dropped to my feet as we dove lower. The plane's engine, now taxed by the evasive maneuvers, made high-pitched sounds that I'd only heard in movies. Every muscle in my body tensed and my heart nearly shot through my chest onto the floor. My fellow passengers were to a person white as sheets. We would know in seconds whether we were going to be hit. I closed my eyes and prayed one last time, "Saint Michael, defend us in battle." An eternity passed in seconds.

Suddenly we leveled off. I sat frozen in my seat still gripping the bar under my legs. It was only after several minutes that I breathed a sigh of relief. When we touched down in Kuwait, I found the major from the Air National Guard who commanded the flight and thanked him. As a matter of fact, I thanked every member of the crew. Before long we were back in the villas at the Kuwait Hilton. Walking through the door of the beachfront house, I paused and stood in the foyer, my bags hanging on my shoulders, my duffle at my feet. I had come full circle. The breeze from the gulf pierced the curtains in the living room. It seemed like forever since I had been there. Yet at the same time, it felt like yesterday. It was like waking up from a long, vivid dream, a disorienting, strange, and emotional dream. The place was the same except perhaps a little more hectic.

I was different. Iraq changed me. Iraq, I think, changed every one of us who spent those testing days and months there. At this point some talking head on television might perk up and say, "Ah! Yet another life marred and irreparably damaged by George Bush's illegal war." Quite the contrary, the changes helped enhance me as an individual, both personally and professionally. It reinforced my values. It redefined my priorities. It showed me a side of existence that made me forever grateful for the life, the family, the friends, and the country I call my own. It strengthened my faith in myself and in God. It taught me how better to handle crisis and adversity.

I've never been one of those people who freaks out at the first sign of trouble. We all know the person in our lives who goes around making everything a Greek tragedy. The coffee maker is broken and the world is coming to an end. That has never been me. I've always prided myself on my levelheadedness and ability to make decisions. I think I inherited that from my father. I learned how to stay positive, focused, and effective in the face of a challenge—and I learned what real challenges are.

Living and working for the Coalition Provisional Authority gave each of us a glimpse into the glory and imperfection of humanity. It made us more cynical, more measured, and more balanced in our view of the possible.

Tragically, lost in the ubiquitous press coverage of the worst of the war was the best of people. It was the small signs of strength, the little acts of enormous courage that were exhibited by Iraqis every day. It was the empowerment that rose for a time from the ashes of a collapsed brutal regime. It was people communicating and working together who never would have before. I saw courage unlike anything I had ever seen before or have ever seen since. I saw selflessness and a commitment to duty that made me stronger. Iraq strengthened my faith in the "supreme worth of the individual," as John D. Rockefeller put it, and that individual's power to achieve great things. That was a reflection not only on the commitment of the brave civilians and soldiers that I met during my travels but also on the Iraqi people.

It is understandable that people looked at this conflict, halfway around the world, and remarked during that time that the Iraqis just didn't seem to want it enough, that they just weren't willing to sacrifice as we were for the benefits of free society. Make no mistake about it, the millions of Iraqis who risked death by marching miles to polling places in 2005 to exercise their right to vote each played a part in liberating their country. Iraqis—Shiite, Sunni, and Kurd—who were willing to serve in the government took enormous risks to rebuild their society during those first months and after. Each Iraqi who worked alongside coalition soldiers and civilians both in the palace and on the streets was willing to give his or her life for Iraq's future. Many did. Those people were far more in number than the terrorists who sought to destroy the hope of Iraqi freedom. They were far greater in number than the press led viewers and readers to believe.

The coalition was there to put itself out of a job, but that didn't mean our moral obligation to continue to provide support and assistance was extinguished when Bremer boarded his plane and came home in June of 2004. We would do right by the Iraqis through the bold surge strategy employed by Bush in 2007. In the years after the CPA transitioned out of Baghdad, we decimated Al-Qaeda, continued to make progress on reconstruction, helped to ensure that the economy grew despite the violence, and saw Iraqis go to the polls three times to complete peaceful transitions of power. It's a story almost never told except by the brave soldiers and civilians who could say that they were there and did their part.

After British Airways delivered me home, I climbed into the black White House sedan sent out to Dulles to pick up Scott and me. As we drove into Washington, I looked out the window in silence, much as I did en route to BIAP a couple of days earlier. There were streetlights and traffic signals and cars that stayed in their lanes. The driver didn't speed up and change lanes under the overpasses to avoid a potential explosive device dropped from above. The highway signs weren't adorned with bullet holes. There were lights glowing in the windows of the buildings and people walking calmly on the sidewalks. It was so orderly, so normal. As we passed the Bureau of Printing and Engraving, I looked up and caught sight of an American flag, waving in the breeze high atop a building. I felt a lump in my throat and thought about how lucky I was to have been given the opportunity to serve, how lucky I was be home again to live and work under that flag. I reflected on what I had just left behind.

We arrived at the black iron gates just beyond the walls of the West Wing. I grabbed my bags and shuffled off past the Eisenhower Executive Office Building to hail a cab home. No one was home when I got there. There was silence. There was solitude. It was over. That was my new reality, but the mission continued unfinished. Over the days and weeks that followed, as I watched the reporting of the escalating violence, I struggled to come to grips with an intense anxiety over the mission. I couldn't help but acknowledge that the administration's reluctance to dedicate adequate troop resources was perhaps irreparably hurting an otherwise noble effort. The press were driving their message of hopelessness, and coverage was getting more lopsided. The body count was rising, and I was regretting my decision to leave as I continued to swerve around even the smallest item in the road, still driving like I was in Baghdad traffic. One morning, the sound of a crashing garbage can out on the street made me jump clear out of bed. There was clearly a time for adjustment.

For those of us who served, the mission became a part of who we are. There will always be a part of me over there. I will take Iraq with me wherever life takes me. We were just ordinary people, asked to do something extraordinary. In so many ways unprepared, we did our jobs against often unforeseen and incredible odds. We were people who believed in what was possible. At times we were facing more than we could bear. As much as the media and critics try to convince people, no one ever said it would be easy. No one ever told anyone that it would take only a year or that it would be without its mistakes. War is never simple. Freedom is never simple. Bush never said that Iraqi democracy would look just like American democracy. What the CPA demonstrated in word and in deed during that critical first year was a commitment to the potential of success, the potential of giving the democratic process a chance to take root in the Middle East, the potential to prevent the establishment of an Islamic caliphate that would spread instability and terror across the globe. The civilians and the soldiers of the CPA proved that we could harness that potential.

Where we failed from a communications standpoint was in our ability to manage expectations while first defining success and then trumpeting progress, using every asset at our disposal. Today, the public has little idea about just what was accomplished in those first months, nor do they realize the significance of those achievements. That public, consequently, can't assess the significant and lasting damage done to those results by our virtual abandonment of Iraq.

In this day and age, it all too often seems like people who believe in something, people with strong commitments, people who choose to have faith are looked upon as gullible and unsophisticated. We see this in the increasingly prevalent attacks on organized religion in the United States and Europe. Iraq had so much to do with faith, potential, and commitment.

Our failure to fight the media war effectively led to losing the war at home. It meant that politicians and opinion leaders today have no compunction about running away from the Iraq mission without thinking about the bigger national security picture, the broader implications for future policy decision-making, or the impact on those who served so nobly. Too often those who served have been allowed to be defined as too naïve to realize they had been duped into believing that the mission was critical to addressing the jihadist threat that we face or that it could actually be accomplished in the first place.

Make no mistake: we are at war and engaged in an ideological battle against ignorance, intolerance, and hate. With great resolve, it will take decades to turn the tide. Praying at the altar of political expediency or offering only what Pope Francis called "declarationist nominalism" in his address to the U.S. Congress in 2015 will not keep this or any free nation safe. It bears repeating that we simply cannot afford to be timid in the face of threats. We move forward, armed with the knowledge that we must protect ourselves, while seeking to bring freedom to others. Our influence, including but surely also beyond our military might, is vital to advancing that cause of freedom. How different that is from the imperialists of the past or the dictators of the twentieth century. How different that is from the terrorists we fight today, who seek to sap the souls from the hearts of men. Those are lessons the media either is loath to learn or willfully ignores for the sake of ratings.

As one by one the members of the CPA boarded planes and left Iraq behind to return to ordinary of life at home, hope was all we could do and feel. The uneasiness we felt was our collective understanding that hope by itself isn't a strategy for real change. We knew that we needed more troops. We knew that this mission was far from complete. From an operational standpoint, Iraq would be in the care of the Iraqis, and the State Department and the coalition forces would still be struggling to forge the peace. It would be years before we upped our game and took the bold steps necessary to turn the tide of violence. In June 2004, Iraq had a long road ahead but had achieved a staggering amount of progress toward building a functional, pluralistic society that could be a contributor to the global community. By 2008, Iraq wasn't out of the woods, but it was far from a failure.

Unfortunately, losing the media and, consequently, the home-front war would do more to imperil Iraq than any terror group or act of commission or omission made during those critical first days. More than the casualty count or any photo of flag-draped caskets, the inability—and at times unwillingness—to articulate and defend effectively this bold mission in the face of powerful, organized critics turned Iraq into political kryptonite. That perception ultimately paved the way for policy shifts that resulted in the increasing and damaging influence of ISIS, Iran, Russia, and other oppressive regimes in a land where so many brave Americans valiantly dared to struggle against the odds for the sake of Iraqi freedom.

EPILOGUE

June 28, 2004, at 10:26 a.m. Baghdad time, the Coalition Provisional Authority handed over power to the Iraqi government—two days early.

The media would suggest that Bremer snuck out of Baghdad. There was no great fanfare upon his return to the United States, although Bush later awarded him the Presidential Medal of Freedom for his work. As the CPA's time as administrator of the country came to an end and the coalition kept its promise to return power to an Iraqi government ready for elections and ratification of a new constitution, the press still wouldn't report the progress. There were too many bombs and too many bodies to give fair time to the fact that the CPA had done what some said would be impossible. Back at home, the 2004 presidential election was in full swing, and there would be far tighter an outcome than there should have been for the man who stood atop the rubble of the World Trade Center three years prior, in part because, although our forces were struggling to push back Al-Qaeda in Iraq, we were clearly losing the media war.

The odds were overwhelming and grew steeper each day. Yet by the time Bremer boarded that C-130 for his last ride out of the country, Iraq—which had lived under the thumb of one of the most brutal dictators in history—had a functioning, pluralistic government (albeit in its infancy), had written and ratified a Transitional Administrative Law, had developed a framework for free elections, had established new political parties, had crafted the most liberal constitution in the Middle East, had reopened its central bank, had stabilized and unified its currency, had introduced a vastly improved health-care system, had created a framework for the return of a strong judiciary, had reestablished diplomatic relations with nations that were once foes, and had begun to grow a new economy. The training of new Iraqi security forces had begun within weeks of the creation of the CPA. Hundreds of schools and government buildings were rebuilt, including hospitals and health care centers.

By the time President Bush left office, after the success of the long-awaited surge in U.S. troops, a constitution had been developed with Shiites, Sunnis, Kurds, and Turkmen at the table. Systems had been created to facilitate an election in an incredibly challenging security environment that saw participation by more than eight million people. Perhaps most important, Al-Qaeda in Iraq had been decimated. By the time Bush left office, the economy of Iraq had increased in size several times over from its time under Hussein. Per capita income had increased between four and six times. Life expectancy also had risen. Security forces had secured much of the country with training and ongoing assistance from the United States.

Despite the consequences of a precipitous withdrawal of troops administered by the Obama administration and our country's insistence on "military strategy via CNN," which left Iraq all but defenseless in the face of ISIS, we also recently saw the fourth peaceful transition of power from one legitimate government to the next in Iraq. It is a feat never before accomplished in the Middle East with the exception of the state of Israel.

We don't think about many of those things today. We only remember what went wrong. There's a consequence for that. Bush's strategy of active deterrence, a broad-based interdiction campaign, and aggressive posture regarding terror networks and states that sponsor them meant that the United States was leading a global fight against a new, often unseen enemy capable of striking anywhere, anytime. Losing the media war and the home-front battle for public opinion sounded the death knell for major components of that effort. The left and even many on the right were forced to respond to a wild shift in the pendulum of public opinion rather than to the realities of the war in which we were engaged. Since Bush left office, we have reverted to a more tepid response to the global threat of terrorism, and any assertion that this has in some way made America and its allies safer simply belies the facts. President Obama's responses to the rise of ISIS, the collapse of

Libya and Yemen, the conflict in Syria, the Paris attacks, and even the first coordinated Islamic terrorist attack on American soil since 9/11, in San Bernardino, have telegraphed to enemies known and unknown that the United States is again a paper tiger. When an American president speaks more forcefully about global climate change than he does about global Islamic terrorism, our national interests will be targeted.

Since my return from Iraq and certainly since the withdrawal of troops, many people have suggested that our departure was justified because the Iraqis didn't want us there. The failure to renew the Status of Forces Agreement (SOFA) between the United States and the Iraqi government is seen as prime evidence for that theory. Of course, a gross oversimplification of the issue would lead to that conclusion. The intellectually honest discussion would focus on the plain fact that the government of Nouri al-Maliki understood that he needed us there. What governments can say publically and what they acknowledge is necessary for their security only privately are often two different things. The Bush administration continued to drive a message that the United States would wind down its mission in Iraq, in part to help build credibility for the Maliki government. But colleagues of mine at the Pentagon and other agencies, as well as those who had served with me at the CPA, understood full well that a robust presence was necessary to help ensure progress generally, to train and assist Iraqi security forces, to fight any resurgence of Al-Qaeda, and to be a watchful eye as an adolescent political system awkwardly matured. It would take time. Obama for his part was able to use Bush's public position to prop up his view that Iraq was a fatally flawed mission and needed to end without regard to the consequences. The 2008 presidential campaign had hinged too much on his promise to make drastic changes in American policy for the forty-fourth president to do anything but cut and run.

President Obama didn't want the SOFA renewal. By the time he took office, Maliki saw the writing on the wall and was already drifting away from the United States into the arms of Iran and Russia. He was already thinking in desperate terms about how to hold the government and the country together without any substantial American help. When up against the wall, he and others reached back to the politics of sectarianism, which fit like an old, worn pair of jeans. Within twenty-four hours of the American pullout, he and his government had fanned the flames of the Sunni-Shiite divide by arresting the country's Sunni vice president and several tribal leaders. Even the *Washington Post* headline the following day read, "Maliki Shatters Iraq." The stage was set for the rise of the Islamic State, or ISIS—or as I like to call them Al-Qaeda 2.0.

As of this writing, France and Russia are perceived to be taking on a greater role in fighting Islamic terrorism than the United States is taking. Large swaths of Iraq and the region are under the influence or outright control of ISIS, which has with great speed and alacrity moved through the Middle East and Africa together with Boko Haram on a brutal march of terror. The soft underbelly of Europe is exposed and, yes, America too is facing a threat not only from the outside but also from within. Only after the Paris attacks has the United States attempted to develop and articulate a coherent and more aggressive strategy against ISIS. In December 2015, Secretary of Defense Ash Carter began new discussions with the Iraqi government about a new wave of American assistance to fight the Islamic State and the White House finally agreed to share the target list of ISIS positions with allies.

Just as the rise of twenty-four-hour cable news and digital media made communicating about war and fighting the battle for public opinion that much harder, some of those mediums have made recruiting, radicalizing, training, and coordinating terror attacks that much easier. It is imperative that we take a more holistic approach to educating Americans about this threat, its causes, and ways to stop it beyond aggressive military action.

Winning this war, as President Bush frequently pointed out, was a generations-long struggle because the countries that help breed this ideology have dealt with oppression and authoritarianism for decades. So how do we fight? First, policymakers—Democrats and Republicans alike—must fight the communications war with every weapon in their arsenal. Information is power, and perceptions created by the use of information become reality. Those are inextricably linked to our ability to implement policy, particularly when that policy will require significant time, resources, and human costs. Our nation needs a new focus on public diplomacy and citizen education about foreign policy. That will be critical toward pushing back against editorial filters on both the right and the left, intellectually dishonest reporting, and uninformed opinions to ensure that what we do vis-à-vis the rest of the world is more accurately contextualized and understood by the American people.

Second, we need Americans to be strong, and we need political leadership to be even stronger in the face of defending our way of life. The day of the San Bernardino terror attack in December 2015, the Obama White House and commentators in the media were calling for more gun laws as a way to stem the violence. Just before the Paris attacks, Obama had indicated his belief that ISIS was "contained." The misplaced priorities and outright obfuscation of the real issues and threats was staggering. It's time for us to get real about the world in which we live. Borders, oceans, and airspace no longer protect us. In the absence of our own will to defend our way of life, we will have acquiescence to a shadow of death that stalks free people.

Third, it is imperative that we foster domestically an opportunity society and that we promote the growth of such societies abroad. Opportunity doesn't mean equal outcomes or government trying artificially to create advancement. It means protecting basic freedoms that are under threat here at home such as privacy, speech, religion, and the right to bear arms. I would add to those the right to obtain a quality education. Those basic freedoms help validate the individual and make us stronger. Economic freedom and opportunity are also vital. So many of the young men and women who are willing to blow themselves up on a bus in Jerusalem or in a market in Baghdad, or shoot up innocent people in California, believe that jihad was worth dying for because they had little else to live for. It doesn't strain the imagination how the environments in the Middle East and Africa can help provide a fertile recruiting ground for terrorist groups who seek pawns willing to sacrifice their lives for their wretched cause. It should also be noted that recruits are also coming from Europe and the United States, albeit when it comes to the latter, they come in much smaller numbers. The social welfare complex in countries like Belgium won't insulate those nations from becoming breeding grounds because government programs don't provide real empowerment and advancement. That's what most people crave. A job is the best social program.

Similarly, it's not hard to imagine areas and groups within our own borders who desire something more, a better life and a chance to advance. As I've traveled around the world and across the country, it has never been clearer that the vast majority of people—regardless of background, religion, socioeconomic status, or political ideology—just want to have a job, earn a living, and provide for themselves and their families. No one has ever said to me, "I just wish the government would come in and give me everything I want and need." That saps the soul of the individual and stunts the growth of the person—and the nation. There are a number of ways to give people real "skin in the game," and accomplishing that goal to a greater extent than we are doing today is a significant weapon against extremism.

In so many ways, it all comes back to communication and the lessons from the media war we fought in Iraq. Al-Qaeda used videos that were shot in a cave. ISIS uses heavily produced films with soundtracks, social media, and grassroots networks. When it came to Iraq, those of us who were attached to the CPA had a right to complain about a liberal editorial bias that ultimately helped denigrate the mission. The Bush administration also failed to counter that bias with sufficient zeal. The fact is that for America and free nations to combat the terror threat or any other that might rise up in the future, the business of journalism and partisan politics at times must yield to facts, realities, and intellectually honest debate and not merely information but also practical knowledge about the world in which we live.

When governments allow policies to be defined by their opposition and the media permit themselves to be little more than mouthpieces for a political agenda, as was the case in Iraq, the result is a decrease in faith in both on the part of the public. Today, according to Gallup, less than half of the American public trusts the media's reporting. A 2015 Pew Research Center survey found that attitudes toward trust in government are far worse, with 11 percent of Republicans and conservative-leaning independents and only 26 percent of Democrats and liberal-leaning independents having confidence in Washington. A lack of credible information from the media and lack of faith in our political system creates a toxic blend that leads to the erosion of citizen-controlled government in the United States. That has repercussions for individual freedoms to be sure, but it similarly has an impact on our foreign policy and our ability to lead on the world stage. Iraq, the War on Terrorism, and the wrath of Islamic extremism are with us still. Just as Iraq was far more than merely a debate over WMDs, the choice today is not merely one of ground troops or no ground troops to engage in the broader conflict. It is whether leaders have the patience, fortitude, and guts to make the tough sell.

INDEX

media bias and sensationalism (*cont.*)
and denigration of CPA mission,
290; and distrust of government,
202–3; and flag protocol, 87–88,
191–92; and infrastructure neglect,
200–202; and judicial reform, 201–
2; and network Baghdad bureau
staffing and operations, 203–6;
and oversimplification, 197–200;
and Ted Koppel, 188; and unethical behavior, 205–6
media relations. *See* press relations
Mehta, Naheed, 33, 137, 163, 239, 243
Mhedi, Abdul, 155
midnight rations ("mid-rats"), 46
Miklaszewski, Jim, 239–40
military reservists, 101–2
Ministry of Justice, 57–61
mission focus, 111–13
Molloy, Marty, 16–17
mortar attacks, 65–66, 74, 114, 146,
220, 251–52, 262
mosques, 49–50, 123–25

National Security Council (NSC),
212–15, 223
NBC news, 94–95, 239–40
Neighborhood Advisory Councils
(NACS), 171
network Baghdad bureaus, 203–6
New York Times, 40, 45, 205, 261, 273
Nidhal, 170, 174–75, 183, 276
9/11 attacks, 2, 5, 14, 16–17, 50, 194,
227–28, 287
NSC (National Security Council),
212–15, 223
numeric accuracy, 143

Obama, Barack, x, 78–79, 85, 158,
200, 202–3, 228, 286–89

Office of Presidential Advance-
ment, 13
Office of Presidential Personnel, 13
Oil for Food Program, UN, 36, 49

Pachachi, Adnan, 266
Pataki, George, 269, 272
Pawlenty, Tim, 269
Perino, Dana, 218
Peshmerga Army, 78–79, 87
Peterson, Pete, 9
post exchange, 256
Powell, Colin, 78–81, 84–85, 88–91,
223
presidential campaign 2000 (U.S.),
16, 18
presidential campaign 2004 (U.S.),
224
presidential campaign 2008 (U.S.),
187
press relations, 135–64; American
face of, 163–64; and Baghdad
road infrastructure project, 147–
51; and BBC, 163; changes in strategy due to increasing violence,
162–64; and circumvention of
CPA spokesperson, 144; and CPA
pecking order, 147; with Foreign
Service Officers, 139–40; and
homesickness, 146; and hometown radio talk shows, 161–62;
and importance of reliable information, 147–51; internal communications between military and
civilians, 144; and internal communications within CPA, 137–39;
and Iraqi Currency Exchange,
158–60; with Iraqi police, 140–
44; and managing expectations,
135–37, 283; and media's interac-